The Bricks before *Brown*

The Bricks before *Brown*

The Chinese American, Native
American, and Mexican Americans'
Struggle for Educational Equality

Marisela Martinez-Cola

The University of Georgia Press
ATHENS

Sociology of Race and
Ethnicity web page

© 2022 by the University of Georgia Press
Athens, Georgia 30602
www.ugapress.org
All rights reserved
Designed by Kaelin Chappell Broaddus
Set in 10.5/13.5 Garamond Premier Pro Regular
by Kaelin Chappell Broaddus

Most University of Georgia Press titles are
available from popular e-book vendors.

Printed digitally

Library of Congress Cataloging-in-Publication Data

Names: Martinez-Cola, Marisela, 1974– author.
Title: The bricks before Brown : the Chinese American,
    Native American, and Mexican Americans' struggle for
    educational equality / Marisela Martinez-Cola.
Description: Athens : The University of Georgia Press, [2022] |
    Series: Sociology of race and ethnicity | Based on author's thesis
    (doctoral - Emory University, 2018) issued under title: The bricks
    before Brown v. Board of Education : a comparative, historical
    study of race, class, and gender in Chinese American, Native
    American, and Mexican American school desegregation cases,
    1885–1947. | Includes bibliographical references and index.
Identifiers: LCCN 2021061641 | ISBN 9780820362021 (hardback) |
    ISBN 9780820362038 (paperback) | ISBN 9780820362045 (ebook)
Subjects: LCSH: Discrimination in education—Law and legislation—
    United States—Cases. | Chinese Americans—Education—Law and
    legislation—United States—Cases. | Mexican Amerians—Education—
    Law and legislation—United States—Cases. | Indians of North
    America—Education—Law and legislation—United States—Cases.
Classification: LCC KF4155 .M369 2022 | DDC
    344.73/0798—dc23/eng/20220331
LC record available at https://lccn.loc.gov/2021061641

This book is dedicated to

My mother, who gave me ambition,

My father, who gave me heart,

My sisters, who give me laughter, and

Greg and David, who give me life and love.

CONTENTS

The Bricks before *Brown*

I, too, sing America.

I am the darker brother.
They send me to eat in the kitchen
When company comes,
But I laugh,
And eat well,
And grow strong.

Tomorrow,
I'll be at the table
When company comes.
Nobody'll dare
Say to me,
"Eat in the kitchen,"
Then.

Besides,
They'll see how beautiful I am
And be ashamed—
I, too, am America.

—LANGSTON HUGHES (1945)

INTRODUCTION

America's history is laden with stories of various groups vying for a spot at "the table when company comes." The history of legal struggle against school segregation in the United States provides an example of how communities respond when confronted with the beauty of the ever-growing and ever-strengthening darker brother who laughs in the face of rejection. But who represents the "darker brother"? Is he Latiné, Asian American, or Indigenous?[1] Is he a she? Is this person rooted solely in the South or making a presence felt through all of America?

Brown v. Board of Education, the case that legally dismantled the "separate but equal" doctrine established by *Plessy v. Ferguson*, has earned its place at the proverbial table. As an example of its eminence, it has been the subject of at least 10 documentaries, more than 150 books or book chapters, and more than 450 peer-reviewed articles or law review articles. The players in this public battle for equality are equally as esteemed. Thurgood Marshall, Robert Carter, Chief Justice Earl Warren, Oliver Brown, and little Linda Brown were all individuals responsible for helping overturn years of established oppressive legal precedents and beginning what became known as the Black Civil Rights Movement. *Brown* is, in a word, iconic and has been covered by equally iconic works such as *Simple Justice* by Richard Kluger, *"Brown v. Board of Education" and the Civil Rights Movement* by Michael J. Klarman, and *Silent Covenants* by Derrick Bell.

Icons, however, cast a very long and wide shadow that can obscure historic contributions, render a myopic view of race without considering the role of gender and class, and deliver a narrative that is linear and uncomplicated. The recent work of Black scholars on those obscured contributions not only adds a critical analysis of class and gender to the discussion of race, but also helps explore how far, deep, and wide the struggle for Black liberation extends. Just as Martin Luther King Jr.'s charismatic presence once overshadowed the critical work of Black women in organizing the Montgomery Bus Boycott, rendered invisible the role of Bayard Rustin in organizing the March on D.C., and limited Rosa Parks's position to a seat on the bus, *Brown* unwittingly conceals many of the legal struggles that occurred before 1954.[2]

Challenging this narrative does not lessen the value of the Black Civil Rights Movement. It expands it, revealing the complexity of the movement. Knowing, for example, of Rosa Parks's role investigating rape cases in the South does not destroy the image and narrative of her standing up for justice by sitting down because she was "tired" that day. It reveals that she had been tired for a very long time and was, as Fannie Lou Hamer put it so plainly, "sick and tired of being sick and tired." Knowing that Claudette Colvin, a young, accomplished Black teenager, was tapped to be "the face" of the movement until she became pregnant out of wedlock does not lessen the work of the NAACP. Instead, it indicates the need for a critical analysis of the influence of middle-class respectability in shaping the deliberate strategy of civil rights organizations.[3] Recognizing the role of these individuals does not diminish the work or memory of the Black Civil Rights Movement, but it reveals that even the most inspiring story is not immune to the effects of patriarchy, homophobia, and classism.

What I have discovered is that the road to *Brown* is lined with "bricks" representing at least one hundred other families who legally challenged segregated schooling in state and federal courts across the country, eleven of which involved Chinese American, Native American, and Mexican American plaintiffs.[4] School desegregation in the United States is filled with the faceless and nameless testimonies of families representing the full racial spectrum of the country. While I describe all eleven cases, this book focuses on three families in California who, across time, contribute to what historians now call the "long civil rights movement."[5]

Those individuals include the Tapes, a Chinese American family in San Francisco who, in 1885, sued the city schools for refusing entry to their eldest daughter, Mamie. There are also the Pipers, a Paiute family from the small town of Big Pine who, in 1924, fought for their daughter Alice to be admitted to the local White school. Finally, there are the Mendezes, a Mexican American family in Los Angeles who, in 1947, almost prompted a Supreme Court case when they sued the school district for refusing entry to their daughter Sylvia.

The Tape, Piper, and Mendez families represent a much more nuanced addition to the grand narrative of segregated schooling in the United States. It is not a story that lines up perfectly with the Black experience. It is a circuitous route that, at times, both challenges and reinforces White supremacy, highlights the role of fathers while obscuring the critical contributions of powerful mothers, and invests in the politics of middle-class respectability as a strategy for success that might have been necessary. Most importantly, these cases reveal that the battle for educational equality requires understanding that its construction began earlier than the 1950s, its boundaries extend beyond the Jim Crow South, and its design was not limited to Black and White.

Adding *Tape*, *Piper*, and *Mendez* to the grand narrative of the Black Civil Rights Movement only enhances the significance of *Brown* in academic as well as personal ways. Academically, these cases reimagine the Black Civil Rights Movement by expanding its boundaries to include the narratives of those *similarly* oppressed by White supremacist institutions. By including their stories, I am not claiming that the experiences of African Americans, Latinés, Native Americans, and Chinese Americans are the same. I am arguing, however, that White supremacy is so efficient in its transmission that there are tremendous similarities among them.

Personally, the book identifies an opportunity for an increasingly diverse America to be invested in the grand narrative of the Black Civil Rights Movement by revealing the place of other non-White peoples in it as well. This generation of students is inspired to protest in response to the racial divisions that have always existed but were amplified and manipulated during and after the 2016 election, the COVID pandemic, and the murder of George Floyd. Today's students want to make history, and their fervent desires can only be enhanced by understanding their own history. The diversification of America, for them, is not limited to Black and White. The Latiné student in Chicago, the Vietnamese student in Atlanta, and the Indigenous student in Oklahoma want to see themselves or members of their groups in books.[6] They are hungry to learn that they are not relegated to the sidelines of social movements but, in fact, have their own place and purpose on the field of racial change in America.

Connecting *Tape*, *Piper*, and *Mendez* to the school desegregation narrative and one another is an intellectually rewarding venture. To fully understand the history of Black segregated schooling, one must also learn the history of Mexican, Chinese, and Indian schools in the United States. To fully understand the racial politics of the Black Civil Rights Movement of the 1950s, one must also study and analyze the racial circumstances of the Chinese in the late 1800s, Native Americans in the 1920s, and Mexican Americans in the 1940s. Traversing two centuries and three racial realities, the ensuing chapters delve into three separate but interconnected disciplinary lenses: law, history, and sociology. All three are necessary for the analysis of school desegregation. Sociology students are often taught that race, class, and gender are social constructs. I contend, and these cases support an understanding, that race, class, and gender are, more accurately, social, legal, and historical constructs.

In chapter 1, I describe the blended theoretical scaffolding required to situate the *Tape, Piper*, and *Mendez* cases generally in the scholarship of race and ethnicity and specifically in the school desegregation movement. Before delving into the specific theories involved, I honor the work of the Black scholars who laid the foundation that makes this kind of scholarly inquiry possible. Framing this intertwined understanding calls for an introduction to two critical theoretical frameworks rooted in intersectionality. The first is a more complicated understanding of CRT and what I refer to as its branches, specifically AsianCrit, TribalCrit, and LatCrit. The second is a blend of the theory of controlling images put forth by Dr. Patricia Hill Collins in her groundbreaking contribution to sociology *Black Feminist Thought*, and the role of the politics of respectability outlined by Evelyn Higginbotham in *Righteous Discontent*. Foregrounding theory invites the reader to embrace the inclusive, intersectional, and interdisciplinary nature of the work, fashioning a comprehensive lens for inquiry that recognizes connections rather than stand-alone stories.

Chapter 2 outlines the legal and historical background of school desegregation efforts since 1849. In providing a rich landscape of the case law, I deliver descriptive statistics of 105 cases discovered through legal research. I identify where and when they took place and generate a map to visualize the school desegregation efforts around the United States. I also summarize eight other Chinese, Native, and Mexican American cases to demonstrate why *Tape, Piper*, and *Mendez* represent the ideal proceedings for in-depth study.[7] An examination of the social and legal circumstances surrounding these cases reveals the genesis of, and connections among, these communities' efforts to achieve educational parity with their White counterparts. Doing so helps to reframe the Black Civil Rights Movement more broadly to represent an increasingly diverse America.

This overarching legal history is followed by chapters 3, 4, and 5, where I introduce the reader to the Tape, Piper, and Mendez families and provide a sociological analysis for each case. The Tapes, whose contributions are often omitted from the school desegregation narrative, are introduced in chapter 3. Progressing from steerage passengers on an ocean liner to individuals leading a lavish lifestyle of wealth, limited influence, and guided assimilation, Joseph and Mary Tape fashioned an extraordinary life for themselves and their children, Mamie, Frank, and

Emily, at the height of the country's anti-Chinese sentiment. So thorough was their Americanization that they had not even considered being rejected by the San Francisco school board, sparking a controversy that culminated in the creation of segregated Chinese public schools. As a precursor to *Plessy*, *Tape v. Hurley* represents the foundation on which the separate but equal doctrine was built. In the Tapes, readers meet a determined father, outraged mother, and exceptionally talented daughter who, according to the literature on Asian Americans and their racial positionality, are threats to labor, model minorities, or racial "middlemen." However, applying the AsianCrit tenets of Asianization and transnational context, I posit that the family's story cannot fit neatly into one or all three of these racial characterizations. Furthermore, using the controlling images, I show how the only middling position taken by Chinese American child Mamie Tape was in between pagans, prostitutes, and poor creatures.

The case of the Pipers, whose contributions have been reduced to a mere remnant of America's racial past, is recounted in chapter 4. Demonstrating the need to decolonize traditional historical methodologies, the family offers a bifurcated narrative comprising two competing stories: The Pipers v. The People. One story, told through legal documents and newspapers, paints the Pipers as willing to sacrifice culture and community in order to be granted citizenship. This citizenship would qualify daughter Alice Piper for entry into White schools. The other story, as told by the Paiute people of Big Pine, bestows a narrative describing the Pipers' deep and abiding connections to the Paiute Nation.

Using the TribalCrit tenets of liminality, assimilation, and autonomy, I show that the Pipers were far from sellouts. Instead, they were subversives manipulating the legal process in order to achieve educational equality. Furthermore, theirs is a story of a community fighting to keep the memory of *Piper v. Big Pine* alive. In 2014, the Big Pine Unified School District and the Paiute Tribe of the Owens Valley erected a life-sized memorial of Alice Piper, the girl who changed history, and not the savage, squaw, or sacrificial maiden she could have become in the U.S. imagination.

Rounding out this historical part of the book is an introduction of the Mendez family, whose case preceded *Brown* to the Supreme Court by seven years. Discussion of the racial identities of Mexican Americans in the United States is often limited to describing Latinés, specifically Mexican Americans, as racial wedges, wearers of cloaks, and bearers of Whiteness. However, using LatCrit tenets of Latino/a essentialism, I attest that the Mendezes' story is one of a Mexican father who went from farmworker to farmer, and of a Puerto Rican mother whose contributions are largely unreported in the historical record. It is also the tale of their daughter, the reluctant representative of a revolution who nevertheless promised to keep the memory of the five thousand families of *Mendez v. Westminster* alive. Far from the *mamacita, malinche,* or mentally inferior educational burden, Sylvia represents the very picture of possibility and promise.

Applying CRT collectively and its branches individually delineates a more robust picture of the complicated case that race constitutes across the different racial groups. The story of race in these instances is not a spotless representation of unity among marginalized groups. To the contrary, it demonstrates that a particular kind of "racial flexibility" was available to Asians, Native Americans, and Latinés in which Black plaintiffs could never partake.

For example, the school board in *Tape* argued that the Fourteenth Amendment was "meant for those of African descent."[8] This reveals the "racial ambiguity" of Chinese Americans in the eyes of the law. In *Piper*, the plaintiffs are referred to as "those of the Aboriginal Race" who had "adopted civilized habits" according to the Dawes Act. The Dawes Act was introduced to give Native Americans a route to U.S. citizenship that could only be achieved through complete assimilation. This circumstance provides insight into the complicated political relationship Native Americans have with the U.S. government because they are both a race and a sovereign nation. In the *Mendez* case, the attorney deployed a legal strategy to avoid being dismissed since Mexicans were classified as White in the Census yet still experienced unequal treatment. Together, these cases both challenge and uphold the U.S. racial hierarchy in ways that are as compelling as they are troubling.

By applying the theory of controlling images, this work explores how the sexual, criminal, and tragic stereotypes of their time both threatened and strengthened Mamie Tape's, Alice Piper's, and Sylvia Mendez's position in the court of public opinion. These daughters were too young to be sexualized, too innocent to be criminalized, and too wealthy to be deemed pathetic. As their social histories will reveal, these families benefited immensely from their middle-class status and used it to secure "tumble proof" plaintiffs. On one hand, the Tapes, Pipers, and Mendezes were not individuals whose livelihood could be threatened. They were entrepreneurial representations of the bootstrap polemic so often attributed to these racial groups. As a result, the families' adherence to "American" ideals could easily be mistaken for complete assimilation. But theirs is an assimilation of convenience, not cultural abandonment. For their cases to be heard, the plaintiffs had to use the language outlined in the laws of the time. Moreover, by centering the role of class, these families reveal that the politics of respectability has roots that are deep and wide, stretching into all racial communities and as far back as the late eighteenth century. Most importantly, the Tapes', Pipers', and Mendezes' struggles demonstrate that resistance comes in various forms and is not always marked by marches and militancy.

Finally, in chapter 6, in addition to summarizing the findings, I suggest future directions for research that could use a comparative Critical Race Theory model. Critical race studies is primed to be pushed past siloed narratives to more meaningful connections among underrepresented communities. There exists a shared history shaped by discriminatory practices designed to subjugate and separate racial communities in the United States. *The Bricks before "Brown"* confirms that the damage to educational equality today is not limited to one racial community and offers people a unique opportunity to learn from one another.

By injecting these cases into the school desegregation grand narrative and treating gender, class, and age as symbiotic with race, I show that these plaintiffs were more than just Chinese American, Native American, and Mexican American. They were fathers and mothers who, like the plaintiffs in *Brown*, utilized their middle-class status to confront a system of inequality that refused to make space for their intelligent, capable, and eager daughters. The Tape, Piper, and Mendez families did not just sit on the side of the road as spectators. Indeed, they were legal agents who contributed to a multiracial, nearly one-hundred-year-long effort to dismantle segregated schooling.

Together, these cases represent an alternate approach to examining the flexibility of race within Latiné, Asian American, and Indigenous communities. From honorary Whiteness to Black Exceptionalism, LatCrit, AsianCrit, and TribalCrit scholars have attempted to carve out a place for non-Black racial groups to identify the issues unique to their communities without interpreting their merit through a Black/White lens. Instead of using "Black Exceptionalism" to describe the well-established field of race scholarship, I offer the phrase "Black Foundationalism" to recognize that the foundation for research regarding race has been built on the rich and varied work established by Black scholars.

Recognizing the foundation of research regarding non-Black racial groups does not preclude one from observing the inherent differences in that research. Indeed, it allows one to characterize new findings as a development of the scholarship rather than challenges to Blackness. This project, for example, began with the question "Since there is a *Brown v. Board*, wouldn't there be a Mexican American, Asian American and Native American equivalent?" Comparing and discussing the meaning of *Tape*, *Piper*, and *Mendez* do not diminish the standing of *Brown*. If anything, these tasks reveal all the twists and turns inherent in the struggle for equality.

CHAPTER 1

Laying the Foundation

> Central to racial thinking is not only the notion that the
> categories of white, black, brown, yellow and red mark
> meaningful distinctions among human beings but also
> that they reflect inferiority and superiority, a human Chain
> of Being, with *white* at the top and *black* on the bottom.
> Determining racial identity was about raising some people
> up that chain to put others down; enslaving some people
> to free others; taking land from some people to give it to
> others; robbing people of their dignity to give others a sense
> of supremacy.
>
> —ARIELA J. GROSS, *What Blood Won't Tell*

The Complicated Case of Race

From Ida B. Wells-Barnett, W. E. B. DuBois, and Frantz Fanon to Patricia Hill
Collins, Kimberlé Crenshaw, and Robin D. G. Kelley, these scholars and countless others have laid the groundwork for much of what we know about race, difference, and inequality in the United States. No race scholars can call themselves
such without having read transformative works like *The Souls of Black Folk*, *All the
Women Are White, All the Men Are Black, but Some of Us Are Brave*, and *Pedagogy
of the Oppressed*.[1] When it comes to social movements, Black scholars once again
created formative works such as *The Origins of the Civil Rights Movement*, *Race,
Reform, and Rebellion*, *Ella Baker and the Black Freedom Movement*, and *Sisters in
the Struggle*.[2] Finally, when specifically examining school desegregation, Michael
Klarman and Richard Kluger may be among the most cited, but Waldo Martin,

Vanessa Siddle Walker, James D. Anderson, and Derrick Bell are just as critical to the canon. All of these scholars and more are the originators of what I call "Black Foundationalism."[3]

While Black Foundationalist scholars settled into their hard-fought spaces in academia, they inspired Latiné, Asian American, and Indigenous scholars to ask hard questions of their own communities. First, where were we during the Abolitionist Movement, the Civil Rights Movement, the Black Power Movement, and the Voting Rights Movement for Women? Did we sit on the sidelines, watch the marches go by, and benefit from the hard work of Black activists? Second, where do our experiences belong in the Black/White binary discussion of race? Studies on racism, discrimination, educational inequality, health disparities, wealth disparities, and poverty are usually examined through a Black lens and inevitably compared to the lives of Whites. Where do the experiences of non-Black populations fall in these discussions? Scholars such as George Sánchez, Judy Yung, and Elizabeth Cook-Lynn were among the early pioneers to begin answering these questions.

Another pivotal aspect of Black Foundationalism was the creation of African American and Black studies departments demanded by Black students and scholars.[4] Those activists inspired other racial groups to demand the creation of Chicano and Latino studies, Native American studies, Asian American studies, and ethnic studies departments.[5] These spaces would produce even richer scholarship that was representative of the worlds intellectuals and protesters were attempting to transform. An unintended consequence of this structure, however, was the building of deep disciplinary divides that very few scholars traversed.[6] Feminist scholars of color attempted to unite these areas in *This Bridge Called My Back: Writings by Radical Women of Color* and *Making Face, Making Soul / Haciendo Caras: Creative and Critical Perspectives by Women of Color*.[7]

A growing community of legal scholars who developed Critical Race Theory would intentionally build bridges between disciplines. They differed from their counterparts outside the legal field in one particular way: the founding CRT scholars were a mixture of Black, White, Latiné, Asian American, and Indigenous individuals. Derrick Bell, Cheryl Harris, and Kimberlé Crenshaw were among the pioneers, but so were Richard Delgado, Mari Matsuda, Neil Gotanda, and Gary Peller. CRT was intended to be an intersectional, interdisciplinary, and inclusive intellectual space before those concepts became the nomenclature of higher education.

As CRT spread into other disciplines, the lives and experiences of African Americans again became central to the discussion of racial inequality in the United States, reinforcing the Black/White binary study of race.[8] CRT schol-

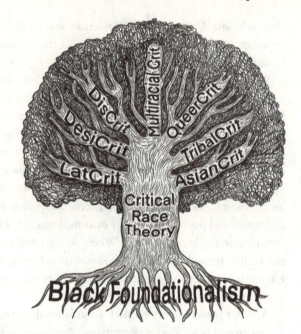

FIGURE 1.1.
Theoretical foundation.

ars have critiqued the Black/White binary, with some even problematically describing it as "hegemonic in nature."[9] The prominence of CRT analysis on *Brown*
alone further perpetuates the racial binary.[10] Put simply, CRT could not capture
the experiences of all people of color. As a result, the theory grew "branches" that
were clearly connected with the base, but necessary to grow the field. Latiné,
Asian American, Indigenous, and like-minded scholars proposed and developed
the following branches: Latino Critical Race Theory (LatCrit), Asian Critical
Race Theory (AsianCrit), and Native American Critical Race Theory (Tribal-
Crit), to name a few (Figure 1.1).[11]

CRT and its branches interrogate the profound differences and meaningful
similarities in how the Tape, Piper, and Mendez families were racialized from 1885
to 1954. These plaintiffs were never quite worthy of the rights afforded to Whites,
and they were not able "to depict themselves and their problems by analogy to
Blacks."[12] Ultimately, examining these cases solely through a Black/White binary
limits the analysis of race and fails to capture the differential racial experiences of
Asian Americans, Native Americans, and Latinés in the United States.

The Problem with the Chains, Spectrums, and Hierarchies

Legal scholar Ariela Gross offers a vivid description of "a human Chain of Being"
that identifies the top and bottom of the chain as White and Black, respectively.
However, the analogy does not discuss the placement or positions of the other ra-

cial links within the chain. While the Gross's analogy delivers a strong visual for the U.S. racial hierarchy, it supports the notion that Asians, Native Americans, and Latinés have a fixed placement and position within the binary of Black and White, inferiority and superiority, or enslaved and free. The same is true when describing race with hierarchies and spectrums.

Yet what *Tape*, *Piper*, and *Mendez* demonstrate is that racial positions are much more flexible. The Black part of the binary will always be constructed against the White part, but Asians, Native Americans, and Latinés are ultimately constructed against both.

Because it puts race at the center of analysis, CRT was supposed to be a solution for explaining these differences. However, as legal scholar Robert Chang explains, "Critical race theory claims that race matters, but has not yet shown how different races matter differently" and, I argue, similarly.[13] I contend that the Black/White binary fails to fully acknowledge or meaningfully capture the experiences of non-Black racial groups. Race scholars are often left to wrestle with where to place the experiences of Asian American, Indigenous, and Latiné people, organizations, and communities. Legal scholars have critiqued the paradigm since the creation of CRT, identifying its limitations through discussions related to constitutional law, school desegregation, interracial marriage, and immigration law.[14]

Sociologists, too, have struggled to even define these racial groups. They have also used static language to describe the position of non-Black racial groups, employing phrases such as "a racial middle,"[15] "racial ambiguity,"[16] "Honorary Whiteness,"[17] "a Caucasian cloak,"[18] a "racial continuum,"[19] "Partly Colored,"[20] and "middleman minorities,"[21] just to name a few. But these characteristics center Whiteness and rank non-Blacks' racial position as less problematic than being Black. It is as if this racial middle represents the Goldilocks equivalent of racism that is not too hard, not too soft, but "just right." Some sociologists have even proposed using color, not race, to analyze inter- and intraracial experiences between and among people of color.[22] I respectfully disagree. Colorism merely sidesteps the complexity of race and fails to acknowledge how the Black/White binary obscures, excludes, and even renders invisible the experiences of the "middleman minorities."

Even Omi and Winant, the creators of racial formation theory and the concept of racial projects, acknowledge that a "bipolar racial discourse tends at best to marginalize and at worst . . . eliminate other positions and voices in the ongoing dialogue about race in the U.S.A."[23] Despite Omi and Winant's call to explore a variety of racial projects, a majority of the sociological and CRT studies on race focus on the Black experience in the United States and the role of White supremacy in maintaining African Americans' economic, social, and cultural inequality. This, however, is not a shortcoming.

Foregrounding of research of Blackness in America is deserved, necessary, and relevant, as it reveals the development, growth, and long-lasting effects of systemic racism in the nation. No other racial groups in the United States were systematically stolen from their countries, shipped across an ocean, and separated from their families to become property and build a burgeoning economy from which they would never benefit. Nikole Hannah-Jones, the architect of the *New York Times Magazine* 1619 Project, explained that the goal of the project was "to reframe the country's history by placing the consequences of slavery and the contributions of black Americans at the very center of our national narrative."[24]

Even so, centering the Black experience does not preclude non-Black racial groups from contributing to the narrative. If anything, Black scholars have invited these stories and challenged race scholars to explore the complex relationships between and within these groups. In *The Conservation of Races*, W. E. B. DuBois wrote, "There is no reason why in the same country and on the same street . . . that men of different races might not strive together for their race ideals as well, perhaps even better, than in isolation."[25] In *Black Feminist Thought*, sociologist Patricia Hill Collins invites scholars to find "points of connection that further social justice projects" between historically oppressed groups.[26] Finally, Dr. Neely Fuller Jr. reminds us, "If you do not understand White supremacy—what it is, and how it works, everything else that you understand will only confuse you."[27] This book is an acceptance of the invitation and the challenge put forth by DuBois, Collins, and Fuller by applying the interdisciplinary, inclusive, and intersectional framework of CRT and its branches to the study of race and the school desegregation movement.

Adding the experiences of Latiné, Asian American, and Indigenous people, families, and communities to the civil rights narrative illustrates the efficacy of White supremacy and its destruction of the principles of racial equality. It provides evidence of the manner in which White supremacy has permeated, affected, and disenfranchised every non-White racial group in the United States. It is no coincidence when similar issues appear in different racial communities. Discussing the social, historical, and legal construction of race in a comparative historical manner, however, requires recognizing the invisibility, complexity, and racial flexibility of non-Black communities.

Using newspaper accounts, judicial records, and secondary research, I show how the racial flexibility of the Tape, Piper, and Mendez families worked both for and against them socially and legally. To accomplish this goal, I summarize the scholarly development and relevant literature of CRT, LatCrit, AsianCrit, and TribalCrit, as well as their analysis of race. Understanding these theoretical branches allows me to apply the relevant tenets of AsianCrit to *Tape*, TribalCrit to *Piper*, and LatCrit to *Mendez* to demonstrate the unique positions of Asian Americans, Native Americans, and Latiné communities along the racial hierarchy over time. Most importantly, I will answer the questions about Latinés', Asian Americans', and Native Americans' role in the fight for educational equality and their place within and outside the Black/White binary.

In discussing these cases, I consider the advice of Gross, who interrogates race through antimiscegenation laws. "We cannot take their legal strategies," she explains, "as a direct reflection of their actual beliefs about their racial or national identity."[28] Claims of citizenship, for example, should not be conflated with calls for Whiteness. Examining the historical record, interviews, and transcripts provides a very different picture of how these plaintiffs understood their racial identities and class positions. These plaintiffs, I argue, present a much more complicated narrative than Whiteness versus racial pride, assimilation versus authenticity, and peril versus preferential status. The overall goal is to provide historic evidence of the racial flexibility afforded to Asians, Native Americans, and Latinés in California that was not available to the other ninety-plus Black plaintiffs who fought segregated schools for over one hundred years.

Exploring the social, legal, and historical construction of race through *Tape*, *Piper*, and *Mendez* disrupts a linear story line that cleanly connects the cases through time. Race as constructed within each case and among all three is, in a word, complicated. As a result, challenging the Black/White binary requires race and legal scholars to embrace this complexity. In an early critique of the Black/White paradigm, legal scholar Juan Perea explains, "Paradigms have limitations. ... Among them is the tendency to truncate history for the sake of telling a linear story of progress."[29] Adding to and comparing the experiences of Chinese Americans, Native Americans, and Mexican Americans in the story of school desegregation in the United States undeniably adds curves, twists, and turns. Ultimately, however, this results in a more profound understanding of the complicated structure of race in America. To provide an example of this complexity, I summarize the development and research of CRT and its branches.

Critical Race Theory and Its Branches

The overall focus of CRT scholars is "studying and transforming the relationship among race, racism, and power."[30] Depending on the author, there are eight to ten tenets of CRT. These, of course, developed over time as scholarship in the field has grown. The original studies of CRT were more theoretical and descriptive, interrogating the role of the NAACP in *Brown*, the function of antidiscrimination laws, the purpose of affirmative action, the promises of the U.S. Constitution, the value of Whiteness, and the intersections of race and gender.[31] The foundation of CRT, as articulated by Derrick Bell, is to recognize that changes in racial policies are rarely born from a desire to right past wrongs. Such policies, he explains, are shaped by capitalism and the White elite's desire to maintain and limit access to status and privilege.

To illustrate CRT, Bell used *Brown v. Board of Education* as his point of analysis.[32] He theorized that the culmination of the 1950s civil rights changes had little to do with attempting to right the wrongs of Jim Crow. Instead, it had to do with the fact that two major wars had ended, the Cold War was a growing reality, and the United States needed to win "the loyalties of uncommitted emerging nations, most of which were black, brown, or Asian."[33] The racial injustices occurring in the country played out on the world's stage and could compromise U.S. interests abroad. Prior to *Brown*, the United Nations General Assembly had unanimously adopted the Universal Declaration of Human Rights in 1948. As the so-called bedrock of democracy, the United States needed to address its own violations of human rights because, according to Bell, "the interest of blacks in achieving racial equality will be accommodated only when it converges with the interest of whites."[34] While controversial at the time, his assertions have since been supported in the literature.[35]

Bell's initial work not only outlines the genesis of CRT but also demonstrates how, since its inception, the Civil Rights Movement generally and school desegregation specifically have been a point of departure for scholars in this area of study. As "revisionist historians," CRT specialists comb through popular U.S. narratives to find hidden aspects of a story, and "to understand the zigs and zags of Black, Latino, and Asian fortunes [by looking] to things like profit, labor supply, international relations, and the interest of white elites."[36]

The following tables identify the corresponding and distinctive tenets of CRT and its branches. The first outlines the founding authors, significant writings, watershed case law, and civil rights organizations and leaders generally affiliated with each theory (Table 1.1). The second table lists the tenets of each branch (Table 1.2).[37] It is not designed to be all encompassing, only to offer a snapshot of the similarities and differences of CRT and its offshoots. In my subsequent analysis, I will apply the theories to the facts of *Mendez*, *Tape*, and *Piper*.

DEVELOPMENT OF LATCRIT

Early LatCrit scholar Juan Perea used equal protection cases such as *Mendez*, *Lopez v. Seccombe* (1944), and *Hernández v. Texas* (1954) to discuss the absence of Mexican Americans within CRT scholarship. Each of these lawsuits involved issues relevant to Black communities as well.[38] *Mendez* involved segregated school-

Table 1.1.
Critical Race Theories' Foundations

	CRT	LatCrit	AsianCrit	TribalCrit
Founding Authors	Derrick Bell Kimberlé Crenshaw Alan Freeman	Richard Delgado Ian Haney López Juan Perea	Robert Chang Neil Gotunda Mari Matsuda	Bryan Brayboy
Significant Cases	*Dred Scott v. Sanford* (1857) *Plessy v. Ferguson* (1896) *Brown v. Board* (1954)	*Mendez v. Westminster* (1947) *Hernandez v. Texas* (1954) *Gonzales v. Sheely* (1951)	*People v. Hall* (1854) *Yick Wo v. Hopkins* (1886) *Gong Lum v. Rice* (1927) *Korematsu v. U.S.* (1944)	*Cherokee Nation v. Georgia* (1831) *Elk v. Wilkins* (1884) *Talton v. Mayes* (1896)
Civil Rights Organizational Affiliation	National Association for the Advancement of Colored People (NAACP)	League of United Latin American Citizens (LULAC)	Japanese American Citizens Council (JACL)	Native American Rights Fund (NARF)
Unique Issues	Impact of slavery One-drop rule	Colonization Legal whiteness Immigration Race vs. ethnicity	Yellow peril Model minority myth Immigration	Colonization Liminal status Blood quantum
Aligned Interests	Race as a social construct Intersectionality Reconstructive Narratives Storytelling Commitment to social justice Connection between race and labor			

TABLE 1.2.
Tenets of Critical Race Theory, LatCrit, AsianCrit, and TribalCrit

Critical Race Theory	LatCrit	TribalCrit	AsianCrit
• Racial inequality is hardwired into the fabric of our social and economic landscape.	• Latino/a essentialism • Latino/a stereotypes	• Colonization is endemic to society.	• Asianization
• Because racism exists at both the subconscious and conscious levels, the elimination of intentional racism would not eliminate racial inequality.	• Storytelling/Counterstorytelling and "naming one's own reality"	• Stories are not separate from theory; they make up theory and are therefore real and legitimate sources of data and ways of being.	• Story, theory, and praxis
• Our racial past exerts contemporary effects.	• Revisionist interpretation of U.S. civil rights law and progress • Critical international and human rights law	• U.S. policies toward Indigenous peoples are rooted in imperialism, White supremacy, and a desire for material gain.	• (Re)constructive history
• Racism intersects with other forms of inequality, such as classism, sexism, and homophobia.	• Intersectionality	• Indigenous peoples have a desire to obtain and forge tribal sovereignty, tribal autonomy, self-determination, and self-identification.	• Intersectionality
• The concept of color blindness in law and social policy and the argument for ostensibly race-neutral practices often serve to undermine the interests of people of color.	• Assimilationism and the colonized mind • Educational issues	• Governmental policies and educational policies toward Indigenous peoples are intimately linked around the problematic goal of assimilation.	• Strategic (anti)essentialism;
• Race is a social construct whose meanings and effects are contingent and change over time.	• Critical social science • Criticism and response	• The concepts of culture, knowledge, and power take on new meaning when examined through an Indigenous lens.	• Transnational contexts

• Racial change occurs when the interests of white elites converge with the interests of the racially disempowered.	• Gender discrimination • Black/Brown tensions	• Theory and practice are connected in deep and explicit ways such that scholars must work toward social change.
• Immigration laws that restrict Asian and Mexican entry into the United States regulate the racial makeup of the nation and perpetuate the view that people of Asian and Latino descent are foreigners.	• Immigration and citizenship • Language and bilingualism	• Indigenous peoples occupy a liminal space that accounts for both the political and racialized natures of our identities.
• Racial stereotypes are ubiquitous in society and limit the opportunities of people of color.	• Separatism and nationalism • Structural determinism	• Tribal philosophies, beliefs, customs, traditions, and visions for the future are central to understanding the lived realities of Indigenous peoples, but they also illustrate the differences and adaptability among individuals and groups.
• The success of various policy initiatives often depends on whether the perceived beneficiaries are people of color.	• Critique of liberalism	

• Commitment to social justice.

ing; *Lopez*, segregated swimming pools; and *Hernández*, jury exclusion. Despite being classified as White in the U.S. Census, Mexican and Mexican American communities in the West and Southwest experienced a de facto Juan Crow, a Mexican version of de jure Jim Crow practices in the South that were socially rather than legally enforced.[39] These cases, however, were not necessarily decided, legally speaking, on race. Instead, the attorneys in the Mexican American cases relied on descent and nationality to frame their equal protection arguments, revealing how race is constructed differently between Black and Latiné communities.

In *Hernández*, for example, an all-White, all-male jury indicted the plaintiff for murder. The plaintiff and his attorneys argued that the indictment was tainted due to jury discrimination because no jurors were Mexicans. The State of Texas argued that, because Mexicans were considered legally White, no actual exclusion occurred. The League of United Latin American Citizens (LULAC), representing Hernández, agreed that Mexicans were White but argued that the discrimination was based on descent or nationality. This decision was no doubt strategic. Had the organization alleged racial inequity its claim would have been thrown out, as in previous Texas cases like *Ramirez v. State* (1931) and *Carrasco v. State* (1936) that tried to prove racial discrimination.

While the strategy worked well enough to make it to the Supreme Court, it added to the confusion of where to "place" Mexicans. In fact, as legal scholar Ian Haney López reveals in his research on *Hernández*, the Supreme Court patently refused to refer to Mexicans as a race or color.[40] Instead, justices determined that discrimination was based "other differences from the community norm" that "might define groups needing the same protection."[41] The court relied on the following evidence to determine that Mexicans were a "group needing the same protection":

> First, people in Jackson County, Texas, routinely distinguished between "white" and "Mexican" persons. Second, business and community groups largely excluded Mexican Americans from participation. Third, until just a few years earlier, children of Mexican descent were required to attend a segregated school for the first four grades, and most children of Mexican descent left school by the fifth or sixth grade. Fourth, at least one restaurant in the county seat prominently displayed a sign announcing, "No Mexicans Served." Fifth, on the Jackson County courthouse grounds at the time of the underlying trial, there were two men's toilets, one unmarked, and the other marked "Colored Men" and "Hombres Aqui" ("Men Here"). And finally . . . there was the stipulation that "for the last twenty-five years there is no record of any person with Mexican or Latin American name having served on a jury commission, grand jury or petit jury."[42]

In examining "differences from the community norm," Haney López correctly concludes that the court was inadvertently arguing that being Mexican was a social construct.[43] Even though the evidence was congruent with practices associated with racial discrimination, Mexicans were still considered White, and the court refused to recognize discrimination based on race. Mexicans were, in a sense, trapped in a racial limbo born of the Black/White binary.

These cases reveal the inability of original CRT to fully capture the racialized experiences of Mexican Americans. Furthermore, CRT could not provide a theoretical explanation for why the court determined race was not an issue in *Hernández* yet *two weeks later* rendered its decision on *Brown* using similar social evidence. Traditional CRT did not have a scholarly space for a group that was "legally White, but socially Mexican."[44]

The differences between the racialized experiences of Mexican Americans and African Americans do not stop there. African Americans, for example, did not have international connections with whom the United States needed to maintain strong relationships. They did not have the United States initiating "Good Neighbor" policies that designated Mexicans as White in order to assuage a foreign government's concern that their citizens were experiencing discrimination.[45] They did not have international worker programs like the Bracero Program, which was critical to the agricultural economy of the United States. Nor did African Americans have the political pull of needing to "make nice" with countries with which it was necessary to maintain relations advantageous in times of war. This irregular treatment and influence from a foreign government could not be captured in the Black/White binary that developed within CRT, thereby inspiring the creation of LatCrit.[46]

Since the appearance of Perea's and Haney López's groundbreaking work, LatCrit scholars from a variety of traditions have continued to examine issues unique to the Latiné population.[47] Scholars have explored such matters as Mexicans and Whiteness,[48] immigration and citizenship,[49] racial tensions between Black/Brown communities,[50] and research focused on Latiné populations beyond Mexicans, such as Puerto Ricans[51] and Cubans.[52] Most relevant to this project, however, is the LatCrit scholarship related to the Civil Rights Movement, segregated schooling, and the unique position of Latinés within the Black/White binary. Mostly historians, legal scholars, and ethnic studies experts have produced such research.

Arguing that Latiné people in the United States are *more* disadvantaged than African Americans, Eduardo Luna uses *Mendez* to point out the erasure of Mexicans and Mexican Americans from the U.S. civil rights narrative.[53] Luna writes, "The Civil Rights Movement and discourse on race/ethnic relations are almost inextricably intertwined with, and exclusively focused on, the contributions and experiences of Blacks. . . . Black historical legal experiences are positioned on center stage, and the experiences of other minority groups are relegated to secondary and inferior roles as stagehands."[54] While I do not agree with Luna's participation in what Angela Davis refers to as the Oppression Olympics, I do appreciate his observation regarding the invisibility of Latiné contributions to civil rights. However, Luna's remarks run the risk of providing fodder for anti-Black sentiment to grow.

Perea, like Bell, interrogates whether cases like *Mendez* resulted in better legal protections and improved schooling for Mexican Americans.[55] In addition to identifying continued discrimination based on race, he also argues that when examining issues related to Latiné populations, one must consider discrimination based on language. "Language discrimination," Perea asserts, "*is* race discrimination."[56] As such, it can be applied to Asian Americans as well. The challenge, of course, is that not all of these ethnic groups are necessarily bilingual.

Other noted scholars have explored segregated Mexican schooling in Texas, as addressed in *Independent School District v. Salvatierra* (1930);[57] Arizona, as concerns *Gonzales v. Sheely* (1951);[58] and unpublished cases in California, such as *Alvarez v. Lemon Grove* (1931).[59] None of this research, however, is analyzed through the lens of sociology, nor does it consider intersectional aspects such as gender and class. This is notable because intersectionality is such a critical component of both CRT and LatCrit. All of the studies, however, wrestle with the racial positioning of Mexicans, and most conclude that Mexicans availed themselves of or embraced their status as Whites, or distanced themselves racially from the civil rights efforts of Black organizations like the NAACP. This limited analysis, which defines the Mexican experience as conforming to the Black/White binary, often overlooks the ambiguous place Mexicans inhabit on the racial hierarchy.

CLOAKS, WEDGES, AND WHITENESS: MEXICANS AND RACE

The treatment of the racial identity of Mexicans is largely built around the argument that this group is related to and assimilated into Whiteness. Sociologists of race and ethnicity and CRT scholars borrow heavily from one another. For example, CRT scholars have adopted sociological concepts such as colorblind racism,[60] racial formation theory and racialization,[61] and White racial frame.[62] Through these scholarly connections, many CRT scholars agree that "each disfavored group in this country has been racialized in its own individual way and according to the needs of the majority group at particular times in history."[63] There are three very specific ways Mexicans and Mexican Americans were racialized: (1) possession of a Caucasian Cloak, (2) formation of a wedge racial group between Black and White, or (3) adoption of some generic form of Whiteness.

Gross explains that Mexicans both denied and challenged Whiteness with the selective deployment of a "Caucasian Cloak."[64] On the one hand, they deployed it to assert their civil rights. If they were indeed White, then they were equal to Whites and should be afforded the same treatment as Whites. On the other hand, White institutions used the cloak to shield themselves from allegations of racism and discrimination, arguing, "Because you [Mexicans] are White, it is not possible to discriminate against you." It was a cloak whose convenience depended on who used it, thereby adding to the racial tug-of-war that Mexicans experienced in the West and Southwest.

The Caucasian Cloak was also very much classed. Mexican American organizations such as LULAC and the American G.I. Forum (AGIF) comprised mostly middle-class, well-resourced members who distanced themselves from Black civil rights efforts and argued for Whiteness. For example, AGIF founder Hector García, in an effort to avoid an association with Black civil rights efforts, declared, "We are not and have never been a civil rights organization" and wrote in another letter, "If we are white, why do we ally with the Negro[?]"[65] Historian Mario García explains that "both middle-class and working-class Mexican Americans joined LULAC, but the middle class dominated leadership positions."[66] Their leadership, too, made several efforts to distance themselves from Black communities, declaring, "Tell these Negroes that we are not going to permit our manhood and womanhood to mingle with them on an equal social basis."[67]

Considering class also reveals that arguing for Whiteness was not necessarily available to all Mexicans. The working-class Mexican farmworker whose skin was bronzed in the burning sun could not wear the cloak. Instead, he was *indio*, mestizo, *cafécito*, or whichever of the several descriptors were deployed by Mexicans to describe darker skin. This mixture of race and class further complicates the race of Mexicans, whose colonized history represents a continuum of color and class made up of both light-skinned, wealthy, landowning elites and the dark-skinned, poor farmworkers who labor on it.[68] Despite the fact that Mexicans included the full racial spectrum, many scholars continued to focus on the construction of and proximity to Whiteness.[69]

In her analysis of the racial status of Mexicans in nineteenth-century New Mexico, legal scholar Laura Gómez attempts to capture the complexity of Mexicans' racial position, but still uses Whiteness as a measure. Gómez agrees with general characterizations that Mexicans constituted an "in between" racial group that represented a sort of "racial ambivalence."[70] She, however, uses the phrase "off white" and describes Mexicans as a "wedge racial group" in her analysis of the racial status of Mexicans in New Mexico during the nineteenth century.[71] In her study, off-white denotes a racial subordination that comes from being almost White. The phrase "wedge racial group" captures how Mexicans distanced themselves from members of races that were lower on the hierarchy, namely Native and African Americans. In a sense, the racial position of Mexicans functioned as a double-edged sword, cutting down Whiteness while simultaneously cutting away color.

Other scholars regularly use the phrase "becoming White" to describe the racial legal journey of Mexicans in the United States, almost suggesting that Whiteness was available to, or could be achieved by, all Mexicans.[72] Quoting James Baldwin, legal scholar Daniel Aaron Rochmes argues that by asserting Whiteness, Latinés were hiding behind "a curtain of guilt and lies."[73] By limiting his analysis to legal arguments, Rochmes misses out on the evidence that could come from the litigants and community members for whom Whiteness was a foreign and inapplicable concept. This, I argue, is what much of the literature on *Mendez* misses: the assertion of a racial identity and the complexity of color within Mexican communities.

The research is also largely constructed in response to rejection by Whites. For instance, consider Perea's concept of the *pobrecito* syndrome.[74] This syndrome appears in teachers' handbooks that describe Mexican students as "lazy" and "dirty and diseased," and that share stories of instructors who refused pupils' hugs "without first inspecting their hair for lice." In their review of the segregated school system of Oxnard, California, David G. García, Tara J. Yosso, and Frank P. Barajas use excerpts from school board meeting minutes to discuss how school officials identified "the brightest and the best [and cleanest] of the Mexican children" by using class and race markers such as hygiene and skin tone.[75] The authors argue that clean, lighter-skinned Mexican children represented a more resourced group and were therefore, in the eyes of White school administrators, worthy of praise and preferential treatment.

The race literature about Mexicans lacks the counternarratives and construction of "brownness," as well as the coalition-building efforts between various race-based organizations, including the NAACP.[76] The agency and community building that developed within the legal battle for educational equality is understudied, limited, or unreported.[77] Much of the evidence presented comes from handbooks, testimonies, and articles written by Whites about Mexicans, not from the community or people themselves. Furthermore, the literature has not progressed much further than exploring and misinterpreting Whiteness as a legal strategy. Even the *Mendez* plaintiffs and their attorney have been mischaracterized as embracing Whiteness.[78] In chapter 5, a review of the transcripts, letters, and interviews reveals a much more complex story of racialization and provides insight into how the plaintiffs racially characterized themselves.

DEVELOPMENT OF ASIANCRIT

AsianCrit was developed at approximately the same time as LatCrit. Just as LatCrit challenged the Black/White binary, so, too, did AsianCrit. Since both theories were advanced at approximately the same time, several scholars wrote about LatCrit and AsianCrit together to articulate their aligned interests, such as language discrimination, restrictive immigration policies, and exclusion from the U.S. civil rights narrative.[79]

Early scholars of AsianCrit Mari Matsuda, Robert S. Chang, and Angelo N. Ancheta introduced and developed this area of study by examining Japanese American and Hawaiian claims for reparations, immigration and nationalization, treatment of Asian Americans during times of war, and deployment of the model minority myth.[80] In contrast to Asians, African Americans were, generally, involuntary immigrants who were denied reparations, not characterized as "the enemy" during times of war, and constructed in direct opposition to the model minority myth.

Similar to Asians, Latiné communities experience language discrimination, unfair treatment under immigration legislation related to their labor, and a connection to a country outside of the United States. Latinés and Asians both represent culturally diverse nationalities; however, Latinés are largely Spanish speaking, whereas Asians are multilingual, both between and within different groups.[81] Both theories address racial tensions with Black communities. These differences and similarities provide an explanation for the much-needed development of AsianCrit.

AsianCrit scholars have also used civil rights issues and the Fourteenth Amendment as a point of analysis. Much of the scholarship regarding the Fourteenth Amendment centers on citizenship rights and racial classification. To discuss these issues, AsianCrit specialists rely on sociology. Ancheta, for example, embraces racial formation theory as well as the concept of racialization.[82] "The racialization of Asian Americans," he explains, "has taken on two primary forms: racialization as non-Americans and racialization as the model minority."[83] As a case in point, challenges to the "Americanness" of Chinese people in the late 1800s began once it was clear that Chinese miners and railroad workers were going to remain in the United States even after their work was completed.

Because the Chinese were characterized as foreign and presented a threat to labor, courts were reluctant to apply the Fourteenth Amendment, resulting in several unfavorable findings involving Chinese plaintiffs. Also, a series of tax cases and legislation taxed Chinese miners and merchants unequally compared with

White miners and merchants. An example of the type of legislation passed began with the following wording: "an Act to protect Free White Labor against competition with Chinese Coolie Labor, and to Discourage the Immigration of the Chinese into the state of California."[84]

One of the earliest Asian American civil rights cases that came before the Supreme Court, *People v. Hall* (1854) involved the right for Chinese to testify as witnesses in legal proceedings. The court ultimately held that the Chinese, as non-Whites, were similar to African Americans and prevented from testifying against whites.

Like Mexicans, Chinese citizens in the United States enjoyed a certain protection from having a foreign government intervene on their behalf. A Chinese consulate was located in San Francisco, local Presbyterian churches hired a lawyer and former judge to lobby the California state legislature, and treaties were negotiated between the United States and China that declared China a "most favored nation."[85] The "most favored nation" status ended once the Pacific Railroad was completed in 1869 and Chinese workers stayed in the United States. What followed was a series of anti-Chinese laws and ordinances that ultimately resulted in the Chinese Exclusion Act of 1882.[86] As a result, the Chinese found themselves fighting for the right to attend White schools (e.g., *Tape v. Hurley* [1885]) and to be afforded protections under the Fourteenth Amendment (e.g., *Yick Wo v. Hopkins* [1886]).

While this is, admittedly, a brief summary of the history of nineteenth-century discriminatory practices against the Chinese in California,[87] AsianCrit scholars argue that this legacy of discrimination is often concealed by the contemporary myth of the model minority, and reinforces a foreign, monolithic narrative of Asian Americans.[88] Unlike African Americans and Latinés, Asians in America are characterized as a population to whom things happen rather than a community that makes things happen. As Sohyun An explains, AsianCrit scholars want to change the civil rights narrative to include events such as the 1903 Japanese farmworker strike; legal challenges to immigration laws such as *U.S. v. Wong Kim* (1898) and *U.S. v. Singh* (1923); and cases involving Japanese Americans who were unjustly, illegally, and unconstitutionally interned in concentration camps, such as *Hirabayashi v. U.S.* (1943) and *Korematsu v. U.S.* (1944).[89]

AsianCrit researchers write to transform the U.S. narrative of civil rights to be more inclusive of the experiences of different racial and ethnic groups in America. Chang observes, "The discourse on race and the law is not as rich or complete as it might or should be. . . . To focus on the black-white paradigm is to misunderstand the complicated racial situation in the United States. It ignores such things as nativistic racism. It ignores the complexity of a racial hierarchy that has more than just a top and bottom."[90] Most relevant to this project, however, is the AsianCrit work regarding school desegregation efforts. In addition to McClain's and Kuo's research on nineteenth-century discrimination case law in California, historians, ethnic scholars, and journalists have more recently expanded the Black/White binary of segregated schooling to include the experiences of Asian Americans in the South.[91]

This historical data has yet to receive direct sociological treatment. This may be due in part to the small number of cases involving Asian American plaintiffs, as well as the contemporary emphasis on the model minority myth and Asian American achievement.[92] Considering that AsianCrit also purports to value intersectionality, much of the literature is presented through the singular lens of race. As the next section reveals, AsianCrit scholarship is largely dedicated to exploring the placement of Asians within the U.S. racial hierarchy.

MINERS, MODELS, AND MIDDLEMEN: ASIAN AMERICANS AND RACE

The focus of AsianCrit on race, it seems, is twofold: to challenge the construction of Asians as (1) perpetual foreigners who do not belong, and as (2) honorary Whites who are used to demonstrate the failures of other non-White groups to achieve "American success." From research on the "yellow peril," represented by miners and miscegenation,[93] to modern-day members of "the racial bourgeoisie,"[94] the racial identity of Asians has been perhaps the most marked by extremes. Once again, heavy borrowing occurs between CRT intellectuals and sociologists represented in the literature.[95] Combining social science definitions of racialization and law, CRT scholars argue, "The dominant society racializes different minority groups at different times, in response to shifting needs" of the dominant society.[96]

This differential racialization of Asian Americans according to shifting needs is most apparent in the legal treatment and fluctuating favored status of the Chinese. The concept of "yellow peril," for example, has been applied to the Chinese, Japanese, Koreans, and Vietnamese during times of war and perceived economic threat;[97] the Chinese in the 1800s;[98] antimiscegenation laws;[99] and Japanese American concentration camps.[100] The group that represented the yellow peril changed according to the favored status of the home country, as demonstrated in the treatment of Filipinos,[101] Koreans,[102] and South Asians.[103] Fear of labor competition underlying the idea of yellow peril lay behind the 1982 death of Vincent Chin, a Chinese American man murdered by two White men laid off from an auto plant, as well as English-only laws and restrictive immigration laws.

The challenge, however, is that AsianCrit scholarship has characterized yellow peril, forever foreigner, and model minority as separate, historically distinct processes. What I contribute to the literature is to show how within one family, the Tapes, all three characterizations can and do exist, often simultaneously. The siloed way AsianCrit is applied runs the risk of creating even more dichotomies within dichotomies. Furthermore, I add to discussion of race by also considering the role of class. As a wealthy, "Americanized" Chinese American family, the Tapes demonstrate how their class failed to protect them from discrimination but also allowed them to sue the school district, as well as challenge the social norms associated with the Chinese of the late 1800s.

DEVELOPMENT OF TRIBALCRIT

TribalCrit is the most recent addition to CRT and is still developing a scholarly repertoire. While Brayboy generates the nine tenets associated with TribalCrit, he is not the only scholar to explore the intersections of race and law within Indigenous communities.[104] Other scholarly contributions in the area of TribalCrit include Torres and Milun's article on the Mashpee Indians, as well as anthropologist Circe Sturm's work on blood politics within the Cherokee Nation.[105]

A pertinent aspect of TribalCrit is that Native Americans have had a "complicated relationship" with the U.S. federal government.[106] This circumstance adds a layer to traditional CRT, which generally only examines race and racism, not political identity. According to Brayboy, Native Americans occupy a "liminal space" that results in possessing a "joint status as legal/political and racialized beings."[107] TribalCrit also acknowledges the overriding and lasting effects of colonization that disappear with the mythical narrative of "the vanishing Indian."[108] These dual layered identities, he argues, are often oversimplified into a singular racialized status.

Native Americans' political, legal, and racially defined relationships lie at the heart of TribalCrit. Because the political and legal relationship is codified, controlled, and legally defined through the Constitution, treaties, and federal statutes, it sets Native Americans apart from African American, Latiné, and Asian American communities.[109] In essence, according to the government, if you are not federally recognized, you do not exist; your identity is not real. "Federally recognized" is the term most often used when listing tribes. No other racial group in the United States has this federal requirement to be acknowledged.[110] Because of these interlocked political, legal, racial, and social definitions of who is or is not Native American, discussions about these individuals' race is limited. There are social, legal, and racial "tests" of authenticity. There are concerns related to assimilation and loss in the fight of cultural survival. Worse yet, there are no questions at all, and Native Americans are significantly absent from discussions of race in the United States.

AUTHENTICITY, ASSIMILATION, AND ABSENCE:
NATIVE AMERICANS AND RACE

Currently, definitions of who is or is not a "real Indian" vary and are politically, legally, and socially determined. Some individuals who can prove through blood quantum evidence that they are at least one-quarter Native American are issued a Certificate of Degree of Indian Blood (CDIB). Individuals who cannot obtain this document are pejoratively called members of the "Outalucks" or the "Wannabe Tribes."[111] Of course, the blood quantum method of identification is not the only way to be recognized. Each tribe/nation has its own requirements for identification, such as matriarchal lineage, paternal descent, tribal vote, residency, or direct lineage, to name a few.[112] Then there are the social definitions of authenticity, such as language fluency, connections with traditions, and level of assimilation of White settler culture.

Tuhiwai Smith argues that Indigenous identities are regulated by the government to its own benefit rather than that of Native Americans. According to TribalCrit, this is a threat to autonomy and self-determination.[113] Tuhiwai Smith writes, "Legislated identities, which regulated who was an Indian and who was not ... who had the correct fraction of blood quantum, who lived in the regulated spaces of reserves and communities, were all worked out arbitrarily (but systematically), to serve the interests of the colonizing society."[114] There were also legally created rules related to landownership that ultimately led to (1) the "removal" of countless Native Americans from their sacred homes and spaces and (2) the reclamation of lands by the government once a tribe lost its federal recognition. This tenet, Brayboy argues, is a result of White supremacists' definitions of landownership, Manifest Destiny, and the Norman Yoke.[115]

In addition to legislating identities and legally defining landownership, nowhere is the government's intent to wipe out an entire population's history, livelihood, and future more apparent than in educational policy. Brayboy explains: "Education in its many forms is imbued with power: power to control young people's bodies, epistemic engagement, curriculum and teaching; power to best determine how education and schooling are utilized and to what end; power to control what kinds of knowledge is shared—or not—when, and where."[116] The goal of the education system established for American Indians was never to empower but to assimilate. "The history of American Indian Education," Brayboy writes, "can be boiled down to three simple words: Battle for power."[117]

In this battle for power, the development of a scholarly narrative from *within* Indigenous communities is paramount. Yet in reviewing the sociological and legal scholarship on CRT, LatCrit, AsianCrit, and civil rights efforts, what clearly emerges is the *invisibility* of research on Native American education and civil rights efforts. Research on or about Indigenous populations is, comparatively speaking, underrepresented in the sociology of race and ethnicity and in critical race scholarship.[118] This reduced presence therefore results in reduced power and recognition.

Conducting adequate research presents another impediment to producing Indigenous scholarship. There exists a lack of formal archives filled with materials generated from specific Indigenous nations. The formality of archival research leaves little room for collective memory and stories passed from one generation to the next. It also fails to consider history that has been "lost or deliberately erased," as historian Jacqueline Fear-Segal and sociologist Susan D. Rose encountered in researching the thirty-nine-year history of Carlisle Indian schools.[119] Unless methodologies are decolonized and come to accept the oral traditions of Indigenous populations, such investigation will remain a challenge. Therefore, my contribution to this literature is simply to expand on it by analyzing *Piper* through the lens of TribalCrit and identifying its unique contributions to the scholarship on race. This requires telling the story of *Piper* as found in archival material (a.k.a. the paper) and as told by members of Paiute Nation in Owens Valley (a.k.a. the people).

Critical Race Theory Meets Controlling Images

The second part of my theoretical framework requires blending theories related to Patricia Hill Collins's controlling images with Evelyn Higginbotham's concept of the politics of respectability.[120] Together, within these stories of school desegregation, Collins and Higginbotham make it clear that gender, class, and age play just as salient a role in education as race does. In fact, they are inextricably connected. The plaintiffs are more than just Chinese, Paiute, and Mexican American individuals. They are Chinese, Paiute, and Mexican American fathers, mothers, and daughters who, in part because of their middle-class status, generated a sympathetic image that portrayed a sense of worthiness not only within the court of law, but also in the court of public opinion.[121] Change any one of these social characteristics, and a different story emerges. Had poor unmarried mothers whose teenage sons were rejected from attending all-White schools brought the cases, would they have been taken as seriously? Whether or not the choice of plaintiffs was intentional, the fact that the fathers were entrepreneurs married to "homemakers" who brought suit on behalf of their accomplished young daughters was meaningful. It was particularly relevant at a time when the Chinese were excluded, Native

Americans were forcibly assimilated, and Mexican Americans were subject to the Juan Crow policies of California. These similar story lines showcase how the enduring markers of race, gender, and class inequality subsist across different racial groups during historical periods of heightened racial animus.

To explore this meaning, I briefly describe the research related to controlling images. Next, through secondary research, I identify the criminalized, sexualized, and piteous controlling images associated with Chinese American women and girls in the late 1800s, Native American women and girls in the early 1920s, and Mexican American women and girls in the 1940s. Through analysis of primary documents—newspaper articles, interviews, and court transcripts of each case—I demonstrate how, through the politics of respectability, these plaintiffs and their attorneys constructed a counternarrative to the controlling images of their time. While I did not uncover direct evidence that suggests plaintiff selection was legally strategic, the cases' respectability narratives are theoretically and empirically relevant to the study of school desegregation.

The Power and Purpose of Controlling Images

Focusing specifically on Black women, Collins identifies and explains how the controlling images of mammies, matriarchs, jezebels, and welfare queens were used in popular culture to disempower, sexualize, criminalize, and disenfranchise Black women. More insidious than stereotypical, "controlling images are designed to make racism, sexism, poverty, and other forms of social injustice appear to be natural, normal, and inevitable parts of everyday life."[122] I would add that such images also make social injustice appear to be deserved, allowing society to blame the victims for their dire circumstances and immorality. This strips away the sense of worthiness and humanity necessary to confer human rights and basic dignity on individuals.

"Within U.S. culture," Collins explains, "racist and sexist ideologies permeate the social structure to such a degree that they become hegemonic."[123] The strongest way these ideologies disseminate in society is through popular culture by inundating the American imagination with relevant images. As bell hooks argues, popular culture is the "primary pedagogical medium for masses of people globally who want to, in some way, understand the politics of difference."[124] Feminist and critical race scholars have identified other gendered controlling images across all forms of media, including but not limited to advertising,[125] film,[126] comic strips,[127] television, and other forms of communications, but they use the phrases "myths" or "stereotypes" to describe them.

There is debate regarding the difference between "controlling images" and stereotypes. While Collins does not explicitly explain the difference, her phrase considers not only the cultural aspects of representations, but also the power such imagery has in shaping policy, justifying oppression, and generating discriminatory practices. I contend, however, that controlling images and stereotypes are more complementary than interchangeable or divergent. Stereotypes are the historically generated descriptive terminology often dismissed as false representations. Controlling images, however, denote an understanding that such representations, while false, possess a power to shape/influence the social structure that results in very real consequences.

Much of the scholarship on controlling images focuses on the specific challenges they pose to Black women, such as the representations of jezebel, mammy, and welfare mother. Sociologist Tanya Golash-Boza, one of the few scholars to specifically discuss controlling images, examines film and television to demonstrate that controlling images are not only raced, but also gendered and classed. In her book *Race and Racisms*, Golash-Boza identifies the controlling images that are Black, gendered, and classed, including the working-class bad bitch, the bad black mother (BBM), and the thug or gangsta, or Black rapist.[128] Taking her analysis a step further, she identifies the controlling images of the butterfly, dragon lady, and threatening foreigner for Asian Americans; the squaw, princess, and savage for Native Americans; and the hot-blooded Latina, maid, and greaser/bandito for Latinés.[129] While Golash-Boza generates a more inclusive list of controlling images, there is still room to identify even more by adding age to the intersectional analysis.

Collins and Golash-Boza identify gendered and classed images, but neither scholar considers the role of age and the possible controlling images related to Black, Latiné, Native American, and Asian girls. The interdisciplinary field of girlhood studies provides useful guidance for explaining how innocence equates with Whiteness. Similar to scholarship on race, much of the research on girlhood studies examines childhood within literature,[130] zines,[131] film and television,[132] historical international media culture,[133] education,[134] and visual culture.[135] Because girlhood studies is firmly rooted in the Black/White binary, most of the controlling images identified in the literature are confined to Topsy-pickaninny-Sambo caricatures that are constructed against the innocence and respectability of White girlhood, as represented by Little Eva in *Uncle Tom's Cabin* or Shirley Temple. It is this construction of racially opposite girlhood that is germane to this study.

In her study on racial innocence, cultural historian Robin Bernstein provides the most compelling explanation for the purpose of girlhood controlling images. Using decidedly sociological language such as "racial projects," "performance," and

FIGURE I.2.
Eva and Topsy, 1908.
Courtesy "Uncle Tom's
Cabin & American Culture"
(Dr. Steve Railton, emeritus
professor of English,
University of Virginia).

"scripts," Bernstein asserts, "Childhood figured pivotally in a set of large-scale U.S. racial projects. . . . Performance, both on stage and, especially, in everyday life, was the vehicle by which childhood suffused, gave power to, and crucially shaped racial projects. Childhood in performance enabled divergent political positions each to appear natural, inevitable, and therefore justified."[136] Innocence, she explains, is constructed through Whiteness. Quoting from *Uncle Tom's Cabin*, Bernstein captures the opposing positions embodied in Topsy and Little Eva (see Figure 1.2): "There stood the two children, representatives of the two extremes of society. The fair, high-bred child, with her golden head, her deep eyes, her spiritual, noble brow, and prince-like movements; and her black, keen, subtle, cringing, yet acute neighbor. They stood the *representatives of their races.* The Saxon, born of ages of cultivation, command, education, physical and moral eminence; the Afric [*sic*], born of ages of oppression, submission, ignorance, toil, and vice!"[137] She observes that racial girlhood represents a line dividing the worthy from the unworthy and the innocent from the immoral. This analysis provides the language necessary to understand how Mamie, Alice, and Sylvia, as representatives of their race, had to portray a certain innocence that mimics White girlhood notions of beauty, intelligence, and purity.

TABLE 1.3.

Sexualized, Criminalized, and Pathetic Controlling Images of Women and Children

Racial Group	Controlling Images	Time Period
Chinese women and girls	Pagans, prostitutes, and poor creatures	1850–1900
Native American women and girls	Savages, squaws, and sacrificial maidens	1887–1925
Mexican American women and girls	*Mamacita, malinche,* and mentally inferior	1920–1948

TABLE 1.4.

Theoretical Foundations of Controlling Images

Racial Group	Controlling Image	Theoretical Foundation
Chinese American women and girls, late 1800s	Pagan	Takaki, Ronald. *Strangers from a Different Shore: A History of Asian Americans.* Updated and rev. ed. New York: Back Bay Books, 1998.
	Prostitute	Yung, Judy. *Unbound Feet: A Social History of Chinese Women in San Francisco.* Berkeley: University of California Press, 1995. Takaki, Ronald. *A Different Mirror: A History of Multicultural America.* New York: Back Bay Books, 2008.
	Poor creature	Jorae, Wendy Rouse. *The Children of Chinatown: Growing Up Chinese American in San Francisco, 1850–1920.* Chapel Hill: University of North Carolina Press, 2009.
Mexican American women and girls, 1940s	Malinche	Ramirez, Catherine S. *The Woman in the Zoot Suit: Gender, Nationalism and the Cultural Politics of Memory.* Durham, N.C.: Duke University Press, 2009.
	Mamacita	Rodriguez, Clara E., ed. *Latin Looks: Images of Latinas and Latinos in the U.S. Media.* Boulder, Colo.: Westview, 1998. Rodriguez, Clara E. *Heroes, Lovers and Others: The Story of Latinos in Hollywood.* Oxford: Oxford University Press, 2004.
	Mentally inferior	Perea, Juan F. 2004. "Buscando América: Why Integration and Equal Protection Fail to Protect Latinos." *Harvard Law Review* 117, no. 5 (2004): 1420–1469. Sánchez, George J. *Becoming Mexican American: Ethnicity, Culture and Identity in Chicano Los Angeles, 1900–1945.* New York: Oxford University Press, 1993.
Native American women and girls, 1920s	Squaw	Hirschfelder, Arlene, Paulette Fairbanks Molin, and Yvonne Wakim. *American Indian Stereotypes in the World of Children: A Reader and Bibliography.* Lanham, Md.: Scarecrow, 1999.
	Savage	Strong, Pauline Turner. *American Indians and the American Imaginary: Cultural Representations across the Centuries.* Boulder, Colo.: Paradigm, 2013.
	Sacrificial maiden	Marubbio, M. Elise. *Killing the Indian Maiden: Images of Native American Women in Film.* Lexington: University Press of Kentucky, 2006.

The Presence and Pervasiveness of Controlling Images

Examining the secondary research on women and children of color in popular culture reveals more controlling images and affirms their historical roots. In this section, I identify prevailing controlling images that emerge from secondary research on Asian, Native American, and Mexican American women and girls, as well as the historical period relevant to each case. Table 1.3 summarizes the prominent controlling images, and Table 1.4 summarizes the literature from which they emerged.

PAGANS, PROSTITUTES, AND POOR CREATURES

The relevant period for *Tape* is the mid- to late 1800s, as Chinese immigration to the United States increased, giving rise to controlling images of Chinese women and girls as pagans, prostitutes, and poor creatures. The presence of Chinese women in San Francisco was small and limited, as there were only 7 women for every 4,018 men in San Francisco.[138] As Chinese immigrated, their labor transformed from a necessity to a threat.

Probably one of the most powerful images of the Chinese in general is that of the heathen. Decades of anti-Chinese sentiment identified the Chinese as "immoral and diseased heathen, and unassimilable aliens."[139] In 1870, for example, noted American author and poet Bret Harte published a poem in the *Overland Monthly* called "The Heathen Chinese." The poem became so popular, as did the phrase, that the *New York Globe* published it twice.[140] As the image below demonstrates, the Chinese of California were characterized as lazy, drunk, violent, and completely hedonistic (see Figure 1.3).

It is at this intersection of time and space that missionaries expressed their deep commitment to enlightening "heathen" Chinese women. Historian Wendy Rouse Jorae, in her research of children in Chinatown, demonstrates how missionaries frequently "contrast between light and dark, cleanliness and filth, or heathenism and Christianity" in their work.[141] A reformer wrote of visiting a Chinese home,

> Setting aside all feelings of loathsomeness born of the repulsive act of this filth and darkness, I entered upon the task of illuminating a soul of corresponding degradation, speaking to her of God's love, pure air and sunshine, contrasting these with her present surroundings. Each succeeding visit found a growing appreciation of my words, 'till finally she became as thoroughly nauseated with her surroundings as myself. To-day we find her in a cheerful room at 822 DuPont Street, which she has thoroughly cleaned, whitewashed and papered.[142]

Such diary entries reveal that heathen Chinese women, while filthy, savage, and diseased, were nonetheless salvageable and, if trained properly, fully capable of

FIGURE 1.3.
"Let the Chinese Embrace
Civilization and They
May Stay," *Harper's
Weekly*, March 18, 1882.

becoming part of respectable American society. Instead of using the phrase "heathen," I will use the synonym "pagan" to describe this controlling image.[143]

The next most pervasive controlling image is that of the Chinese prostitute. According to historian Ronald Takaki, locals called prostitutes "*lougeui*" ('always hold her legs up') and *baak haak chai* ('hundred men's wife')."[144] In the 1870s, most of the prostitutes were either stolen by a brothel owner or sold by their parents "for as little as $50 and then resold in America for as much as $1,000."[145] Without legal or diplomatic representation, they entered into service contracts with clauses like this one: "If Ah Ho shall be sick for any time for more than ten days, she shall make up by an extra month of service for every ten days' sickness."[146] Due to menstrual cycles, illnesses, or even unwanted pregnancies, such stipulations extended contracts indefinitely.[147] According to historian Judy Yung, Chinese prostitutes were characterized "in books, magazines and newspapers as ... 'reared to a life of shame from infancy' ... [and] ... guilty of disseminating vile diseases capable of destroying 'the very morals, the manhood and health of our [read White] people.'"[148]

The final controlling image most prevalent in the narrative about Chinese women and girls is that of the pathetically poor creature. These figures were called *mui tsai*, which in Cantonese means "little sister."[149] The *mui tsai* were largely responsible for serving the home in any capacity an owner saw fit, including caring for children, cleaning the home, and being "on call" at any time of the day or night.[150] Under a Confucian ideology, these young girls were to be submissive and obedient to their "father at home . . . husband in marriage . . . and eldest son when widowed."[151] Furthermore, because these girls could not carry on the family lineage, they were at risk for being "sold, abandoned, or drowned during desperate times."[152] This fact largely explains why *mui tsai* were mostly little girls. Census data confirms that in 1880, the time closest to the *Tape* trial, many Chinese children in San Francisco were either at home or working as servants, cooks, or gardeners (see Table 1.5).[153]

At this time, the benevolent, maternal missionaries rallied to "rescue" these poor creatures. According to historian Peggy Pascoe, the most powerful image in missionary writings, literature, and reports is that of the "Chinese slave girl."[154]

TABLE 1.5.
Occupations of Chinese Children in San Francisco, 1860–1880

Occupation	1860	1870	1880
At home / none listed	67 (63%)	444 (29%)	708 (48%)
At school	0	21 (1%)	82 (6%)
Servant/cook/gardener	4 (4%)	498 (32%)	322 (22%)
Laundry/washman	1 (1%)	179 (12%)	89 (6%)
Cigar maker	0	188 (12%)	60 (4%)
Clothing manufacturer	1 (1%)	5 (<1%)	52 (4%)
Shoe/slipper factory	0	42 (3%)	23 (2%)
Laborer	20 (19%)	49 (3%)	42 (3%)
Prostitute	0	66 (4%)	33 (2%)
Miscellaneous	13 (12%)	54 (3%)	63 (4%)
TOTAL	106	1,546	1,474

From *The Children of Chinatown: Growing Up Chinese American in San Francisco, 1850–1920*, by Wendy Rouse Jorae, published by the University of North Carolina Press, © 2009, www.uncpress.org. Used by permission of the publisher.

Missionary women answering the call to rescue young girls sold into domestic service capitalized on this portrayal. Determined to interrupt the "hateful practice of buying and selling their [Chinese] women like so much merchandise," missionaries often made these girls the target of their rescue operations.[155]

The controlling images of the pagan, the prostitute, and the poor creature represent two distinct and extreme representations of Chinese women and girls. Chinese women are sexualized and criminalized, while Chinese girls are infantilized. In chapter 3, you will find that Mamie Tape, as the lead plaintiff of *Tape v. Hurley*, was neither. Instead, she occupied a respectable position where she was too young to be a sexual object or a hardened criminal and too wealthy to be a poor creature.

SAVAGES, SQUAWS, AND SACRIFICIAL MAIDENS

The relevant period for the *Piper* case is from 1887 to 1924, when the controlling images of Native American women included savages, squaws, and sacrificial maidens.[156] These years were marked by two significant and related events relevant to this case: the Dawes Act of 1887 and the creation, implementation, and subsequent failure of Indian boarding schools. All of these efforts were ultimately made to assimilate, dissolve, or destroy tribal nations and transform Native Americans into "American" citizens.[157]

In considering this change in U.S./tribal educational policy, one must also consider the cultural climate in which such programs were generated and transformed. Due in large part to the interdisciplinary field of Native American studies, new scholarship has emerged on cultural representations of Native Americans, ranging from children's toys to films. These kinds of portrayals provide insight into the "relationship between media content and cultural schemas."[158] Furthermore, "exploring the cultural continuities and changes that are an intricate part of critical periods in history furthers our understanding of the interconnections between symbolic and social relations."[159] A review of the literature on cultural production of Native American imagery allows us to consider the social relations that emerge in the struggle for educational equality.

Much of the scholarship on stereotypical representations of Native Americans assumes the figure in question is male.[160] Nevertheless, there are a number of studies that focus specifically on women and children. In *Killing the Indian Maiden*, women's studies scholar M. Elise Marubbio analyzes over thirty-four films in which Native American women appear.[161] While she names a variety of "types," including the squaw, the hag, the celluloid princess, and the sexualized maiden, her analysis of thirteen films made between 1908 and 1931 is devoted to Native women depicting "the helper" and "the lover." Marubbio observes that both portrayals are "innocent, attached to an exotic culture, and linked to ritual and the American landscape; she [the helper or the lover] yearns for the white hero or western European culture; and she sacrifices herself to preserve whiteness from racial contamination."[162] These representations symbolize both "the possible merging of the two [cultures] and the differences between them."[163] The main difference between the two, Marubbio explains, is that the helper figure is usually killed, while the lover figure takes her own life.

Helper films such as *The Broken Doll* (1910), *Red Wing's Gratitude* (1909), and *Iola's Promise* (1912) set up a savage/civilized dichotomy in which a White settler or settlers help an Indian maiden who is abused by her tribal family. In return for their kindness, the helper warns the benevolent Whites of an impending attack at the hands of her tribe. Her reward for this act of heroism is death. In the ensuing melee, she is tragically killed, usually by her own kind. "The sympathy created for the Indian girl . . . reinforces how very dangerous Indians are to each other and, by extension, to whites."[164]

Lover films, on the other hand, seem to follow the story established by playwright Edwin Milton Royle in *The Squaw Man*. The play opened in New York in 1905, became a national touring show in 1906, and returned to Broadway in 1907 and 1908.[165] Cecil B. DeMille adapted the plotline in three feature-length films. Marubbio summarizes one of them, *The Kentuckian: Story of a Squaw's Devotion and Sacrifice* (1908) as follows:

> The text tells us "Ward Fatherly is the son of a wealthy and indulgent Kentuckian" who finds himself in trouble for killing a man in a duel. He escapes to the "Western frontier, whither he has gone incog, working as a miner." Here he meets a young Indian girl, who rescues him when "a couple of low-down Redskins" knife him. "She drags the wounded Kentuckian to her tipi and nurses him back to health. *The inevitable happens*—they are married. A lapse of several years occurs and we find the little family—the Kentuckian, his Squaw, and a little son—living in blissful peace." A friend arrives to give Ward the news that he has inherited his father's estate and must return immediately to the East. "He feels, on the one hand, that he cannot take his Squaw back and introduce her into society of his set, and on the other, he knows it would break her heart to leave her. No, no. He must give up all and stay where he is. . . . The Squaw realizes the situation. She must, for her love for him, make the sacrifice, which she does by sending a bullet through her brain, thus leaving the way clear for him—a woman's devotion for the man she loves."[166]

While the reasons differ, in all three films the "Indian girl" kills herself to set her lover free and give her mixed-race child the chance to live in "civilized" society. These films identify the emotional, physical, and cultural price to be paid when social boundaries are crossed. Only the death of the Native character resolves the problem and restores racial order.

It is also important to remember that these films were made during great pol-

icy changes regarding Indian schools. At the time, "federal Indian policy maintained a distinct paternalistic attitude toward Native Americans, who were lagging
in the evolutionary march from savagery to a more civilized state."[167] These kinds
of films highlighted the miserable failure of the assimilationist policy of the federal government. Furthermore, these movies celebrated "a mythic paradigm of the
frontier West."[168] Within this myth, "the Celluloid Princess stands metonymically
for Native American acquiescence to the sovereignty of the United States . . . and
her death [represents] an unavoidable consequence of western expansion and
conquest."[169]

Scholars have also found a wealth of information in children's picture books.
Mary Gloyne Byler, a member of the Eastern Band of Cherokee Indians of North
Carolina, analyzed six hundred books for young readers that were specifically
about Native Americans.[170] While I have yet to find her original research, Byler's
introductory remarks are often reprinted in scholarly analysis about Native representations in juvenile literature.[171] Her critique gives me an idea of the kinds of
types reflected in children's books. She concludes,

> There are too many children's books about American Indians. There are too many
> books featuring painted, whooping, befeathered Indians closing in on too many forts,
> maliciously attacking "peaceful" settlers or simply leering menacingly from the back-
> ground; too many books in which white benevolence is the only thing that saves the
> day for the incompetent, childlike Indian. . . . Non-Indian writers have created an im-
> age of the American Indian that is almost sheer fantasy . . . sustaining the illusion that
> the original inhabitants deserved to lose their land because they were so barbaric and
> uncivilized.[172]

Finally, the diaries, photography, and newspaper accounts of the children of
Carlisle Indian School provide yet another form of cultural object to identify
controlling images. As previously explained, beginning in the late 1800s and into
the early 1920s, the renowned Carlisle Indian Industrial School in Pennsylvania
spurred the growth of industrial schools around the country. These institutions
were dedicated to developing an Indian women's education program that corre-
sponded with the overall mission of Indian schools. Many of the students were
young Indian girls who were taken from their homes and families on the reservation, placed with White families, housed in boarding dorms, and taught to become good homemakers to help their future husbands fully assimilate.[173] This
transformation from "savage to civility" was captured in a series of famous before-
and-after photographs (see Figures 1.4 & 1.5).

In her reading of these famous photographs, visual arts scholar Laura Wexler outlines how the school successfully transformed its "Native girls" into imitations of middle-class White women. Wexler describes how "the spontaneous and

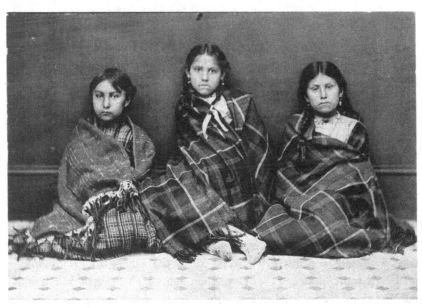

FIGURE I.4.
Carrie Anderson, Annie Dawson, and Sarah Walker on arrival at Hampton, Va., 1872.
Courtesy of the Peabody Museum of Archaeology and Ethnology, Harvard University,
2004.29.5634.

FIGURE I.5.
Same girls fourteen
months later, 1872.
Courtesy of the Peabody
Museum of Archaeology
and Ethnology, Harvard
University, 2004.29.5635.

revealing postures of the first image are long gone . . . overridden by the impera-
tive to dress up the Indian children in White children's outfits, place their hands
upon White children's games, set their limbs at White children's customary an-
gles . . . [creating replicas] of the ideal image of Victorian girlhood."[174]

In their book on a girls' basketball team from the Fort Shaw Indian School,
Linda Peavy and Ursula Smith provide numerous accounts of the public's fascination with young Indian girls.[175] Contemporary descriptions of the girls are mythical, almost reverent, and definitely pleased with the "progress" these formerly
savage youths demonstrated under the guidance of White caretakers. In observing the players' schoolwork, a journalist for the local newspaper noted, "[It was]
a great surprise to those . . . who have been more used to thinking [of] the Indian
and the scalping knife than . . . of the Indian and the slate and pencil."[176] While
these young girls were in a very different part of the country from Alice Piper, it
is telling that they possessed the heavy responsibility of changing the minds of the
public. One display of academic excellence, it seems, was enough to transform
these young savages to schoolgirls.

While these young Native basketball players demonstrated that it was possible to be "civilized," they were also allowed to be celebrated and even desirable.
Under a headline that touted a game as "White Girls against Reds," another local reporter wrote, "What . . . may be said [about] a team of Indian girls?"[177] He
went on to describe the athletes as "strong and lithe" as well as "comely," predict-
ing, "A great number of white boys will cheer for the dark-complexioned maidens," a combination of "half-breeds" and "full-blooded" Indians.[178] It seems the
young women's complexion and blood status were important, perhaps explaining
why White boys would applaud. Interracial interactions between White men and
Indian women were commonplace and even normal.[179] Young White boys could
cheer on Indian maidens, but would they be encouraged to support mulattos,
mestizos, or Mongolians?

More recently, Fear-Segal and Rose have invited readers to experience intimate,
sometimes painful firsthand accounts of life with the Carlisle Indian School.[180] In
describing the Carlisle school, Scott Momaday writes, "It is a kind of mythic memory in the American mind. Perhaps it is an extension of the Wild West, which is so
gaudy and predictable in the dime novels and stock Hollywood films. The crucial
difference, of course, is that the Indians who take the field are not fabled warriors
like . . . Sitting Bull. They are children."[181] To save this "savage race," the philosophy was to begin the assimilation progress early and educate children about respectability as represented by Whiteness. In one account after another, Fear-Segal
and Rose capture the singular failure this experiment represented when it came
to America's policy toward Indigenous people. This was the fiasco that preceded

Piper. Attorneys for the Native American Legal Rights Fund (NARF) described the impact of these boarding schools in the following manner:

> Cut off from their families and culture, the children were punished for speaking their Native languages, banned from conducting traditional or cultural practices, shorn of traditional clothing and identity of their Native cultures, taught that their cultures and traditions were evil and sinful, and that they should be ashamed of being Native American.... They returned to their communities ... as deeply scarred humans lacking the skills, community, parenting, extended family language and cultural practices of those raised in their cultural context.[182]

The closure of Indian boarding and industrial schools left behind children who represented proverbial sacrificial lambs, stripped of their innocence and culture for the so-called greater good.

Like the helper and lover images in Hollywood films, these young girls represent the sacrifice White society required for them to be deemed acceptable, worthy, and pure. However, instead of sacrificing themselves through tragic death or suicide, these young girls were required to sacrifice their families, homes, and customs in order to "kill" their tribal identity and affiliations for the promise of equal opportunity. Photographs, newspaper accounts, and Indigenous reclamations provide examples of the Native American struggle for legitimacy in the eyes of White America. These young women represent a fraction of the thousands of Indian children who tried, but ultimately "failed," to adopt the norms, values, beliefs, and definitions of "civilized" society.[183] In chapter 4, I explain that these experiences provide insight into the low expectations for Indian children's educational achievement and high expectations for their assimilation and denial of their Indigenous heritage and identities, providing important insight into the relevance of *Piper.*

MAMACITAS, MALINCHES, AND MENTALLY INFERIOR

The relevant period for *Mendez* is from the late 1920s to 1948. Massive immigration from Mexico and major changes in United States–Mexico relations involving the Mexican repatriation efforts of 1929–1930, the 1939 Good Neighbor Policy, and the Bracero Program of 1942 characterize these years. Mexican Americans' high levels of participation in World War II also mark this era. Furthermore, two significant events dominate Los Angeles newspapers just before the *Mendez* trial: the 1942 criminal trial of *People v. Zamora,* also known as the "Sleepy Lagoon murder case," and the infamous 1943 Zoot Suit Riots.

As for Mexican American women and girls from the 1920s to 1940s, I rely on the analysis of women's studies, American studies, and Chicano studies scholars and historians to identify and describe the *mamacita*, *malinche*, and mentally inferior controlling images. As with Chinese women and girls, scholarship shows how Mexican women and girls were racially othered with sexualized, criminalized, and infantilized controlling images.

The first and probably most well-known controlling image is that of the "spicy senorita," or the *mamacita*. Sociologist Clara Rodriguez explains Hollywood's hunger for this figure in her review of Latinos in film and one Mexican actress in particular: Lupe Vélez.[184] Because Vélez was bilingual, she was one of the few Mexican actresses able to cross over into American films in the 1940s as the industry moved from silent movies to "talkies."

A comedic actress, Vélez played a character that spoke in highly exaggerated, broken English and was prone to fits, temper tantrums, and frequent outbursts in Spanish. The press described her as "just a Mexican wild kitten."[185] A simple review of the titles of her films demonstrates the popularity of Vélez's *mamacita* persona: *The Girl from Mexico* (1939), *Mexican Spitfire* (1940), *Mexican Spitfire out West* (1940), *Mexican Spitfire's Baby* (1941), *Playmates* (1941), *Mexican Spitfire at Sea* (1942), *Mexican Spitfire Sees a Ghost* (1942), *Mexican Spitfire's Elephant* (1942), and *Mexican Spitfire's Blessed Event* (1943). Her character, Carmelita, was a "hot-blooded, south-of-the-border Latina" and a "feisty, in-your-face hot tamale, defiant of traditional conventions and seemingly independent of male and industry controls."[186]

The next controlling image is that of the *pachuca* or the *malinche*. In Mexican folklore, *La Malinche* was an Indigenous woman who helped the Spanish conquer Mexico by serving as translator to Spanish conquistador Hernán Cortés and offering her body as the vessel for creating a new mestizo (mixed) race. The term *malinche* refers to troublemakers, race traitors, and temptresses. Historian Catherine Ramirez identifies the 1940s zoot suit–wearing *pachucas* of Los Angeles as the modern-day *malinches*.[187]

In 1940s Los Angeles, the public was very familiar with the zoot suit because of the 1942 Sleepy Lagoon murder case and the 1943 Zoot Suit Riots. In a time when the country was rationing heavily for the war, the zoot suit was considered excessive, indulgent, and unpatriotic. *Pachucas*, female zoot-suiters, were also subject to public scrutiny. They were not only criminalized but also highly sexualized by the White and Mexican press. The *pachucas'* general look involved tight-fitted clothing, ratted bouffant hair, and heavy makeup with dark lipstick. As Ramirez explains, "They appeared to betray middle-class definitions of feminine beauty and decorum."[188] The women were also undesirable within the Mexican community. In an article from the local Spanish-language newspaper, *La Opinión*, a writer reported, "*Las malinches* wore *'falda negra y muy corta'* [very short black skirts], that they painted their faces—in particular their lips and eyes—*'en una manera escan-*

dalosa' [in a scandalous manner] and that they punctuated their racy ensembles with a bushy head of matted hair soaked in grease."[189] What the newspaper described was the fact that the controlling image of the *malinche* violated the politics of respectability among Whites *and* Mexicans.

The final controlling image, and the most damaging one to the pursuit of educational desegregation, is that of the mentally inferior Mexican child. This image dominated the discourse on education in the 1940s. Juan Perea explains how teachers used genetic determinism to conclude that Mexican American children are less intelligent than White children. He calls this the *pobrecito* syndrome, writing, "Mexican American students are considered to have low intelligence and inferior academic potential, as measured by 'intelligence tests' of questionable validity."[190] He further demonstrates how the mentally inferior stereotype continues to manifest even today: "Current research demonstrates that Latino students continue to be tracked toward vocational and technical courses . . . [and] are systematically overrepresented in classes for the educable mentally retarded."[191]

The supposed mental inferiority of Mexican children also arose from a perceived lack of cleanliness (i.e., the dirty Mexican stereotype). Historian George Sánchez describes the reasoning behind the dirty Mexican stereotype as written in a 1929 manual called *Americanization through Homemaking*: "Sanitary, hygienic, and dietetic measures are not easily learned by the Mexican. His [*sic*] philosophy of life flows along the lines of least resistance and it requires far less exertion to remain dirty than to clean up."[192] Perea also describes how the persistence of these attitudes even years after *Mendez*, stating, "Many Anglo teachers and parents advocated for mandatory baths for 'dirty Mexican kids because it will teach them how it feels to be clean.'"[193]

Like the controlling images of Chinese American women, and girls, the *mamacita, malinche*, and *mentally inferior* figures are also sexualized, criminalized, and pitiable. Applying these images to *Tape, Piper*, and *Mendez* reveals the way the families involved in the cases contradicted the conventions of their time, particularly when you add class to the analysis. Therefore, these plaintiffs throw into question the observation by Toni Morrison that "definitions belong to the definers, not the defined." In these cases, it appears that the families and their attorneys, by adhering to the politics of respectability, might have exercised a limited form of agency in projecting their public personas.

Fighting Fathers, Missing Mothers, and Pretty Little Plaintiffs

Situating the Tape, Piper, and Mendez families within the proper sociological context requires a foray beyond poverty and pity into middle-classness and the intersectional politics of respectability. For example, we learn from *Brown* that gender and class mattered. For years, the explanation for selecting Oliver Brown as the lead plaintiff was that the decision was alphabetical. If that were the case, then *Briggs*, *Belton*, or *Bolling* would have been the lead case. *Briggs*, however, involved young Harry Briggs Jr. and his working-class parents who were forced to move to Florida as a result of racial intimidation. *Belton* comprised two cases brought forth by two mothers, Ethel Louise Belton and Sarah Bulah, on behalf of their daughters. *Bolling* was also brought by a mother, Sarah Bolling, on behalf of her junior high school–aged son Spotswood Bolling Jr. In an interview, Linda Brown recalled that her father was selected because he was the only man among the plaintiffs, as well as a minister, thus serving the politics of respectability.[194] These gender and class dynamics in *Brown* guide my reading of the role of gender, race, age, and class in *Tape*, *Piper*, and *Mendez* with regard to not only the lead plaintiffs, but also their parents.

The fathers in *Tape* and *Mendez* were consistently highlighted in historical accounts of the cases. Joseph Tape was prominently featured in the *Daily California Alta*. Even though he played a critical role in building the suit and testifying in court, Gonzalo Mendez was always identified in the newspapers as one of five fathers involved in the proceedings. However, Pike, the father in *Piper*, was not as prominent in newspaper accounts of the case. Nevertheless, the three fathers' presence in the media and role in the court cases might simply have been the result of an already patriarchal society where men were legally recognized as "the head of the household." Yet the prevailing controlling images for men of color were rarely that respectful. Mexican, Chinese, and Indigenous men were characterized as violent, sexualized, emasculating, or savage.[195] In these legal cases, they were cast in the much more relatable masculine role of the protective, loving father. Class played an unspoken role, however. Joseph Tape's, Gonzalo Mendez's, and Pike Piper's socioeconomic status transformed them into protective, loving, *middle-class* fathers defending their daughters.

Where are the mothers in this story line? Historically, mothers have been and continue to be critical, often tragic figures in social justice narratives. Their images are permanently etched in historical memory. Mamie Till wailing over the casket of her murdered son Emmett. A widowed Coretta Scott King sitting in a pew and comforting a young Bernice. An utterly despondent Lily Chen being shuffled out of a courthouse where the murderers of her only child, Vincent, received an insultingly light sentence—a $3,000 fine and three years of probation. An inconsolable Luz Salazar barely able to stand by Ruben's casket after his death at the hands of the Los Angeles during the National Chicano Moratorium March. Collectively, these mourning mothers became the reluctant reminders of the consequences of racial hatred. They transformed their tragedies into movements.

In school desegregation cases, though, the mothers are decidedly missing. Leola Brown appeared in a public family photograph, but she was never quoted in a newspaper or photographed with Linda. In fact, the public did not hear from Leola Brown Montgomery until the sixtieth anniversary of the case during an interview with Linda Brown.[196] Similarly, Mary Tape, Annie Piper, and Felícitas Mendez were relegated to a behind-the-scenes supportive role when their contributions were just as valuable to the success of their cases. They wrote letters, organized families, worked tirelessly, and launched movements. In the meantime, their daughters, Mamie, Alice, and Sylvia, occupied a harsh spotlight as central characters in their very public legal proceedings. Exploring the role of these fathers, mothers, and daughters reveals a significant shortcoming in the scholarship of school desegregation: the lack of an intersectional analysis. Deploying an intersectional approach deepens our analysis of the theater behind the school desegregation movement. The marked presence of the fathers, the absence of the mothers, and the impermeable innocence of the lead plaintiffs all contributed to an elaborate performance of respectability.

The fathers were cast as men who fought for the rights of their little girls. Mothers were conspicuously absent. I argue that it is not coincidental that the lead plaintiff in each case was a little girl. In all the proceedings, younger boys were available to serve as lead plaintiffs. There was Frank for Mamie, and Gonzalo for Sylvia. Alice was the only girl out of the original seven plaintiffs in her case. If, theoretically, youth could evoke more sympathy, then why were these boys overlooked? I suggest that the thought of little Mexican, Indigenous, and Chinese boys sitting next to little White girls stoked the very public horror over racial mixing. Young girls were less threatening, perhaps innocent, and definitely not as dangerous. The Tape, Piper, and Mendez daughters were Americanized replicas of racial innocents who could be rescued from immorality and inferiority. Newspapers, interviews, and transcripts concerning *Tape* and *Mendez* yielded the most information on the families. Though a few articles were published about *Piper*, those reporters discussed the case in a very general way and unfortunately omitted the description necessary to ascertain how Pike, Annie, and Alice Piper were perceived by the public.[197] Still, the *Piper* opinion and photographs of Alice Piper later in her life are very telling, providing some material about the family generally and Alice specifically.

What my research demonstrates is a pattern of criminal and sexual controlling images for women and pathetic, inferior, and victimized controlling images for girls. In exploring "patterns of representation and modes of portrayal across gender, age, [and racial] groups," I follow research similar to that of sociologists Ashley Mears, Shyon Baumann, and Kim de Laat.[198] This effort helps race and civil rights scholars consider the "cultural continuities and changes that are an intricate part of critical periods in history [that] further our understanding of the interconnections between symbolic and social relations."[199] Within chapters 3 through 5, I demonstrate where and how these images were used in and around the cases. More importantly, I show how, through the display of middle-class respectability and youthful innocence, the plaintiffs and families were able to sustain a respectable position between the problematic and the pathetic racialized, gendered, and "low-class" imagery. With the theoretical scaffolding of Critical Race Theory, its branches, and controlling images firmly in place, I can outline the book's structure.

CHAPTER 2

The 105 Bricks before *Brown*

> School houses do not teach themselves— piles of brick and
> mortar and machinery do not send out men. It is the trained,
> living human soul, cultivated and strengthened by long study
> and thought, that breathes the real breath of life into boys
> and girls and makes them human, whether they be black or
> white, Greek, Russian or American.
>
> —W. E. B. DUBOIS

In the acclaimed documentary *The Road to "Brown,"* director and writer William
Elwood recounts the celebrated tale of how Charles Houston, chief counsel of
the NAACP, worked tirelessly and strategically to dismantle school segregation
and Jim Crow practices. Understandably, the documentary focuses exclusively on
Plessy v. Ferguson and the Jim Crow South. However, in the spirit of recognizing what historians call the "long civil rights movement," the proverbial road to
Brown begins long before the storied 1950s.[1] In addition to those cases studied by
legal scholars, historians, and education experts, there are at least 105 others reported in either state supreme courts or federal appellate courts.[2] This chapter offers a historical and legal review of the various attempts to dismantle the practice
of "separate but equal" since 1849. These cases demonstrate that the road to *Brown*
was long, anfractuous, determined, and, most importantly, paved with the multiracial contributions of at least eleven lawsuits involving Chinese American, Native
American, and Mexican American plaintiffs, inclusive of *Tape*, *Piper*, and *Mendez*.

The overall goals of this chapter are three-fold. First, I provide a brief social
history of the growth and development of the common school and explain when,
where, and how it departed from its egalitarian roots and split into two racially

defined paths marred by segregation beginning in 1849. Second, I demonstrate that the legal fight for educational equality began before the 1950s, existed beyond the South, and was not limited to the Black/White racial binary by providing descriptive statistics and geographical locations of cases filed before *Brown*. Third, I identify all the cases involving Mexican, Chinese, and Indigenous plaintiffs to show why *Tape*, *Piper*, and *Mendez* are ideal for study. While my research reveals over 105 cases, all of which deserve further analysis in their own rights, describing the facts, analyzing the strategies, and surmising the significance of all of them is beyond the scope of this analysis. Nevertheless, in identifying these lawsuits, I enthusiastically yet unknowingly welcomed an entire area of study.

The Legal and Historical Beginnings of "Separate but Equal"

The creation of the common school in the 1830s marked the beginning of the struggle for educational equality. Tied to the country's economic development, the U.S. early education system was deeply interconnected to labor needs. The result was an education that was either agrarian in nature and designed to teach children to take over the family farm, or rooted in apprenticeships to learn a trade. The growth of wage labor and an increase in foreign trade and investment steadily drove out the small business owners and independent farmers. "In 1820, for every person working in manufacturing and distribution, there were six people engaged in agriculture; by 1860, this figure had fallen to three."[3] Furthermore, from 1846 to 1856, over 3.1 million mostly Irish immigrants arrived in the United States with little to offer but their labor.[4] As a unit of production, the family was replaced with manufacturing largely related to the textiles and shoe industries.

The largest company in the United States, Merrimack Manufacturing of Lowell, Massachusetts, was perhaps the most influential force in the creation of mass public education. Eager to establish a school system, firm owner Kirk Boott invited young minister Theodore Edson to move to Lowell and start a school.[5] A central school board was created comprised mostly of businessmen and professionals, the academic year was lengthened, sequential grades were created, and school attendance became compulsory. At the state level, a board of education was formed in 1837 and was led by Horace Mann, the father of common schools. In Mann's mind, education in Massachusetts would know "no distinction of rich and poor, of bond and free." He said of the school system, "Without money and without price, it throws open its doors and spread the table of its bounty, for all the children of the State."[6] It was a vision of the common school rendered by political cartoonist Thomas Nast in 1870 and depicting children of every race and culture holding hands (see Figure 2.1).

FIGURE 2.1.
"Our Common Schools
as They Are and as
They May Be," *Harper's
Weekly*, February 1870.

Common schools, then, spread across the country. Wherever there were large amounts of wage labor, a common school would inevitably follow. Simultaneously, the persistence of slavery generated the Abolitionist Movement and developed a growing community of free Blacks in the North.[7] While the vision for the common school was that it be a space where all children were welcomed and educated, African Americans were routinely marginalized and excluded. Northern and midwestern states established separate schools for Black children that were often underfunded, ill equipped, and overlooked.[8] According to historian Ronald Takaki, an individual observed, "The colored people are ... charged with want of desire for education and improvement, yet, if a colored man comes to the door of our institutions of learning, with desires ever so strong, the lords of these institutions rise up and shut the door."[9]

This history explains why the first school desegregation case is *Roberts v. Boston* in 1849, marking the beginning of the legal journey to *Brown*. This seems fitting particularly since the first common school originated in Massachusetts.[10] On behalf of his daughter Sarah, Benjamin F. Roberts filed a lawsuit against the city of Boston in 1849 for violating an ordinance that stated, "Every member of the [district] committee shall admit to his school, all applicants, of suitable age and qualifications, residing nearest to the school under his charge, (except those for whom *special provision* has been made,) provided the number in his school will warrant the admission."[11] Similar to today, schools were established and managed by districts. The *Roberts* opinion declared, "For half a century, separate schools have been kept in Boston for colored children and the primary school for colored children in Belknap street was established in 1820." According to the opinion, the schools for Black children were more than 2,100 feet from Sarah Roberts's residence. To attend that school, she would have passed five White schools along the way. Roberts applied to a White school "nearest her residence" and was rejected four times.[12]

Using the "special provision" language of the ordinance, the school committee refused her admission on the "ground of her being a colored person." Committee members successfully argued that the distance from Sarah Roberts's home to Belknap Street was an inconsequential issue, and that admitting her to any school satisfied the requirements of the law. More importantly, they also argued, "The teachers of this [colored] school have the same compensation and qualifications as in other schools in the city."[13] This case was, in essence, precursor and precedent for *Plessy* and the separate but equal doctrine.

Despite famed attorney Charles Sumner's impassioned plea that "prejudice is the child of ignorance. It is sure to prevail, where people do not know each other," Chief Justice Shaw remained unconvinced.[14] In his opinion, he upheld the decision of the school district. However, he prophetically wrote, "It is urged, that this maintenance of separate schools tends to deepen and perpetuate the odious distinction of caste, founded in deep-rooted prejudice in public opinion. This prejudice, *if it exists*, is not created by law, and probably cannot be changed by the law."[15] And so began the legal struggle to prove Shaw wrong. *Roberts* represents a haunting foreshadowing because the legal arguments used against Sarah Roberts would be viciously recycled over one hundred years later to deny the same rights to Linda Brown. The legal fight for educational equality began with an abolitionist and his daughter and ended with an activist and his daughter.

From *Roberts* to *Plessy* (1849–1896)

Between *Roberts* and *Plessy*, at least twenty-five lawsuits were filed throughout the country, spreading through the Midwest (Ohio, Iowa, Michigan, Indiana, and Kansas) to the West (Nevada and California) and eventually the South (Louisi-

TABLE 2.1.
Pre-*Plessy* (1896) School Desegregation Cases

Case	Year	Race	Gender	State	School	Result
Roberts v. Boston	1849	B	F	Mass.	Common	L
van Camp v. Board of Education	1859	B	M	Ohio	Common	L
Clark v. Board	1868	B	F	Iowa	Elementary	W
Workman v. Board of Education of Detroit	1869	B	M	Mich.	Elementary	W
Garnes v. McCann	1871	B	B	Ohio	Common	L
Stoutmeyer v. Duffy	1872	B	M	Nev.	Common	L
Ward v. Flood	1874	B	F	Calif.	Common	L
Corey v. Carter	1874	B	B	Ind.	Common	L
Dove v. Independent School District	1875	B	M	Iowa	Elementary	W
Smith v. Keokuk	1875	B	M	Iowa	High School	W
Lewis v. Board	1876	B	B	Ohio	Intermediate	L
Bertonneau v. Board	1878	B	B	La.	Common	L
Board of Education v. Tinnon	1881	B	M	Kans.	Common	W
Longress v. Board	1882	B	B	Ill.	Common	W
King v. Gallagher	1883	B	F	N.Y.	Common	L
Mitchell v. Gray	1884	B	M	Ind.	Common	L
Tape v. Hurley	1885	A	F	Calif.	Elementary	W
People v. McFall	1886	B	B	Ill.	Elementary	L
Peair v. Board	1889	B	B	Ill.	High School	W
Wysinger v. Crookshank	1890	B	M	Calif.	Elementary	W
McMillan v. School Committee District	1890	N	B	N.C.	Common	W
Knox v. Board	1891	B	F	Kans.	Elementary	W
Lehew v. Brummell	1891	B	B	Mo.	Common	L
Hare v. Board	1893	B	M	N.C.	Common	L
Martin v. Board of Education	1896	B	B	W.Va.	Common	L

ana and North Carolina) with mixed and inconsistent results. Some cases were won but most were lost (Table 2.1).[16] Furthermore, a "win" did not imply victory against school segregation because a victory in court did not necessarily translate to legislative support.

These cases also exposed the deep racial divides across the country and revealed that the dichotomous view of North/South as progressive/conservative on issues of race reflected an oversimplified narrative. While Iowa, Michigan, Kansas, and Illinois consistently sided with plaintiffs in school desegregation cases, New York, Massachusetts, Ohio, Indiana, and Missouri planted their loyalties with school boards that advanced a separate but equal doctrine. In fact, the first southern case did not emerge until 1878, almost thirty years after *Roberts* and fifteen years after the passage of the Thirteenth and Fourteenth Amendments.

This racial divide is best captured by Iowa and Ohio, states representing both sides of the ideological spectrum. In Iowa, three separate school districts attempted to maintain segregated schooling and were denied before the passage of the Fourteenth Amendment, after the passage of the Fourteenth Amendment, and at the elementary and high school levels. Those cases were, respectively, *Clark v. Board* (1868), *Dove v. Independent* (1875), and *Smith v. Keokuk* (1875). *Clark* tested the newly passed state constitution that allowed for "equal common school privileges to all."[17] The state supreme court went to great lengths to describe Iowa's evolution of school law from "the dark phase" that required "total exclusion of colored children." The justices ultimately held, "All the youths are equal before the law, and there is no discretion vested in the board of directors or elsewhere, to interfere with or disturb that equality."[18]

A few short years later in 1875, *Dove* and *Smith* were filed by the same attorneys to expose a ploy at the elementary and high school levels. In both cases, the school districts attempted to keep Black children out of White schools on the basis that there was "no room." At this point, they made an argument based on space rather than race. However, the administrators in *Smith* insisted on discussing race, arguing in over thirty pages, "The citizens of the city and district are opposed to mixed schools, and to admit colored pupils with the white would destroy the harmony and impair the usefulness of the high school."[19] In comparison, the court's opinion was only a paragraph long, citing *Clark* and holding that the plaintiff could not be excluded because of his color.

Ohio, on the other hand, made it quite clear before and after the passage of the Fourteenth Amendment that all schools could, should, and would be racially segregated. The three Ohio cases were *Van Camp v. Board* (1859), *Garnes v. McCann* (1871), and *Lewis v. Board* (1876). In *Van Camp*, the plaintiff's father alleged that because he was only one-half African, two of his children were less than three-eighths African and therefore eligible to attend the local White school. The court first ruled that the rules of blood quantum were about "classification and not exclusion" designed to distinguish children who possessed "any visible taint of African blood."[20] Eleven years later, after the adoption of the Fourteenth Amendment, another attempt at legal action in the state concerned a father who tried to send his children to a White school closest to their home. The court found that a "joint district for the education of colored children" was created to accommodate colored children living in the White district. Because the court found that "no substantial inequality of school privileges" existed between the schools, the creation of and requirements for a "colored" school did not violate the Equal Protection Clause.[21]

Five years later, a Black father made application for his children to attend the White intermediate school closest to their home, arguing that they had to walk four miles past schools that that were closer to their home to attend the school for "colored children." The state supreme court of Ohio made its support for segregated education abundantly clear: "It is not possible for all the children to live in one spot, so as to place them all equally distant from the school. They cannot all live on a circle having the school-house in the center."[22] The state did not integrate schools until the enactment of the Ohio Civil Rights Act of 1959, five years after *Brown*.

While I am unsure of what made Iowa such a legally progressive state and Ohio such a racially divided state, other scholars have shared their relevant knowledge through a variety of law review articles.[23] In total, however, these earlier court cases support an observation made by Malcolm X regarding segregated schooling. When asked about the boycott of segregated schools in New York in a 1964 television interview, he replied, "It proves you don't have to go to Mississippi to find a segregated school.... It shows that the problems that the white liberals have been pointing the finger at the southern segregationists and condemning them for exist right here in New York City."[24]

Ultimately, many of these cases prepared the way for *Plessy* by setting a precedent for "separate but equal" before it became the law of the land. Even so, only a handful of cases were specifically cited in *Plessy*. They were *Roberts v. Boston* (1849), *Garnes v. McCann* (1871), *Ward v. Flood* (1874), *Bertonneau v. Board* (1878), *King v. Gallagher* (1883), and *Lehew v. Brummell* (1891). There is nothing particularly unique about these cases except that the states in which they were argued (Massachusetts, Ohio, California, Louisiana, New York, and Missouri) represent various geographic regions of the United States. As shown in Table 2.2, the most cited pre-*Plessy* cases were *Roberts, Garnes, Ward*, and *King*, with the following post-*Plessy* cases in common: *Martin* (1896), *Plessy* (1896), *Wong Him* (1902), *Gong Lum* (1927), *Weaver* (1933), *Corbin* (1949), and *Briggs* (1951).

Table 2.3 shows that *Crawford* (1913), *Gong Lum* (1927), *Corbin* (1949), and *Briggs* (1951) almost all cite the same pre-*Plessy* cases as precedent. All four cases cite *Roberts, Ward*, and *McMillan*, but *Gong Lum, Corbin*, and *Briggs* cite the exact same cases. Once again, the only pattern appears to be geographical, with cases

TABLE 2.2.
Most Cited Pre-*Plessy* Cases (1896–1954)

Roberts (1849) Mass.	Garnes (1871) Ohio	Ward (1874) Calif.	King (1883) N.Y.
Stoutmeyer	Cory	Tinnon	Lehew
Longress	Lewis	Longress	Martin
King	Tinnon	Mitchell	Plessy
Lehew	Longress	Tape	Wong Him
Martin (W.Va.)	King	Wysinger	Reynolds
Plessy	Mitchell	Lehew	Tucker
Wong Him (Calif.)	McMillan	Martin	Piper
Reynolds	Lehew	Plessy	Gong Lum
Crawford	Martin	Wong Him	Weaver
Tucker	Plessy	Reynolds	Gaines
Piper	Wong Him	Dameron	Graham
Gong Lum (Miss.)	Reynolds	Crawford	Corbin
Weaver (Ohio)	Gong Lum	Piper	Carr
Pearson	Weaver	Gong Lum	Briggs
Graham	Pearson	Weaver	Belton
Mendez	Graham	Pearson	
Corbin (Va.)	Corbin	Graham	
Carr	Carr	Mendez	
Briggs (S.C.)	Briggs	Corbin	
		Briggs	

TABLE 2.3.
Most Post-*Plessy* Cases Using Pre-*Plessy* as Precedent

Crawford (1913) Oreg.	Gong Lum (1927) Miss.	Corbin (1949) Va.	Briggs (1951) N.C.
Roberts	Roberts	Roberts	Roberts
Clark	Garnes	Garnes	Garnes
Workman	Stoutmeyer	Stoutmeyer	Stoutmeyer
Ward	Ward	Ward	Ward
Dove	Bertonneau	Bertonneau	Bertonneau
Tinnon	King	King	King
Longress	Wysinger	Wysinger	Wysinger
McMillan	McMillan	McMillan	McMillan
Knox	Lehew	Lehew	Lehew

representing the North, South, Midwest, and West. To my surprise, of all the pre-*Plessy* subsequent citations, *Clark* (1868), the first case in which a plaintiff won, was the only case cited in *Brown*.

From *Plessy* to *Brown* (1896–1954)

After *Plessy*, the campaign for equality remained focused on the K–12 education system. Apparently, it was not until 1933, with *Weaver v. Board of Trustees of Ohio State University*, that activists began a two-pronged approach by adding higher education to the strategic battle. The literature largely credits the NAACP with this legal strategy.[25] However, the data makes it clear that the strategy was deployed much earlier than the 1950s, when the NAACP filed suit.

In this case, Doris Weaver, asked the Ohio State University to admit her to housing made available for "students pursuing the course of Home Economics."[26] Relying on *Roberts*, the court denied her request asserting, "The purely social relations of our citizens cannot be enforced by law; nor were they intended to be regulated by our own laws or by the state and Federal Constitutions."[27] The Supreme Court of Ohio supported the university's argument that it had offered Weaver special and equal housing that would allow her to complete her educational requirements. Courts across the country reached similar results as plaintiffs sued to gain admission to colleges, law schools, graduate schools, and other professional schools (Table 2.4).

However, in areas lacking separate but equal facilities, attorneys found overwhelming success (Table 2.5). With such chaotic, contradictory findings, it is no wonder that *Brown* emerged as the final answer to questions of fairness and equality. While the pattern attributed to legal strategy is fairly well known, the geographic and racial composition of the cases merit closer study.[28]

When school desegregation cases preceding *Brown* are examined in their totality, two very clear patterns emerge that reinforce the relevance of *Tape*, *Piper*, and *Mendez*. First, the legal battle for racial equality was not just Black/White. While African American plaintiffs accounted for ninety cases, five cases involved Native American plaintiffs, four involved Asian American plaintiffs, and two involved Latiné plaintiffs (Table 2.6). The mere presence of these cases invites inquiry.

Second, the race for educational equality was not strictly a battle between the North and South. The South accounted for 42 percent of the cases, and the North was responsible for 24 percent. This means that over a third of the cases took place outside of the North/South binary. Specifically, approximately 23 percent of the cases took place in the Midwest, and 11 percent in the West. Over a third of the cases took place beyond the eastern half of the country. What's more, the win/loss patterns of the regions are remarkable.

TABLE 2.4.
Higher Education Cases and States with Unfavorable Results

Colleges	State	Law Schools	State	Graduate Schools	State
Boyd v. Board (1950)	Fla.	*Gaines v. Canada* (1938)	Mo.	*Bluford v. Canada* (1940)	Mo.
Maxey v. Board (1950)	Fla.	*Wrighten v. Board* (1947)	S.C.	*Michael v. Witham* (1942)	Tenn.
Toliver v. Board (1950)	Mo.	*Fisher v. Hurst* (1948)	Okla.	*Finley v. Board* (1950)	Fla.
		Lewis v. Board (1950)	Fla.		
		Epps v. Carmichael (1950)	N.C.		
		Hawkins v. Board (1952)	Fla.		

TABLE 2.5
Higher Ed.ucation Cases and States with Favorable Results

Colleges	State	Law Schools	State	Graduate Schools	State
Parker v. University (1950)	Del.	*Pearson v. Murray* (1936)	Md.	*Kerr v. Enoch* (1945)	Md.
Board v. Tureaud (1953)	La.	*Sipuel v. Board* (1948)	Okla.	*Johnson v. Board* (1949)	Ky.
Bruce v. Stilwell (1953)	Tex.	*Wilson v. Board* (1950)	La.	*McCready v. Byrd* (1950)	Md.
Wichita Falls JC v. Battle (1953)	Tex.	*Sweatt v. Painter* (1950)	Tex.	*McLaurin v. Regents* (1950)	Okla.
Constantine v. Institute (1954)	La.	*McKissick v. Carmichael* (1951)	N.C.	*Gray v. University* (1951)	Tenn.
		Gray v. University (1951)	Tenn.		

TABLE 2.6.
Racial Composition of Cases

	Black	Indigenous	Asian American	Latiné	Total
Number of Cases	94	5	4	2	105
Percent	89%	5%	4%	2%	100%

TABLE 2.7.
Regional Distribution of School Desegregation by Wins/Losses

State	Wins	Losses	Total
SOUTHERN STATES			
Alabama	0	2	2
Arkansas	0	2	2
Florida	0	6	6
Kentucky	1	2	3
Louisiana	3	1	4
Mississippi	0	3	3
North Carolina	2	5	7
Oklahoma	2	1	3
South Carolina	0	3	3
Tennessee	1	2	3
Texas	3	1	4
Virginia	2	1	3
West Virginia	0	1	1
SOUTHERN TOTALS	14	30	44
% Wins vs. % Losses	32%	68%	
NORTHERN STATES			
D.C.	1	4	5
Delaware	3	1	4
Indiana	0	3	3
Maryland	3	2	5
Massachusetts	0	1	1
Michigan	1	0	1
New York	0	2	2
Ohio	0	4	4
NORTHERN TOTALS	8	17	25
% Wins vs. % Losses	32%	68%	

TABLE 2.7. (*continued*)

State	Wins	Losses	Total
MIDWESTERN STATES			
Kansas	8	2	10
Missouri	2	5	7
Iowa	3	0	3
Illinois	3	1	4
MIDWESTERN TOTALS	16	8	24
% Wins vs. % Losses	67%	33%	
WESTERN STATES			
California	5	2	7
Arizona	1	2	3
Nevada	0	1	1
Oregon	1	0	1
WESTERN TOTALS	7	5	12
% Wins vs. % Losses	58%	42%	
ALL CASES	44	58	105

As demonstrated in Table 2.7, the North and South won and lost cases at relatively the same rate (32 percent versus 68 percent). However, in the Midwest, the pattern flips—67 percent of the cases were won, and 33 percent were lost. In the West, the win/loss record was considerably closer (58 percent versus 42 percent) In observing the 11 cases involving non-Black plaintiffs, 4 were filed in the South (North Carolina and Mississippi), and the remaining 7 all occurred in the West (Arizona, Oregon, and California). The geographical spread, regional breakdown, and names and dates of the cases are also represented in Figures 7–10. There are 105 cases represented in the figures, as they include the cases filed with *Brown*, which are designated with a star. The 11 cases with non-Black plaintiffs are designated with a triangle.

Given the U.S. racial hierarchy, there were only two legal options available for Native American, Latiné, and Asian American communities. The first, as demonstrated by *McMillan, Crawford, Moreau, Gong Lum*, and *Tij Fung*, was to distance themselves racially from African Americans. The second, as argued in *Piper, Peters, Tape, Wong Him, Mendez*, and *Sheely*, was to demand the same rights afforded to Whites without receiving the full benefits. A review of these cases reveals the forever floating and forgotten racial middle of a society that does not quite know where to place Asian Americans, Indigenous nations, and Latiné Americans on the Black/White binary or in the history of racial politics in the United States.

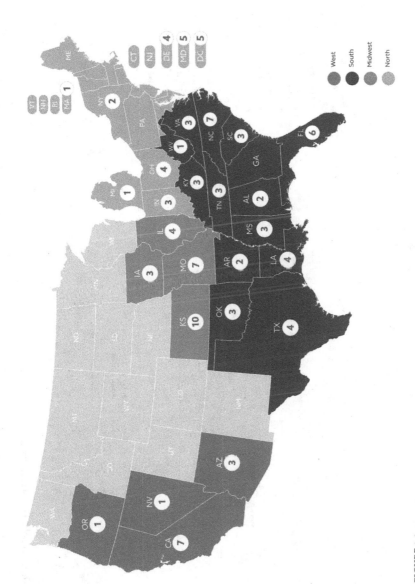

FIGURE 2.2.
Geographic distribution of cases.

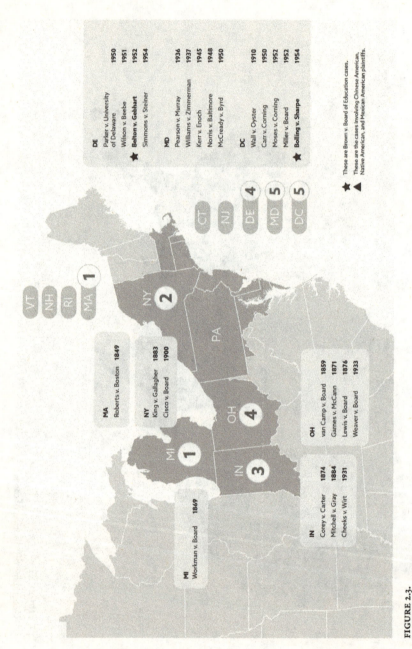

FIGURE 2.3.
Northern school desegregation cases.

MA
Roberts v. Boston — 1849

NY
King v. Gallagher — 1883
Cisco v. Board — 1900

MI
Workman v. Board — 1869

IN
Corey v. Carter — 1874
Mitchell v. Gray — 1884
Cheeks v. Wirt — 1931

OH
van Camp v. Board — 1859
Gaines v. McCann — 1871
Lewis v. Board — 1876
Weaver v. Board — 1933

DE
Parker v. University of Delaware — 1950
Wilson v. Beebe — 1951
★ Belton v. Gebhart — 1952
Simmons v. Steiner — 1954

MD
Pearson v. Murray — 1936
Williams v. Zimmerman — 1937
Kerr v. Enoch — 1945
Norris v. Baltimore — 1948
McCready v. Byrd — 1950

DC
Wall v. Oyster — 1910
Carr v. Corning — 1950
Moses v. Corning — 1952
Miller v. Board — 1952
★ Bolling v. Sharpe — 1954

★ These are Brown v. Board of Education cases.
▲ These are the cases involving Chinese American, Native American, and Mexican American plaintiffs.

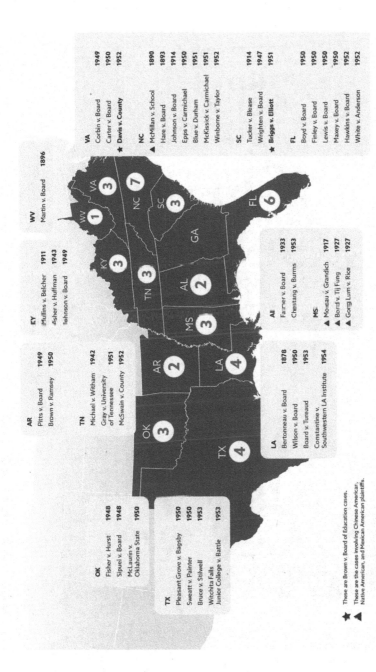

WV
Martin v. Board   1896

KY
Mullins v. Belcher   1911
Fisher v. Huffman   1943
Johnson v. Board   1949

AR
Pitts v. Board   1949
Brown v. Ramsey   1950

TN
Michael v. Witham   1942
Gray v. University of Tennessee   1951
McSwain v. County   1952

OK
Fisher v. Hurst   1948
Sipuel v. Board   1948
McLaurin v. Oklahoma State   1950

TX
Pleasant Grove v. Bagsby   1950
Sweatt v. Painter   1950
Bruce v. Stilwell   1953
Witchita Falls Junior College v. Battle   1953

LA
Bertonneau v. Board   1878
Wilson v. Board   1950
Board v. Tureaud   1953
Constantine v. Southwestern LA Institute   1954

AL
Farner v. Board   1933
Chestang v. Burns   1953

MS:
▲ Moreau v. Grandich   1917
▲ Bond v. Tij Fung   1927
▲ Gong Lum v. Rice   1927

VA
Corbin v. Board   1949
Carter v. Board   1950
★ Davis v. County   1952

NC
▲ McMillan v. School   1890
Hare v. Board   1893
Johnson v. Board   1914
Epps v. Carmichael   1950
Blue v. Durham   1951
McKissick v. Carmichael   1951
Winborne v. Taylor   1952

SC
Tucker v. Blease   1914
Wrighten v. Board   1947
★ Briggs v. Elliott   1951

FL
Boyd v. Board   1950
Finley v. Board   1950
Lewis v. Board   1950
Maxey v. Board   1950
Hawkins v. Board   1952
White v. Anderson   1952

★ These are Brown v. Board of Education cases.

▲ These are the cases involving Chinese American, Native American, and Mexican American plaintiffs.

FIGURE 2.4.
Southern school desegregation cases.

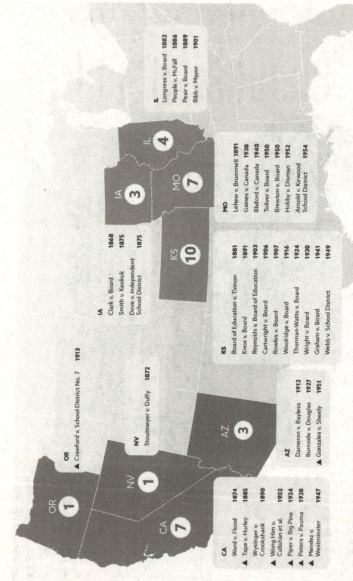

OR
▲ Crawford v. School District No. 7   1913

IL
Longress v. Board   1882
People v. McFall   1886
Peair v. Board   1889
Bibb v. Mayor   1901

IA
Clark v. Board   1868
Smith v. Keokuk   1875
Dove v. Independent   1875
School District

NV
Stoutmeyer v. Duffy   1872

MO
Lehew v. Brummell   1891
Gaines v. Canada   1938
Bluford v. Canada   1940
Toliver v. Board   1950
Brewton v. Board   1950
Hobby v. Disman.   1952
Arnold v. Kirwood   1954
School District

KS
Board of Education v. Tinnon   1881
Knox v. Board   1891
Reynolds v. Board of Education   1903
Cartwright v. Board   1906
Rowles v. Board   1907
Woolridge v. Board   1916
Thurman-Watts v. Board   1924
Wright v. Board   1930
Graham v. Board   1941
Webb v. School District   1949

AZ
Dameron v. Bayless   1912
Burnside v. Douglas   1927
▲ Gonzales v. Sheely   1951

CA
Ward v. Flood   1874
▲ Tape v. Hurley   1885
Wysinger v.   1890
Crookshank
▲ Wong Him v.   1902
Callahan et al.
▲ Piper v. Big Pine   1924
▲ Peters v. Pauma   1928
▲ Mendez v.   1947
Westminster

▲ These are the cases involving Chinese American,
Native American, and Mexican American plaintiffs.

FIGURE 2.5.
Midwestern and western school desegregation cases.

The Native American Bricks

In addition to *Piper*, at least four Native American cases regarding school desegregation preceded *Brown*.[29] They began in the late nineteenth century and ended in the early twentieth century, coinciding with the demise of Indian boarding schools throughout the United States and an influx of Native American students into deeply unprepared public school systems.[30] The cases were argued in their respective state supreme courts but never made it to the U.S. Supreme Court. There are several explanations as to why, including, but not limited to, policy changes, insufficient funding for appeals, or favorable outcomes at the lower level. Taken together and presented in chronological order, these lawsuits interrogate how the courts racialized Native Americans in ways both promising and problematic. What these proceedings show is how the plaintiffs, school boards, and state courts used anti-Blackness, citizenship status, assimilation, blood quantum evidence, and even landownership to racialize Native Americans in ways that the traditional dichotomous sociological treatment of race in the United States does not capture.

MCMILLAN V. SCHOOL COMMITTEE OF DISTRICT NO. 4 (1890): NEGRO . . . NOT INDIAN

Decided in North Carolina in 1890 even before *Plessy*, this first case reveals the troubling relationship between Native Americans and African Americans in Robeson County, North Carolina. There were three schools in District No. 4: one White, one colored, and another Indian. "Famously tri-racial," Robeson County housed roughly equal populations of Native Americans, Whites, and African Americans.[31] The Indian schools, created in 1885, were for individuals who declared themselves "descendants of the friendly tribe of Indians known as Croatans."[32] The Croatan Act created the Native school after the Census identified enough Croatans to garner a separate institution. Prior to the act's creation, Croatan children attended the "colored" school. Shortly before trial, in 1888, the state legislature amended the law specifically to exclude "all negroes to the fourth generation" from White and Indian schools.[33]

Nathan McMillan, whose wife was Croatan and whose home was within the district of both the Croatan and colored schools, sent his children to the Croatan school. On August 18, 1888, he received a note from the school dismissing his children because they were considered Negro.[34] McMillan ignored the order and continued to send his children to class until they were refused entry. He then requested admission from the state board of education. The superintendent, J. A. McAllister, issued the following note: "It is ordered by the Board of Education that Nathan McMillan be assigned to Croatan District No. 4 and the committee of said district are hereby directed to receive his children."[35]

During the trial, the superintendent testified that the memorandum was not meant to be an official order. According to the record, "It was [written] simply to try to arrange the differences between [the schools]."[36] Even after presenting the note, the school refused entrance to the McMillan children again, arguing that prior to the Croatan Act's creation, the Croatans were identified as mulattos, not Negros. In this case, mulattos were mixed race. The McMillan children, school officials argued, were neither Croatan nor mulatto and were therefore ineligible. After this refusal, McMillan filed suit.

McMillan did not argue that separate schools were unconstitutional or that the legislature did not have the power to create them. Instead, he argued that his children were classified improperly. He distanced himself racially from Blackness in order to be identified as colored or mulatto. Evidence the school introduced at trial showed that Nathan McMillan was a former slave whose father was White and mother Black, thereby making his children ineligible to be pupils. McMillan contended that he was mulatto, not Negro, making him the same racial background as Croatans. In a move that seems absurd today yet was commonplace in trials involving racial identification, "McMillan's son was 'exhibited to the jury' so that they might make a judgment on his racial background."[37]

The issue under appeal centered on the definition of "within the fourth degree." The court explained the phrase's meaning as follows: "If, by tracing back four successive generations, through father or mother, we reach a negro ancestor of the plaintiff's children, then they are excluded."[38] McMillan's attorney argued, "Generation, as used in the statute, means a single succession of *living* beings in natural descent."[39] Unconvinced by his argument, the court agreed that the McMillan children, by virtue of their father, were Negro and not Indian. The judge upheld the jury's answer to the third question and supported the finding that the plaintiff's children were neither colored nor Indian. The court also found that the state board of education did not have the authority to override state law. Therefore, the superintendent's "order" held no power. The fact that the McMillan children were at least one-half Croatan because of their mother was never discussed in the opinion. It is not clear whether they were recognized as members of the Croatan Nation. However, since it was the Croatan school that rejected the McMillan family, it can be surmised that no claim for membership existed.

CRAWFORD V. SCHOOL DISTRICT NO. 7 (1913): WHOLLY WHITE

Approximately twenty years later, William Crawford filed suit in Oregon on behalf of his daughters Naoma and Juanita (ages eight and nine, respectively). This case provides an example of the investment in Whiteness via assimilation. Crawford's daughters attended the local White school for at least two years. Then, in 1912, the local school board established a separate school for "Indian children and children that were part Indian."[40] It is remarkable that provisions were made for youths who were "part Indian" in light of the antimiscegenation rampant in the country.[41] Racial mixing between Whites and Native Americans, however, was much more acceptable than racial mixing between Blacks and Whites.[42] Once the Indian school was created, its officials directed a teacher to refuse Naoma and Juanita Crawford admission on the basis that they were "part Indian."[43] So strong was the desire to separate the races that the institution turned away children who traversed their halls, played with their children, and learned from their books for two years.

Crawford and his wife testified that they both had fathers who were White and mothers who were Indian. Crawford also offered evidence that, while they owned land in the nearby reservation, he and his spouse did not live there and had "voluntarily adopted the customs, usages and habits of civilized life."[44] According the Dawes Act, this made the Crawford girls American and state citizens and therefore eligible to attend the White schools. The Oregon Supreme Court accepted the evidence; stated, "These children are half white, and their rights are the same as they would be if they were wholly white"; and compelled the school to admit them.[45] This particular finding is an example of a clear departure from the "one-drop rule" unfailingly applied to African Americans.[46] Instead, this decision represents what historian Paige Raibmon calls the "one-drop theory of civilization."[47]

Once again, the plaintiffs did not argue that separate schools were unconstitutional, only that their children were U.S. citizens and therefore allowed to attend the White school. Even though the Crawford family did not challenge the constitutionality of separate schools, the state supreme court dedicated the remainder of the opinion to making it clear that separate schools were constitutional and necessary. In the *Crawford* opinion, the court advised, "The states may enact laws providing for the establishment of separate schools for colored children, whether black or red, but such schools must be equal. . . . But in this state we have no statute expressly providing for the establishment of separate schools for colored children."[48] Because no state law existed allowing for the creation of separate but equal schools, the court held that the school board did not have the authority to create a separate school on its own. By 1922, however, the state legislature, dominated by members of the KKK, ensured that local school boards were granted such power.[49] However, the courts conveniently considered those efforts to be more anti-Catholic than racist.[50]

Crawford offers an example of a plaintiff who technically "won" the case but lost the cause. As we will see in other cases, courts were less arbiters of justice and more legislative advisers, giving local school boards the proverbial blueprints for creating segregated schooling. This was not simply post-*Plessy* practice, but a tradition that began before the official doctrine of separate but equal.

MOREAU V. GRANDICH (1917):
"A SLIGHT STRAIN OF RED BLOOD"

The next case, *Moreau*, was decided in 1917 by the Mississippi Supreme Court and reveals the irrationality behind the state's "race laws." So entrenched and deep seated was racial animus in Mississippi that not even a tremendous loophole in the law could stop its impact. Antonio Grandich and his wife, married for over twenty-five years, filed suit on behalf of their four children to keep them at the White public school of Bay Saint Louis. According to the opinion, the children had been attending that school until 1914, when the trustees deemed them colored and therefore ineligible to be pupils.

In response, the Grandich family put forth two arguments. First, the school board overstepped its authority in determining that the Grandich children were colored. As a result, the family sought the right to sue the school board in court and have the decision reversed. The lower court concurred with the Grandiches and agreed to hear the case. Next, the family's counsel argued that while laws governing education did designate separate schools for "children of white and colored races," the Mississippi marriage law affirmed that the Grandich children were White and therefore eligible to attend the White school. Under the Mississippi marriage statute, marrying people with one-eighth or more Negro blood was unlawful. Since the Grandich parents had been allowed to marry under Mississippi law, it meant that they were neither colored nor Negro but White.

The school board argued that identifying a child as colored was a power that lay within the reach of the school board, its superintendent, and the state board of education. The plaintiffs, therefore, did not have a right to "appeal" the school board's decision to the courts. The Grandiches' remedy was to appeal to the superintendent and then to the board of education. Because they had not even exercised their administrative appeals, the board argued that the family should not be allowed to pursue legal appeals. Even if the plaintiffs could appeal to the courts, the school board argued that the record made it clear that the children were colored because they were ultimately of Negro descent. But the lower court agreed with the Grandich family and compelled the school to admit their children.

The school appealed and pled its case to a circuit court judge. The circuit court judge agreed with the Grandich family's argument that if they were White under marriage law then they were certainly White under the education law. The attorney for Grandich family, J. H. Leathers, argued that if their marriage was recognized as a marriage between two White people, then the Grandiches' children could not be classified as colored. He argued, "Would it not be folly to say nothing of the injustice of it, for the legislature to have thus provided that such marriages may have the legal status of white marriages, and then have intended that if children are born as a result of such marriage, the court shall hold that they are colored children and of the colored race[?]"[51] Furthermore, he argued, the children had been admitted into the White schools until 1914, before the school board determined they were "colored" and therefore ineligible. The circuit court also ruled in favor of the family.

The school board appealed to the state supreme court and argued its case before Justice Ethridge. The attorney for the school devoted a great deal of argument to specifically defining "colored," relying mostly on the "usual common acceptation of said word."[52] Quoting the *Standard Dictionary*, the lawyer argued that colored was defined as "of a dark skinned or noncaucasian race; specifically, in the United States. Of African descent, wholly or in part."[53]

Antonio Grandich and his wife claimed that they were White with only "a slight strain of red blood," and that their children were thus entitled to attend the White school near their home. The Grandiches also argued that the youths' expulsion from the school "resulted in irreparable damages, humiliation, and disgrace, [from] being classed as members of the colored race."[54] More importantly, the family contended that the school board had no authority to act as a judicial authority to determine whether a student was colored.

To prove the Grandich children's Whiteness, testimony centered on the race of their great-grandmother Christiana Jourdan. Attorneys argued that she was an Indian woman married to a White man and that her descendants intermarried with Whites. The family's counsel said of the children, "[They] are as fair as members of the white race, and there is nothing in their personal appearance to indicate the presence of negro blood." This meant that they were less than one-eighth colored and therefore White by law. Attorneys did not explain precisely what in Christiana's personal appearance would have demonstrated the "presence of negro blood."[55]

The school board presented evidence that Christiana was a "negro, classed and associated with the negroes at church and other social gatherings," and that two of her daughters intermarried with "negroes."[56] Witnesses said that her appearance was "griff," or "a shade lighter than negro," and that "she had negro hair, was dark or ginger-cake color, and ... associated ... with negroes exclusively."[57] Furthermore, when Christiana and her children attended church, they "sat with the negroes."[58]

Using personal appearance and social relationships to determine race was a common method in law. Hair texture, skin color, and nose width were often the markers to measure Blackness.[59] As shown in the *McMillan* case, people's bodies were frequently used as exhibits for judges and juries. Perhaps one of the most outrageous body displays came in the 1924 *Rhinelander v. Rhinelander* annulment proceedings. New York scion Kip Rhinelander sued to annul his marriage to Alice Rhinelander on the grounds that she had concealed her race.[60] Her attorney recommended she strip down to the waist, arguing that because the marriage had been consummated, Kip Rhinelander should have known she was Black. Unfortunately, the tactic worked, and a jury of White men voted against the famously wealthy Rhinelander family. The question remains: What did these attorneys expect the judges and juries to see? These were the commonsense notions of race coupled with devasting junk science about race.[61] The jury never revealed what they saw to make them decide in Alice's favor. However, historians Earl Lewis and Heidi Ardizzone argue that, in accordance with racial tropes regarding Black women, jurors must have determined that her breasts, shape, or skin color were somehow different underneath her clothing.[62] The idea behind the disrobing was that if they had consummated their marriage, Kip would have seen Alice naked and therefore "should have known" she was Black.

In *Moreau*, the judge made two legal conclusions. First, he determined that the marriage statute had no bearing on the separate school statute. "Both sections," he explained, "reflected the purpose of the Constitution makers to provide for a separation of the races in the state."[63] The marriage statute was created to prevent "the evils of bastardy from falling upon children."[64] Under the separate school provisions, the judge held that "the Constitution makers must be assumed to have used those [racial] terms according to their fixed and settled meaning in this country. The word 'white' defined means member of the white or Caucasian race, and the word 'colored' means, not only negroes, but persons who are of the 'mixed blood.'"[65] Finding that the lower court had erred, the state supreme court reversed the decision and excluded the Grandich children from attending the White school. At the hands of the law, the Grandich children were unfortunately victims of the "evils of bastardy" that the law was designed to prevent in the first place. They children no doubt served as a cautionary tale because , through no fault of their own, they were denied access to the school they had known for years.

While *Moreau* refers to "a slight strain of red blood," the opinion never indicates the Grandiches' tribal affiliation. However, because the case originated in Hancock Country, it is likely that the quotation refers to the still federally recognized Choctaw Tribe of Mississippi.[66] While I am not certain what percentage of the population of Hancock County consisted of Choctaws, in the eyes of the court, there was no distinction between Black and Choctaw.

Prior to the case, the Choctaws were fighting for federal recognition on behalf of "full-blooded Mississippi Choctaws, speaking the Choctaw language."[67] The Choctaws of Mississippi, however, were far from "full-blooded," and many did not know the language. The *Gulf Coast Progress*, a Mississippi newspaper, argued that the Choctaw "represented all shades and colors, running from *the real Indians* to the coal-black, thick-lipped, flat-nosed, kinky-headed Negro."[68] Antonio Grandich's mixed blood was enough to disqualify his children as White.

PETERS V. PAUMA (1928): RACE VERSUS LAND

The final Native American school desegregation case, *Peters v. Pauma School District*, was tried in 1927 in San Diego, California. The father, Max Peters, filed suit on behalf of his son Wesley. Because of the *Piper* decision, the school district could not deny Wesley admission based on race. Instead, the district argued that it could deny him admission because he lived on a reservation and was thereby required to attend the reservation school. If it was determined that Wesley did not live on an Indian reservation, then the school, under *Piper*, would be required to admit him. Therefore, the question of who owned the land was the main legal issue in this case. Interestingly, the government, represented by U.S. district attorney Samuel W. McNabb and assistant U.S. district attorney Ames Peterson, found it necessary to file an amicus brief.

The court reviewed the "ownership" history of the land where the Peters family lived. "Originally a large Spanish Grant" passed on to the Mexican government, via Jose Serrano, in 1844, the land was then "patented" as "planting grounds for the use and benefit of said Indians."[69] In 1889, the land grant passed to Francis Mora, who quitclaimed it to the government in 1899 "for the use and benefit of the Mission Indians."[70]

The lower court found that Max and Wesley Peters resided on the reservation but lived "in the manner of other American citizens in the vicinity."[71] The record does not outline what the "manner of other American citizens" means. On appeal, the government argued that the Peterses did not live on an Indian reservation and were therefore allowed admittance to the White school. The government also claimed that the Mission Indians were not a federally recognized tribe. All the while, Mission Indians were "allowed to" live on and use the land for agricultural purposes. The school district contended that because the Mission Indians had lived on the land for so long, it was in fact and in practice an Indian reservation. The court disagreed, holding that a reservation must be established by an act of Congress, a treaty, or an executive order. "Custom or prescription" does not constitute ownership.[72]

In this particular case, it appears that land trumps race. If the court had held

that the land was an Indian reservation, it would have made way for the Mission
Indians to claim ownership of the land and gain federal tribal recognition, with
all the accompanying responsibilities of the U.S. government to the tribal nation.
While the school was trying to exclude him based on race under the guise of reservation ownership, Wesley Peters and the government argued that he did not live
on a reservation and had adopted a "manner of American citizens." Land, as the
old saying goes, is supreme. Furthermore, to maintain its ownership and shirk its
responsibilities to the Mission Indians, the United States deliberately interfered in
local politics as this was the only case where the U.S. government filed an amicus
brief.

WERE THESE PRECEDENT-SETTING CASES?

Some of these cases set legal precedent for future school desegregation cases, illu-
minating the ways in which they represented bricks before *Brown*. *McMillan* and
Grandich were cited in *Gong Lum v. Rice* (1927), a school desegregation case out of
Mississippi involving a Chinese American plaintiff. *McMillan* and *Grandich* were
also cited in *Briggs v. Elliott* (1951), the South Carolina case that became one of the
five cases subsumed in the *Brown* decision. *Crawford* was cited by *Pearson v. Murray*, a 1936 case out of Maryland where a Black student was denied acceptance into
law school, and *Graham v. Board of Education*, a 1941 case involving the segregation of Kansas's junior high schools. *Peters* was never cited again, likely because it
was about landownership and not race.

The Chinese American Bricks

The three cases besides *Tape* involving Chinese American plaintiffs began in the
late 1800s. Each represents the unique temporal and regional experiences of Chinese Americans in the United States. Similar to the Native American cases, the
opinions in these proceedings reveal the complicated position of Chinese Americans in the racial binary. Unlike the Native American cases, however, they involve
no government directive or responsibility to the community as a whole, leaving
Chinese Americans to drift vulnerably in the binary of Black/White. What these
cases demonstrate is that the Chinese were simultaneously shunned by Whites
and no different from African Americans under the law.

WONG HIM V. CALLAHAN (1902): LEGISLATION UPHELD

Relying on the Fourteenth Amendment, the next attempt to legally challenge separate Chinese schools was *Wong Him v. Callahan* (1902). The Wong Him family
of San Francisco attempted to enroll their daughter in the local White school and

were turned away based on her race. California law assigned "to the trustees of school districts the power to establish separate schools for children of Mongolian or Chinese descent."[73] The family alleged that the statute was in direct conflict with the Fourteenth Amendment. In their complaint, the plaintiffs argued that the maintenance of separate schools resulted in "discrimination that is arbitrary, and the result of hatred for the Chinese race."[74]

Citing *Roberts*, the court explained that it played no role in the affairs of the state and the motivations of its lawmakers. "If the law does not conflict with some constitutional limitation of the powers of the state legislature," Judge De Haven wrote, "it cannot be declared invalid."[75] Furthermore, according to legal scholar Joyce Kuo, because *Wong Him* argued that the separate schools were inconvenient, and not that they were unequal, the court did not find a violation of the Equal Protection Clause. Consequently, it upheld the "separate but equal" doctrine established by *Plessy*.

Historian Charles Wollenberg asserts that, beginning as early as 1905, the segregation policy toward the Chinese became less strictly enforced in California.[76] Over the years, Chinese parents, wealthy Chinese merchants, and Chinese American educators challenged the educational policy. More Chinese American children were steadily admitted into White or "mixed" schools as a result.[77] By 1936, "the 'Chinese school' no longer officially existed," and any predominantly Chinese schools were blamed on residential segregation rather than the enforcement of policy.[78]

THE SETTLED LAW OF THE SOUTH

From the late 1800s to the early 1920s, a surprisingly strong Chinese presence emerged in the South. Historians attributed this growth to the pull of economic forces established by the growing cotton industry.[79] The Chinese either directly immigrated into Mississippi from the Guangdong Province, left the "Golden Mountain" and other ethnic enclaves of California to pursue work as farm laborers, or joined the ranks of the growing grocer population in the South. According to psychologist John Jung, southern cotton plantation capitalists at the Memphis Convention of 1869 "considered a proposal to have contractors hire Chinese laborers to replace blacks to punish them for acting like free men."[80] Their toil, therefore, was not only desired, but also used to punish Black men and women after the demise of slavery. These workers, Jung explains, may also represent the remnants of the completed Texas and Yazoo Railroad. Regardless of the reasons and circumstances that brought the Chinese to the Delta, by the 1920s the area's relatively small population of 211 people was about to make two disastrous contributions to constitutional law that solidified segregation. The 1927 cases involving the Tij Fung and Gong Lum families signaled a seismic departure from the legal wrangling of the West. In these cases based in the Mississippi Delta, all pretense and coded language disappears.

GONG LUM V. RICE (1927):
CONSTITUTIONALLY COLORED

The first and arguably most powerful case, *Gong Lum v. Rice* (1927) has the distinction of being the only school segregation case involving non-Black plaintiffs to make it to the Supreme Court. In *Gong Lum*, the plaintiff's daughter, Martha, was initially admitted to a local White school, only to be sent home at noon and told she was not allowed to return. When asked why Martha was refused admission, the school board affirmed that she was excluded based on her race. According to the board members, she was classified as colored under the law and required to avail herself of the colored school nearest her home.

Martha Lum's attorneys presented a convoluted argument to the Mississippi Supreme Court. On the one hand, they argued that the racial classification system was a product of White supremacy and, as a result, discriminated against anyone who was not White. On the other, they asserted that this unjust classification system wrongly identified the Chinese as colored. Finally, the plaintiff's lawyers contended that because she was not colored and there were no Chinese schools in the state, Martha was therefore entitled to admission to the White school.

The Mississippi Supreme Court disagreed. It classified Martha Lum as colored and explained that the state was under no obligation to create separate schools for every race. As a Chinese citizen of the United States, Martha was afforded the ability to attend an equally situated school for colored children and thus not denied equal protection. The additional concern or reason for separate schools (i.e., the maintenance of White purity) was a moot point so long as the law satisfied *Plessy*.

The Gong Lum family appealed their case to the U.S. Supreme Court only to be disappointed with the decision. First, the court affirmed that the creation and maintenance of separate schools was settled law. Second, the justices affirmed and agreed with Mississippi's classification of Chinese as colored. In a unanimous decision, Chief Justice Taft wrote, "Most of the cases cited [by the plaintiffs] arose, it is true, over the establishment of separate schools between white pupils and black pupils, but we cannot think that the question is any different . . . between white pupils and the pupils of the yellow races."[81] Decided on November 21, 1927, *Gong Lum* made it clear that the Chinese were not White under the law, but were clearly colored under the Constitution.[82] While journalist Adrienne Berard touts *Gong Lum* as "the first fight to desegregate schools in Jim Crow South," the case also strengthened the color line enforced by Jim Crow.[83] It follows that *Gong Lum* is less of a civil rights triumph and more of a win for White supremacy because Chinese plaintiffs attempted to racially distance themselves from Blacks in the South. These complicated contributions to an understanding of race are more fully explored through analysis of each case.

BOND V. TIJ FUNG (1927): SUBSTANTIALLY SIMILAR

Filed at nearly the same time as *Gong Lum*, *Tij Fung* deployed a different yet similarly unsuccessful approach. In *Tij Fung*, plaintiff Joe Tin Lun was a fourteen-year-old "good, clean, moral boy," and a native-born citizen of China. He sought entry to the Dublin consolidated school for Whites and was denied admission. Like *Gong Lum*, *Tij Fung* argued no separate school for Chinese children had been established for Joe to attend. Unlike *Gong Lum*, however, *Tij Fung* argued that Joe was guaranteed admission to the local White public school under the Burlingame Treaty of 1868. The plaintiff's counsel argued that the treaty trumped local laws because it established a reciprocal relationship between China and the United States that granted its citizens the right to attend the public schools located within each country. Attorneys also alleged racial discrimination against Chinese students in general. However, the petitioners problematically argued, "Because a Chinese child is living in the state, it is entitled to equal protection of the law ... and to *force it to associate with colored children* or to not attend the white school is discrimination."[84] This is another tragic example of racial distancing deployed by non-Black plaintiffs in cases involving discrimination.

While the county superintendent admitted that Joe Tin Lun was turned away based on his race, the school board maintained that *Gong Lum* established the Chinese as colored under the law and not entitled to attend White schools. When the plaintiffs argued that the separate schools were unequal, the court responded by stating, "We belong to that class of people who believe that there are no two things created exactly alike. Things are similar to each other. So it is with schools. They have a similarity, but it is certain that no two schools in Mississippi ... are exactly alike."[85]

In one opinion, the Mississippi Supreme Court established that sufficiently "similar" satisfied the constitutional requirement of equality. Moreover, the court unapologetically argued that segregation was, in fact, established to protect "the colored races ... [and] promote the peace, quietude, and happiness of all the races ... [so that] ... the prejudices and passions engendered by race consciousness might be avoided."[86] According to the justices, the purpose of the Mississippi Constitution was to "preserve the purity and integrity of the white race, and prevent amalgamation, and to preserve, as far as possible, the social system of racial segregation."[87] *Gong Lum* and the precedent set by *Plessy* held that the reason for creating separate schools was not important so long as the separate schools were equal in all respects.

Together, these cases essentially erased the Chinese identity in the South and, like *Moreau*, lumped any race that was not White into the category of "colored." Educational historian Eileen H. Tamura argues that *Gong Lum* "brought [Chinese racial] in-between-ness into public debate and thereby transformed their [Chinese Americans'] status from invisible to visible."[88] I respectfully disagree.

In the *Gong Lum* and *Tij Fung* decisions, three truths became abundantly clear. First, despite their efforts to the contrary, the courts did not recognize the Chinese as a separate and distinct racial group. They were very clearly lumped in with African Americans under the label "colored" and not separated into their own category. Second, the Chinese, like African Americans, drew the disgust, ire, and hatred of Whites in the South. Third, and perhaps most unfortunately, the court cases provided fodder for the division between two racial groups that should have been allies.

As all three cases suggest, Asian Americans occupied a problematic middling position within the racial hierarchy of the United States.[89] On one hand, they were a convenient token used to shame and antagonize African Americans. On the other, they were clearly rejected by White society as foreigners who threaten White purity.

The Mexican American Bricks

A search of federal and state legal databases reveals two published cases involving Mexican American plaintiffs: *Mendez v. Westminster* (1947) and *Gonzales v. Sheely* (1951). The emergence of only two cases demonstrates the challenges inherent in legal research. For example, secondary research reveals the existence of several other cases, namely *Del Rio Independent School District v. Salvatierra* (1930) and *Delgado v. Bastrop Independent School District* (1948), both based in Texas, and *Alvarez v. Lemon Grove School District* (1931), based in California.[90] These cases, however, have received treatment in other books and articles.[91]

The position of Mexican Americans in California, Arizona, and Texas during the 1940s and 1950s explains the emergence of legal challenges to segregated schools. Poor treatment of day laborers, the criminalization of Mexican American youths, the mistreatment of returning Mexican American servicemen from World War II, and the segregation endured by Mexican Americans in the West and Southwest all came to a head during this period. While Mexicans were, at their insistence and in accordance with the Treaty of Guadalupe Hidalgo, classified as White based on citizenship, they were not necessarily afforded the same treatment and rights as Whites.[92] Policies and laws were still in place to limit voting by language and required placement in English learning programs.[93] Classification did not imply cooperation on the part of Whites in the United States. While African Americans in the South lived under *de jure* Jim Crow laws, Mexican Americans in the Southwest and West were recipients of a socially sanctioned segregation practice of Juan Crow.[94]

Historian Mae Ngai illustrates this enmeshed relationship between citizenship, race, and immigration when it comes to Mexicans and Mexican Americans. Describing the relationship between the U.S. agricultural industry and Mexican labor as "imported colonialism," she correctly identifies the mechanism through which Mexicans and Mexican Americans became "racialized" beginning as early as the 1920s.[95] That mechanism was an immigration policy designed to supply the seemingly endless need for cheap labor for an expanding agricultural market.

Mexicans and Mexican Americans became commodities that were subject to the laws of supply and demand. In the 1920s, a shortage of labor inspired the development of guest worker programs to serve the ever expanding and seasonal nature of the agricultural industry. In the 1930s, shortly after the Depression, immigration policy "repatriated" four hundred thousand Mexicans, only to be followed by the creation of the Bracero Program during World War II to bring them back.[96] In a sense, the immigration policy of America as it pertains to Mexicans was marked by "we need you, we need you, we need you" inevitably followed by "go back, go back, go back." The physical value of racialized bodies of Mexican laborers increased and decreased according to the market demands. Mexicans' personal value, however, was measured as either worker or wetback, but never citizen. It was against this foundation of pity, greed, and anti-Mexican sentiment that *Gonzales* was situated in history.

GONZALES V. SHEELY (1951)

In *Gonzales*, the Gonzales and Curiel families of Arizona sued the Tolleson school district of Maricopa County on behalf of their children, Gloria and Mary Ellen Gonzales, and Faustino Jr. and Dora Curiel. Three hundred other students and their families joined the lawsuit. The Tolleson school district acknowledged that it did create separate schools for Mexican children. Officials argued that the schools were not only equal to White schools, but also necessary because Mexican children were "retarded" in their ability to acquire and master English. The school district purportedly administered a "test" to measure a child's mastery of English but failed to produce credible evidence of such tests.

In *Gonzales*, Justice Ling also methodically laid out the following findings of fact:

- This segregation resulted in an injury to the plaintiffs that was "continuous, great, and irreparable ... [and] affect[ed] their health, rights, and privileges as citizens of the United States."
- The school board's contention that Mexican children were "retarded in learning English" was not enough of a reason to segregate an entire population of children even if they were just learning English.
- Such segregated practices, "foster[ed] antagonisms in the children and suggest inferiority among them where none exists."
- The tests the school board put forth as evidence of Mexican inferiority were "generally hasty, superficial and not reliable."
- Most importantly, the judge stated, "There is substantial inequality in the accommodations accorded [Mexican children] when compared to the facilities and accommodations afforded White children."[97]

Justice Ling concluded, "[The school board's] conduct of segregating public-school children of Mexican descent ... is discriminatory and illegal and is a violation ... of the Fourteenth Amendment."[98] In addition to *Mendez*, Ling cited the *McLaurin* (1950) decision, which found that the Equal Protection Clause was violated simply by placing an African American student in a separate room because of his racial origin. If that action was a violation of the Fourteenth Amendment, Ling concluded, the creation and maintenance of an entirely separate school system was even more of one.

While *Gonzales* signaled a victory for Mexican American children, the victory did not carry over to African American communities. Despite Ling's acknowledgment of the constitutional connection between *McLaurin* and *Gonzales*, Arizona school districts continued segregating African American children until May 13, 1954, four days before the *Brown* decision, when the Mesa school district of Maricopa County announced that children could attend whichever school was in their district "regardless of race or color."[99] This lag in equity exposes the slow and unequal progression of justice through the racial hierarchy of the United States.

Education scholars such as Jeanne M. Powers and Lirio Patton attempt to distinguish *Gonzales* from *Mendez* by arguing that the *Gonzales* court made a more explicit, unqualified case against segregation and "embraced a social science critique of racism."[100] A deeper review of the legal and social history of the *Mendez* case in the following chapter demonstrates that the arguments put forth in *Gonzales* would not have been possible without *Mendez*. One thing that both cases share is a citation in the NAACP's brief in *Brown*. However, they are not cited in the actual *Brown* opinion, which explains their relative obscurity. While shrewd, David Marcus's legal strategy in *Mendez* unfortunately contributed to the divide between Black and brown, where one was seen as a race and the other as an ethnic identity.

Why Not *Crawford*, *Gong Lum*, and *Gonzales*?

I am often asked why I did not select *Crawford*, *Gong Lum*, and *Gonzales* for my case study. After all, *Crawford* is more cited than *Piper*, *Gong Lum* is a Supreme Court case whereas *Tape* is only subsequently cited four times, and *Gonzales* is lesser known than *Mendez*. My answer is twofold. First, *Crawford* and *Gong Lum* do not argue racial discrimination on the basis of the plaintiffs' identity. The Crawford family successfully argued that their daughters were White, and the Gong Lum family unsuccessfully argued that their daughter was not Black. This project requires a clear argument for racial discrimination, not for racial inclusion with Whites or exclusion with African Americans. Gonzales, while a strong candidate for study, came after *Mendez*, and the judge in that case relied heavily on *Mendez* in his opinion. Second, *Tape*, *Piper*, and *Mendez* all occurred in California, which allows me to keep the law consistent while I explore race, class, gender, and age. Admittedly, *Tape* is not cited as much in subsequent cases, but that is only because it is a pre-*Plessy* suit. As a result, *Wong Him* (1902) became the most cited Chinese American proceeding in California. Despite its numerous citations, *Tape* is ultimately the case that created separate Chinese schools in the United States. Finally, *Crawford*, *Gong Lum*, and *Gonzales* represent three different legal jurisdictions and social histories.

Patterns Revealed

The U.S. public school system was designed with democratic principles of equality in order to provide access for all. However, like *Roberts v. Boston* (1849) makes clear, its beginnings were not properly laid to withstand discrimination. It appears that *Plessy* and *Brown* do not represent the beginning and the end of segregated schooling. I argue, and this legal timeline demonstrates, that two distinct roads toward educational equality exist. The first road leads to *Plessy*, with various states implementing "separate but equal" before it became legal doctrine. The second road leads away from *Plessy* toward *Brown*. It was a road that, in hindsight, represented more of a speed bump rather than the end of a doctrine.[101]

Reviewing the dates, locations, courts, and gender and racial identity of the plaintiffs of each case separately and then collectively reveals an elaborate and compelling pattern. First, the cases before *Brown* were not limited to the South or the 1950s. The contributions to these structures of inequality came from all around the country and all across time, demonstrating the length, depth, and breadth of the Civil Rights Movement throughout history. From Massachusetts to California, the bricks that lined the path to *Brown* were the result of families, communities, and attorneys around the country taking a stand against injustice beginning as early as the mid-1800s.[102]

Second, the 105 bricks that line the road to *Brown* reveal that the road is multi-racial. While Chinese Americans, Native Americans, and Mexican Americans also desired and demanded equal protection and treatment under the law, they rein-forced the U.S. racial hierarchy. The fact that 89 percent of school desegregation cases involved Black plaintiffs shows how African Americans have been, are, and continue to be pushed toward the bottom of the U.S. racial hierarchy but remain the vanguard of the battle for equality. As unwilling immigrants into the United States, theirs is a history of 476 years of systemic, legal, and overt forms of racism and discrimination that cannot and have not been undone in the over fifty years since the passage of the civil rights laws of 1965.

As a description of the eight cases represented by Chinese Americans, Native Americans, and Mexican Americans plaintiffs reveals, most of those actions were rooted in legal arguments that characterized the racial divide as Black/non-Black. The result of this anti-Blackness strategy, I argue, is the solidification of a system of inequality that strategically places Asian, Indigenous, and Latiné racial groups above African Americans but always below Whites. In reality and in practice, however, the racial divide is overwhelmingly White/non-White. However, White supremacy is most effective when it convinces the oppressed that they are supe-rior to one another yet never equal to White. These cases did not necessarily le-gally "touch" because most of them failed to cite one another. They were, however, part of the legal history whose findings simultaneously advanced and retreated the fight toward educational equality. Collectively, these cases paved the road to *Brown* and were ultimately bonded with the mortar of oppression.

CHAPTER 3

Tape v. Hurley—the Omitted

History is not the past. It is the stories we tell about the past.
How we tell these stories—triumphantly or self-critically,
metaphysically or dialectically—has a lot to do with whether
we cut short or advance our evolution as human beings.

—GRACE LEE BOGGS

The year is 1884 in the city of San Francisco. An eight-year-old child, excited about enrolling in her new school, holds tightly to her brother's hand as her father holds tightly to hers. She is too overwhelmed by the number of children around her ... children who are going to be her future classmates and maybe friends. Her eyes trace the school walls, and she is in awe of the building nearest her home. She is too distracted to see what her father sees ... confused looks, quiet whispers, and the stern look on the face of the woman with whom he must interact to enroll his children in the school.

He is familiar with that look. He saw it when he first arrived. He saw it despite training his tongue to say the misshapen large words that fell rather than flowed from his mouth. He saw it every time he was called on to translate for the local consulate and businesses. He was accustomed to the register of mixed assessments of his appearance. He looks Chinese, but he is not dressed like "the Chinese." He is wearing a suit ... a nice suit ... an expensive suit. The little children he has in tow are quiet, respectful, and uncommonly un-Chinese.

The little girl is snapped from her worshipful gaze of the school by the loud voice of a woman and the terse voice of her father. She can tell he is angry because his grip on her hand has tightened, but his voice is calm, even, and determined. The words emerge like the blurry photographs her mother sometimes takes. They are not clear, but you know what the picture captures. White. School. Filthy. Chinese. Go home.

She notices that other parents begin to look over to her family and whisper among themselves. Unlike her father, she is not used to this treatment. Her friends and their families come over to her house, play in her yard, worship with her in church.

Her father pulls her toward him as she frantically grasps her brother's hand. Where are we going? What happened? Why are we leaving? All these questions must flood her little mind, but they are all questions she is too smart to pretend not to know the answers to. She and her little brother Frank cannot attend this school because they are Chinese. This school does not want them. They return to their beautifully situated home on 1769 Green Street, an affluent part of San Francisco just outside of Chinatown. Her father arranges a meeting with the Honorable F. A. Bee, the Chinese consul of San Francisco. All the while she and her brother are left to wrestle with a complicated answer to a relatively simple question: Where do we go to school tomorrow?

While this account is not explicitly written in the California newspapers of the late 1800s, it is a scene constructed from the letters, interviews, and newspaper accounts of the time when Joseph Tape, an "Americanized" Chinese man, attempted to enroll his children in the school nearest their home. This chapter informs and introduces the first of three disparate but connected worlds: that of a Chinese American family in the 1880s, a Native American family in the 1920s, and a Mexican American family in the 1940s, all struggling for educational equality. Through the legal system, they brought forth the following cases, respectively: *Tape v. Hurley* (1885), *Piper v. Big Pine* (1924), and *Mendez v. Westminster* (1947). These legal battles have been omitted, forgotten, or eclipsed in the historical narratives of school desegregation. In providing the social and legal history of *Tape*, *Piper*, and *Mendez*, a clearer picture emerges of the ways in which individual acts of social inequality became structural in the United States.

The Tapes—the Omitted

The story of Joseph Tape attempting to enroll his child in school begins in 1869, when Jeu Diep immigrated to the United States from Skipping Stone Village in Xinning County, Guangdong Province, in southern China. Born in 1852, Jeu Diep was approximately seventeen years old when he arrived in San Francisco's port. His name was Americanized to Joe Tape or Joseph Tape. While the details of his story are not clear, historian Mae Ngai writes that Joseph Tape lived his life as a houseboy delivering milk for Matthew Sterling, a wealthy businessman. His delivery route included the home where he would eventually meet and wed his wife, Mary.[1]

Mary was born in 1857 in northern China, near Shanghai, and immigrated to the United States in 1868 when she was just eleven years old.[2] While the specific circumstances of her immigration are also unknown, the fate of many Chinese girls her age was domestic service, slavery, or prostitution.[3] She lived alone for five months in San Francisco's Chinatown before being "rescued" by the San Francisco Ladies' Protection and Relief Society, a middle-class women's service organization that built and managed an orphanage in Chinatown.[4] While it is not clear what Mary's life was like during those first five months in the streets of San Francisco, the society's mission was to "render protection and relief to strangers, [and] to sick, and dependent women and children," suggesting that she needed protection.[5] In 1871, she came under the guardianship of the society by way of Samuel Loomis, head of the Presbyterian Chinese Mission. He introduced Mary to the women who would change the course of her life.

While it had not yet created an official orphanage for Chinese girls, the San Francisco Ladies' Protection and Relief Society served as an orphanage for White children whose parents were struggling to provide basic, necessary care. During their meetings, the society would deliver a member report on weekly visits to the orphanage. On April 4, 1871, the minutes indicated, "Mr. Loomis made application to have the two Chinese girls put under the guardianship of the Society."[6] For some unknown reason, "the two Chinese girls" became "the Chinese girl," suggesting that something happened to the second girl that caused her to disappear from the record. Perhaps another service agency "adopted" her. She might have run away. Her name and fate never appear in the minutes. Hers is a story that joined those of the nameless children that were relegated to the margins of the already marginalized Chinatown. The Chinese girl who remained eventually abandoned her Chinese name and adopted the Irish name of the beloved head matron of the orphanage, Mary McGladery. Young Mary, the Chinese girl with an Irish name, ultimately became the beneficiary of an incredibly extraordinary life.

Mary's life trajectory was quite different from the tragic fate of so many Chinese women in the late 1800s. Becoming the ward of a missionary agency did not always result in a reprieve from racial hatred. In her study of Protestant women and their work with Chinese mission homes, historian Peggy Pascoe writes that Chinese wards' experience of racialism was mixed.[7] While some individuals adhered to a strict racial hierarchy, others believed that the adoption of "Victorian values of piety and purity" made Chinese women the perfect example of the successful civilization of the racial other. Mary, in her short time with the Ladies' Protection and Relief Society, demonstrated the latter phenomenon. While she did not divulge very much about her time in the orphanage in later interviews with the San Francisco *Morning Call*, the meeting minutes of the society reveal a few previously unknown interactions that showed that she was a protected and valuable member of the orphanage community.

The July 7, 1873, meeting minutes describe a remarkable event that must have been deeply meaningful to Mary's understanding of equality. Society members reported as follows: "Mrs. Hill visited fourth week; found the cook unwilling to submit to the Matron in allowing the Chinese girl her turn in the kitchen; so she was discharged, as was the laundress for the same reason. It was decided that the Chinese girl should assist in the kitchen and the laundry in turn with the others."[8] Imagine what it must have been like for a young Chinese girl to be flatly rejected by the cook and laundress, deemed unworthy to even touch the food or clothing of White children. Did the women look at Mary with the same hostility and loathing that she likely encountered as she wandered the streets of San Francisco? She could change her name, her circumstances, and her religion, but she could never change her race. Still, at a time when anti-Chinese sentiment was arguably at its highest, the society stood up on her behalf in the face of bigotry.

According to the minutes, there was no discussion of the issue; the decision to fire the cook and laundress was swift and certain. These acts clearly sent the message that Mary was just as valuable as the White children in the home. She was to be treated no differently. Perhaps this incident helped to shape the sense of equality and justice that she would need later.

Mary was also trusted with the other children. In the August 5, 1873, minutes, the society reported, "The Chinese girl had sole charge of the nursery dining room, Mrs. Harvey being sick. . . . [She] seemed patient and methodical with the babies."[9] In a home with over 150 children at any given time, this was a tremendous responsibility, and Mary's service stood out. She lived with the San Francisco Ladies' Protection and Relief Society for a total of five years, during which time she learned English, acquired "American manners," and assisted in recruiting orphaned Chinese girls. In evolving from "the Chinese girl" to Mary McGladery, her life was transformed from one of needing protection to one of providing protection for others.

It was also during her time at the orphanage that Mary met and eventually married Joseph Tape.[10] It is likely that they courted under the watchful eye of the Presbyterian Church, whose benevolent efforts were often tied to the Chinese community.[11] Reverend Loomis, the man who "rescued" Mary, married the couple on November 16, 1875, in the First Presbyterian Church, which allowed White guests to attend. Joseph Tape stopped working for Matthew Sterling and went on to become a drayman delivering goods from the San Francisco ports. Shortly thereafter, in 1876, the Tapes welcomed their first child, Mamie Hunter, who was named after her father's favorite pastime.[12] She was also the only child who was given a Chinese name, Yuen Heung, which translates to "distant fragrance."[13] The family's sec-

FIGURE 3.1.
The Tape family, 1885
(Joseph, Emily, Mamie,
Frank, and Mary, L–R).
Courtesy of Mitchell Kim.

ond child, Frank Harvey, was born in 1878, and Emily, the third, arrived in 1880. Gertrude, the last child, was born in 1890, well after the case.

Why Mamie was the only child given a Chinese name is uncertain. Perhaps as their wealth increased, so, too, did the Tapes' assimilation and distancing from Chinese customs and practice. While they continued to serve the Chinese community, Joseph and Mamie Tape adopted an "American" dress and lifestyle, as demonstrated in their family photograph, where their wealth and warmth are on display (Figure 3.1). They donned decidedly Victorian-style Western clothing and used a fancy backdrop, setting themselves apart from popular Chinese photographs of the time that featured women in Chinese garb with tightly bound feet and men with queues or long, braided ponytails. Instead, the Tape family hired the professional services of Brown Photography, whose studio was situated in the wealthy part of San Francisco on Kearny Street.

Nonetheless, in all the opulence and stillness, the photograph is a beautiful display of love and family. Joseph has Emily on his lap, and Mary has Frank on hers. In a culture typically associated with favoring males over females, this switch speaks volumes of the balance within this family. Furthermore, Joseph and Mary are seated as equals. The husband is not set higher than the wife. Mamie, the eldest, tenderly holds Frank's hand, and it seems that she may be holding her mother's hand behind his back. While they all lack smiles, it is only because in the early years of photography, the subject needed to stay perfectly still for an extended period of time. As a result, a still face is easier to hold than a smile.

Assimilated, Not Acceptable

Living in White neighborhoods, adopting Americanized and expensive pastimes (e.g., hunting, painting, and photography), attending White churches, and maintaining friendships almost exclusively with Whites, Joseph and Mary Tape were an example of the classic assimilated immigrant "success story." As poor immigrants who became wealthy newcomers, the Tapes represented the kind of family that bootstrap polemics use as proof that the American Dream is achievable for everyone, except for one significant detail. The family was Chinese at a time when the Chinese of California experienced a deluge of adverse judicial decisions. In *Ho Ah Kow v. Nunan* (1879), Chinese men were ordered to remove their queue/braid. *People v. Hall* (1954) forbade Chinese to testify against White men. And most importantly, there was *Ward v. Flood* (1874), which forbade Chinese from attending the state's public schools and prohibited educational discrimination of the basis of race.

It was shortly after the passage of the Chinese Exclusion Act of 1882 that Joseph, described as "an Americanized Chinaman" in the local newspaper, sought the admission of his daughter to Spring Valley Primary School and was refused.[14] According to the *Daily Alta California*, she was denied entry because she was not considered a citizen of either the United States or California despite being American born. The headline of the article, "No Chinese Need Apply," made it clear where the Tapes stood in the public eye. Because of his connection to the Chinese consul as a translator, Joseph approached the Chinese consulate, which decided to help "test the matter in the Courts" via a writ of mandate.[15] Attorneys request a writ of mandate or a writ of mandamus when a plaintiff needs a judge to review a decision made by an administrative body. In this case, the Tapes asked the court to review the decision of the school board and order it to admit Mamie Tape as a primary school student. This legal action did not require a formal trial or recorded testimony. It was handled via legal briefs and affidavits filed by both parties. (See appendix A for chart demonstrating the relevant parties to the case.)

Chinese consul Frederick Bee and state superintendent of public instruc-

tion William T. Welcker engaged in correspondence where Bee "urged that under the law and the ruling of the recent decision by Justices Field, Sawyer, Sabin
and Hoffman, all Chinese children born in the country were entitled to public
instruction."[16] Bee was among a group of White lawyers who worked on behalf of
Chinese workers and organizations.[17] The law that he referenced in his letter was
Political Code §1667, which read, "Every school, unless otherwise provided by the
law, must be open for admission of *all children* between six and twenty-one years
of age, residing in the district" (emphasis mine). The justices to whom the consulate referred were members of the U.S. Superior Court of San Francisco. They had
recently handed down a critical decision regarding the citizenship of American-
born Chinese children via *In re Look Tin Sing* (1884). *Look* was a case involving
a Chinese American boy who was born in California but was sent to China for
his education when he was nine years old.[18] Upon his return five years later, the
port authorities refused him entry. His parents, with the help of the Chinese consulate, filed a writ of habeas corpus on his behalf. They claimed that, under the
Fourteenth Amendment, he was a citizen of the United States and California and
thereby not subject to the Chinese Exclusion Act of 1882. Therefore, he was entitled to the rights and privileges afforded all citizens.

Before rendering his opinion in *Look*, Justice Fields explained that this decision
was bigger than managing Chinese immigration. "If you depart from the plain
wording of the statute," he explained, "you will close the rights of citizenship upon
thousands of native born persons of Irish, English, and German parentage."[19] In
fact, in the opinion itself, Justice Fields argued that the citizenship clause of the
Fourteenth Amendment was created to overrule the *Dred Scott* case. Did this decision affirm the citizenship of African Americans and Chinese Americans? Al-
ternatively, did it recognize that such a ruling would jeopardize European American citizenship? In this declaration, there seemed to be an inherent protection of
Whiteness even if it meant also protecting non-Whites.

Although it was clear that both state law and judicial precedent were on the
Tapes' side, the decision was not well received by the board. In a letter published
in the *Daily Alta California* on October 10, William Welcker, the superintendent
for public instruction, rejected the court's finding for three reasons. First, he explained that he was not required to follow a simple newspaper account of the
hearing. Second, the *Look* case was not specifically about schools. Finally, the federal courts had no say over state matters. While his first two arguments were legally groundless, he was correct in that the San Francisco Board of Education held
the ultimate authority over school issues.

Agreeing with Welcker, Andrew Jackson Moulder, the superintendent of public instruction in San Francisco, made his case to deny entry to Mamie Tape at an

October 21 school board meeting. While most board members agreed with the action, they encountered surprise opposition from director Dr. Charles Cleveland, an ardent supporter of Chinese exclusion laws and vocal opponent of Chinese immigration. According to the *Daily Alta California*, Cleveland "was in favor of extending the privileges of the public schools to all native-born children irrespective of race or color."[20] Two other board members joined him to vote against the measure. Nonetheless, the following resolution was proposed and passed with a vote of eight to three: "*Resolved*, That each and every Principal of the public schools throughout the city and county under the jurisdiction of the Board of Education [are] ... hereby absolutely prohibited from admitting any Mongolian child of proper school age or otherwise, either male or female, into such school or class." Violation of this order, board members warned, would result in immediate dismissal. The order passed, but the Tapes would not be deterred.

The Tape family again attempted to enroll Mamie in Spring Valley Primary School. Principal Jeannie M. Hurley denied her entry as directed by the school board. With the help of their attorney, William F. Gibson, and the support of the Chinese consulate, the Tapes filed a writ of mandate with the Superior Court of the City and County of San Francisco the following day. At the hearing, Judge James McGuire ordered an alternate writ of mandate for the board members to admit Mamie to the school or provide an explanation for their refusal to do so by Friday, November 14.[21] In response, the board moved to quash the writ and argued that she could not be admitted because she was vicious, filthy, and dangerous to the other students because she carried contagious or infectious diseases. Under California Code §1667, these were legitimate "public health" reasons for excluding an individual regardless of race. The school also argued, "The mingling of the Mongolian and Caucassian [*sic*] races in the public school will be fraught with disastrous consequences to *our* civilization and to *our* institutions."[22] There were no such legal grounds for this assertion.

An Unvictorious Victory

Judge McGuire's opinion was released January 9, 1885, and reported in the *Daily Alta California* the next day. He ruled in favor of Mamie Tape, supporting the argument that, in conflict with the Fourteenth Amendment, she was denied entry to school simply because she was Chinese. According to McGuire, state law made public school available to all races. To do otherwise, he noted, would be "unconstitutional and void."[23] Hidden within this masked support of the Fourteenth Amendment, however, was a blueprint for how to restrict constitutional protections for the Tapes.

McGuire explained that, according to state law, schools were always meant to be open *unless* there were provisions for creating separate schools. McGuire ultimately agreed with Spring Valley Primary School's argument that racial commingling would be catastrophic, but he clarified, again, that without legislative action, he could not assert his judicial power. "This Court," he wrote, "has no power to avert a danger which springs from the absence of *necessary* laws."[24] While this opinion seemed to support a win for the Tapes, it simultaneously advised the board, in no uncertain terms, that any racial restrictions could only be handled through the legislature.

Once again, despite the holding, it was clear that the Chinese were not welcome in White schools. "Moulder," the *Daily Alta California* reported, "is strongly opposed to the admission of Chinese children into our already crowded schools and will probably contest the case to the bitter end."[25] The mention of "already crowded schools" was no doubt a precursor to race and space politics common throughout the school desegregation movement. The argument shifted from racial reasons to administrative/budgetary ones. In contending that there was no room and no funding to serve the influx of students into a school, Moulder attempted to sidestep the issue of race. It was this argument, among others, that the board engaged in a public appeal to the California legislature for separate Chinese schools while the ruling was under legal appeal. During the appeals process, the board members still refused Mamie's entry to the school.

At the school board meeting following the court's decision, Moulder read another letter from Welcker that addressed what the press dubbed "the Chinese Problem."[26] In the missive, Welcker argued that the Fourteenth Amendment, which addressed citizenship and equal treatment, did not apply to the Chinese. "Every intelligent person knows," he wrote, "that the Fourteenth Amendment was intended for persons of African descent."[27] I address this argument more thoroughly later in the chapter.

Despite weak constitutional arguments, the true sentiment regarding the Chinese in California emerged in the Welcker letter. Arguing that free public education would encourage Chinese immigration, the state superintendent asserted that the Chinese would do anything to learn English. "They have attended Sunday Schools and even pretended to be converted to Christianity in order to learn English," he wrote.[28] No matter how Americanized, the Chinese were unacceptable. The Tape family, in all their wealth and status, were still unacceptable. According to Welcker's statement, even Chinese Americans' Christianity was a ruse to take advantage of a system created and sustained by the White citizens of San Francisco. Therefore, to "protect public schools from disaster," the board disagreed with the court's ruling and ultimately decided to appeal the decision. The full text of the letter was also reported in the *Sacramento Daily Record Union* the following day. This decidedly front-page news reached the state capitol.

The board appealed its case to the California Supreme Court, and the court published its decision on March 3, 1885. Justices relied on *Ward v. Flood* (1874), where they had previously made this determination: "*Except where separate schools are actually maintained* for the education of colored children ... all children of the school district, whether white or colored, have an equal right to become pupils at any common school organized under the laws of the State."[29] Furthermore, in 1880, the California legislature passed a law that read, "Every school, unless otherwise provided by law, must be open for the admission of all children between six and twenty-one years of age residing in the district." Therefore, because separate Chinese schools did not exist, and the law provided that public schools were open for "all children," the board was compelled to admit Mamie Tape to Spring Valley Primary School. The Tapes won their case yet again.

However, like McGuire before him, Judge Sharpstein issued an opinion in which he essentially advised the school district to lobby the legislature if it wanted the law changed. He explained that while his hands were legally constrained by the law, "the legislature not only declare[d] who shall be admitted, but also who may be excluded."[30] Sharpstein also argued, "Where the law is plain and unambiguous, whether it be expressed in general or limited terms, *the legislature should be intended to mean what they have plainly expressed*."[31] Once again, the court clarified that, unless the law was changed, it could not prohibit Mamie Tape's admission to school. If, however, the legislature allowed local school boards to determine a need for separate schools, those local entities were free to deny Mamie entry. But they would have to establish Chinese schools.

The decision was reported in the news immediately thereafter, and the board, specifically director J. H. Culver, petitioned the legislature to create a bill that bestowed authority on local school boards to create separate schools for Chinese children. One month later, the board began discussing and planning a separate school for Chinese children within the boundaries of Chinatown. However, Moulder and Culver both objected to spending public funds to create it. At the April 1 board meeting, Culver made the case that, despite the rulings, California schools should remain White: "If we have patriotism, if we have love for our fellow men, the Caucasian race, if we have any regard for the 50,000 children ... placed our charge, we should cry halt."[32] While it was not clear exactly what he proposed as a solution, he used vivid military imagery to argue that the board should, like the Spartans against the Persians, "never be polluted by these barbarian hordes."[33]

Culver's appeal was dripping with disdain and disgust for the Chinese. He declared that ten thousand "Mongolian monster[s]" were working feverishly to steal labor, and that Mamie Tape was "the apex of a triangle whose base [was] unknown."[34] Finally, Culver called on the board and the citizens of San Francisco to exclude "this foul element" who were "worse than pests."[35] Though hyperbolic in his assertions, Culver used catastrophic, monstrous, and diseased language as evidence that Mamie Tape and children like her were unwelcome, unwanted, and intolerable.

Shortly thereafter, Joseph, with judicial order in hand, applied again for Mamie to attend the school. This time, Hurley denied her admission on the grounds that she did not present vaccination records "properly signed by a respectable physician."[36] The headline "Mamie Tape Outwitted" epitomized the pride the public took in deterring an eight-year-old from her education.

In response, the board called a special meeting to discuss the creation of a Chinese school. In addition to discussing the facility's location, they agreed to pay Miss Thayer, the principal of the Chinese school, over $100 per month, which was over three times as much as a nearby principal was paid. Why the increased salary? Moulder explained that Thayer deserved extra pay because this assignment "would not be very pleasant at this time; she would have to go through Chinatown and be thrown constantly among children of a foreign race."[37] This, effectively, was tantamount to hazard pay.

It was also during this meeting that Moulder proclaimed, "The people of this city and State have been often abused by the tirades of such cranks as Henry Ward Beecher, De Witt Talmage, and Bob Ingersoll for their exhibitions of race prejudice."[38] Henry Ward Beecher was a preacher who was known for his advocacy of the Chinese. During visits to California, he "gave lectures and interviews deriding the opposition to the Chinese and accusing Californians of gross exaggeration regarding the danger of Chinese immigration."[39] He and Thomas De Witt Talmage, an American Presbyterian minister, both wrote or spoke out against anti-Chinese legislation put forth in Congress and politicians' attempts to restrict vessels to fifteen Chinese passengers.[40] While not a religious man, Robert "Bob" Ingersoll was a well-known local lawyer who vigorously defended and supported equal rights for all races.[41] The fact that these men's names were even uttered demonstrated the powerful influence clergy and allies held over the politics of the day.

After securing vaccination records, the Tapes once again attempted to enroll Mamie at Spring Valley Primary School. This time she was turned away because the classes were "full." Gibson, the Tapes' attorney, subsequently threatened to file for contempt. Moulder, the board, and Hurley explained that Mamie could attend any school created for Chinese students. The Tapes then alleged that the alternate school was too far from their home. This "distance argument" was a foreshadowing of what would become a common theme in future school desegregation cases. Many plaintiffs would try and fail to argue that inconvenient or even dangerous distances were legitimate reasons to allow entry into more conveniently located

White schools. Unfortunately, as Joseph Tape and his attorney made these pleas, "carpenters began the work of fitting the school room" for the Chinese school.[42]

The Chinese school opened the following Monday, April 13, 1885, with only six children in attendance, including Mamie and Frank. A reporter for the *Daily Alta California* identified the Tape children as "a pair of little heathens" and described the room in vivid detail, calling it a "fully equipped American class."[43] Despite the fact that Mamie and Frank were U.S. citizens, the word "Americans" was synonymous with "White" in this report.

In the afternoon, four more children came to the school, and the reporter observed, "The youngsters all speak good English."[44] The same, however, could not be said for the journalist. Nevertheless, it was clear that Mamie was the focus of the article, which described her as "the most intelligent member of the class."[45] The detail used to depict her dress was particularly fascinating. All the other children wore "Chinese costume," except for Mamie. Mamie was "gorgeously attired in American clothes, including pink stockings and a light-colored leghorn hat, provided with an ostrich plume of *immense* proportions."[46] One can only imagine how Mary dressed her daughter that morning with the knowledge that she would be on display. Her family was captured in the public eye for the better part of a year, all the while accused of false Christianity, described as heathens, and likened to catastrophic events like waves, floods, wars, and plagues.

Still, even the young girl's fancy and elaborate dress could not insulate her from slights and stereotyping. Superintendent O'Connor visited the school and "tested" Mamie by asking her for the definition of "newspaper," an interesting choice of word considering the presence of the press. The *Daily Alta California* journalist described her reaction: "She looks puzzled for a few seconds, then quickly answers, 'a tidings sheet.'" Instead of being impressed, the reporter wrote that Mamie's reply was obviously coached. Directly contradicting his earlier description of Mamie's intelligence, he wrote, "From the answer it is apparent that most of her information is a result of drilling."[47] This was all laid out on the front page for all of San Francisco to witness. As San Franciscans consumed these newsworthy events, accounts like this one must have shaped and contributed to the contention that the Tapes, and by extension the Chinese community, could never truly be Americans.

A Mother's Wrath

With all of those eyes transfixed on the Tapes, the final story printed about the family was telling. On April 16, 1885, the *Daily Alta California* published "a verbatim copy" of a searing letter from Mrs. Mary Tape addressed to the school board

(Figure 3.2). The editors did not correct the numerous spelling and grammatical errors. Perhaps this was intentional, making Mrs. Tape (and, by extension, her children) appear unintelligent and unworthy of the White school. A reader could further conclude that Mrs. Tape did not have mastery over English, or that she was so angry she wrote without regard for grammatical rules. The strong vocabulary and generous use of exclamation points supports the latter contention. Nevertheless, Mary Tape filled her letter with outrage that mimics the fierce rhythm of Sojourner Truth's "Ain't I a Woman" speech. In it, the indignant mother turned many of the board members' arguments against them. For example, she questioned their Christianity by asking, "Do you call that a Christian act to compel my little children to go so far to a school that is made in purpose for them."[48]

She also argued that board members had "expended a lot of the Public money foolishly," especially considering their reluctance to spend tax money on the school in the first place. Mrs. Tape consistently deployed the imagery of men picking on a little girl, demonstrating the obvious power imbalance inherent in the case. She referred to Mamie as "my little child . . . one poor little Child . . . [and] little Mamie Tape," using "little" to describe her daughter's age and size.[49] For almost a year, Mamie was the face of a reviled population demanding equality, dignity, and a recognition of citizenship. By consistently describing her as little, Mary staged Mamie as the innocent victim of the big, bad Superintendent Moulder, for whom she reserved her most direct and acerbic accusations. Directly addressing Moulder, Mary wrote, "It seems to me Mr. Moulder has a grudge against this Eight-year-old Mamie Tape [*sic*]. . . . May you Mr. Moulder never be persecuted like the way you have persecuted little Mamie Tape."[50] Though notions of assimilation and allegations of racism took up most of the letter, Mrs. Tape's "momma bear" instincts were on full display.

She directly accused the White men of racism and suggested that Mamie, a Chinese American child, represented more of the American ideal than they ever could. Just as the San Francisco Ladies' Protection and Relief Society fired the kitchen worker and laundress who refused to work with Mary when she was a ward, Mary stood up for her daughter years later. In examining this letter within its historical context, Mrs. Tape's words directly attacked these White male administrators. Even in the face of legislative defeat, this mother still wanted the public to know that it was these men, and not the Tapes, who were un-Christian, foolish, and un-American.

In addition to the *Daily Alta California*, the letter was printed in the *Sausalito News* and the *Marin County Journal* on June 11, 1885. Why it appeared almost two months after the original story's publication is uncertain. What is certain, however, is that *Tape v. Hurley* captured the public's imagination. It was a watershed

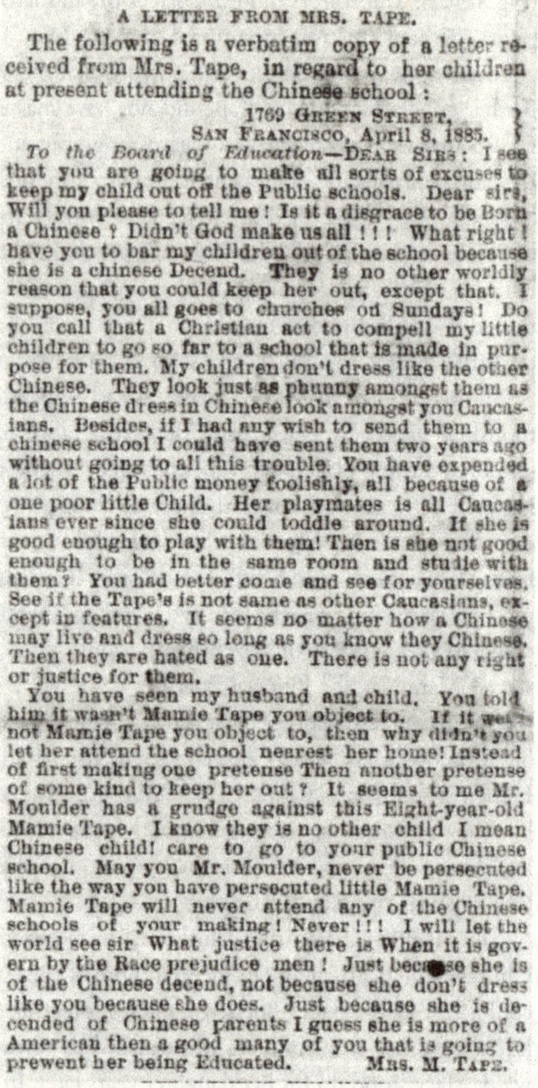

FIGURE 3.2.

A mother's letter, *Daily Alta California*, April 16, 1885, 1.

A LETTER FROM MRS. TAPE.

The following is a verbatim copy of a letter received from Mrs. Tape, in regard to her children at present attending the Chinese school :

1769 GREEN STREET,
SAN FRANCISCO, April 8, 1885.

To the Board of Education—DEAR SIRS : I see that you are going to make all sorts of excuses to keep my child out off the Public schools. Dear sirs, Will you please to tell me ! Is it a disgrace to be Born a Chinese ? Didn't God make us all ! ! ! What right ! have you to bar my children out of the school because she is a chinese Decend. They is no other worldly reason that you could keep her out, except that. I suppose, you all goes to churches on Sundays ! Do you call that a Christian act to compel my little children to go so far to a school that is made in purpose for them. My children don't dress like the other Chinese. They look just as phunny amongst them as the Chinese dress in Chinese look amongst you Caucasians. Besides, if I had any wish to send them to a chinese school I could have sent them two years ago without going to all this trouble. You have expended a lot of the Public money foolishly, all because of a one poor little Child. Her playmates is all Caucasians ever since she could toddle around. If she is good enough to play with them ! Then is she not good enough to be in the same room and studie with them ? You had better come and see for yourselves. See if the Tape's is not same as other Caucasians, except in features. It seems no matter how a Chinese may live and dress so long as you know they Chinese. Then they are hated as one. There is not any right or justice for them.

You have seen my husband and child. You told him it wasn't Mamie Tape you object to. If it was not Mamie Tape you object to, then why didn't you let her attend the school nearest her home ! Instead of first making one pretense Then another pretense of some kind to keep her out ? It seems to me Mr. Moulder has a grudge against this Eight-year-old Mamie Tape. I know they is no other child I mean Chinese child ! care to go to your public Chinese school. May you Mr. Moulder, never be persecuted like the way you have persecuted little Mamie Tape. Mamie Tape will never attend any of the Chinese schools of your making ! Never ! ! ! I will let the world see sir What justice there is When it is govern by the Race prejudice men ! Just because she is of the Chinese decend, not because she don't dress like you does. Just because she is decended of Chinese parents I guess she is more of a American then a good many of you that is going to prevent her being Educated.   MRS. M. TAPE.

event in history that laid the groundwork for *Plessy v. Ferguson* (1896) before that case even established the doctrine of "separate but equal," which remained the law of the land until 1954.

Tape v. Hurley itself was not mentioned or revisited again until the *Sacramento Union* published an eleven-line retrospective called "Twenty-Five Years Ago Today."[51] It was printed on page six, indicating how inconsequential the story was to the newspaper editors. The Tapes reappeared in the press approximately seven years later in an interview with Leland Gamble of the San Francisco *Morning Call.*

This interaction did not mention the case, but its significance is addressed later in the chapter.

Legal scholar Joyce Kuo argues that *Tape v. Hurley* "symbolized a new era of activism through the legal system."[52] Still, the story of *Tape*, its participants, and its significance disappeared into the annals of legal history, largely omitted from the school desegregation narrative.[53] There may be several reasons for its omission. First, *Tape* was a pre-*Plessy* decision. Once *Plessy* became the "law of the land," and *Wong Him* was decided in 1902, the legal findings and significance of *Tape* were moot. Second, there were far more legal cases involving Black plaintiffs that set stronger precedent than those involving non-Black plaintiffs, including *Roberts* (1849), *Garnes* (1871), *Ward* (1874), and *King* (1883). It may have been too easy to dismiss the significance of a case involving a Chinese American plaintiff when there were so many stronger, similarly situated cases involving Black plaintiffs. Third, because it was never appealed to the federal courts, *Tape v. Hurley* did not gain the same legal significance reserved for circuit and Supreme Court cases. These are all solidly legal reasons for its absence in the canon of civil rights law generally and school desegregation law specifically.

I argue, however, that the reason for *Tape*'s exclusion is rooted in a much deeper issue related to Asian Americans' perceived proximity to Whiteness within U.S. race relations. Outside of Japanese American concentration camps, civil rights scholarship largely fails to consider the past experiences of Asian Americans due to their modern-day perception as "model minorities."[54] This exclusion, I believe, is ultimately rooted in the misinformed opinion that the past discrimination of Asian Americans did not result in the same persistent, long-term, and systemic oppression experienced in Latiné and Black communities and is therefore historically insignificant. I hope the Tapes and their story demonstrate otherwise.

ASIANCRIT AND *TAPE*

An analysis of the *Tape* case and the Tapes as a family reveals how the racialization of Asians mixes with the politics of respectability and contributes to the variability of Asians' placement on the racial hierarchy. In one legal case and with one family, Asians move from not belonging on the color line to being forever foreigners and then model minorities. The Tapes' very public legal journey, I contend, reflects the AsianCrit tenets of Asianization and transnational contexts.

Asianization builds on the treatment of race under CRT by adding the convenient, incongruent treatment of Asian and Asian Americans as the "yellow peril," "forever foreigners," and "model minorities." As my research demonstrates, the Tapes experienced all three treatments. First, school officials declared them to be outside the protections of the Fourteenth Amendment's Equal Protection Clause, arguing it was only applicable to African Americans. Second, newspapers regularly characterized them as threats to an "American" way of life. Third, journalists, and the Tapes themselves, described their family as more American than Americans.

A review of the historical record, however, reveals how ascribing a singular treatment to the Tape family fails to consider the complexity with which they were racialized. In 1885 San Francisco, it seems the Chinese were ranked below African Americans on the racial hierarchy and stood outside the Black/White binary of race altogether. AsianCrit provides an explanation for this "flip" in the racial hierarchy. Specifically, it has been called "unevenly oppressed" as well as a "flexibility of convenience."[55]

First, school officials, despite the lower court's ruling, determined that the Chinese were not beneficiaries of the Constitution. In the initial case, Judge McGuire ruled that Mamie Tape was protected under the Fourteenth Amendment. On January 10, the *Daily Alta California*, under the headline "Judge Maguire Says They Have Same Rights as Others," printed a verbatim copy of the judge's opinion: "The only reason urged against her [Mamie Tape's] admission is that she was born of Chinese parents. In other words, because she is descended from the Chinese branch of the Mongolian race, she is excluded by law from participating in the benefits and privileges of free public education, which are by the same law accorded children of all other races—white, black, and copper-colored."[56] While Maguire did not define "copper-colored," it is clear from his opinion that he referred to the Chinese children of the state. Later in the week, in a letter read during a school board meeting, state superintendent Welcker announced, "There is not an intelligent man or woman in the United States ... who does not know perfectly well that the Fourteenth Amendment was intended for persons of African descent, and particularly for the protection of those who had been born in slavery. No thought was had of the Chinese in the matter; indeed [*sic*] had there been such thought, undoubtedly an exception would have been made against them."[57] The Fourteenth Amendment, school officials argued, "is confined to those within the sphere of Federal citizenship."[58] This wording was a classic states' rights argument.

This declaration, however, is fraught with contradictions. On the one hand, it is an acknowledgment that such protections were afforded to African Americans, despite numerous state laws and ordinances in California and around the country designed to limit them.[59] On the other hand, the Chinese were excluded from what little protections that did exist. Even though the court had to rule in the Tapes' favor, the decision still managed to lobby for the right to create separate Chinese schools.

In addition, school officials often characterized the Tapes as threats to Whites and America, which was consistent with representing Asians as "forever foreigners" and part of the "yellow peril." While most of this language was ascribed to two individuals, state superintendent Welcker and San Francisco superintendent Culver, they were two men in positions of power whose words could be and were translated into law. Recall that in their petition to the lower court, the attorneys for the schools argued that mixing Chinese and White students would be catastrophic "to *our* civilization and to *our* institutions."[60] The "our" in this proclamation is not indicative of a generalized notion of San Francisco civilization or institutions. It is a claim of ownership that accompanies Whiteness and separates "our" (read White) world from their Chinese world. Even Judge McGuire wrote that he had no power to "*avert a danger*" until the law was changed.[61] Superintendent Welcker went on to ask, "Shall we neglect *our own children* for the Chinese?"[62] In this query, the "our" is much more explicit and clearly constructed against the Chinese other. Finally, in supporting the decision to appeal the case, Superintendent Welcker explained that it was the responsibility of the school board "to protect public schools from *disaster*."[63]

Throughout the public reporting of the trial, the Tapes were consistently referred to as "the Chinese Problem" or "the Chinese Trouble" in headlines.[64] Newspapers and school officials used the following language to refer to the Chinese generally and the Tapes specifically:

- "Preventing children of the Caucasian race from coming into contact with their objectionable neighbors."[65]
- "Admitting Chinese will demoralize our schools."[66]
- "Our classes will be inundated by Mongolians. Trouble will follow."[67]
- "Dreaded and the most insidious enemy we have."[68]
- "Long, sinuous, blue-bloused, wooden-shod, stealthy treading Mongolian monster."[69]
- "Insects and pests that threaten the products of the husbandman."[70]
- "An evil an [*sic*] hundred times more to be dreaded than worm or weevil or phylloxera."[71]
- "A moral blight that no skill or science can cure."[72]
- "This blight, this cancer on our otherwise fair city."[73]

Violence-laden words like "disastrous," "danger," "problem," "enemy," and "trouble" were constructed against the repeated use of the word "our" to delineate a clear line between Whites and Chinese. As a result, it seemed as if the Chinese were not only a different race, but they were also inhuman, akin to insects, pests, fictional monsters, and a devastating cancer.

In addition to being characterized as yellow peril, Chinese were often described as unwelcomed foreigners who were incapable of assimilation. In a letter published in a Sacramento newspaper, San Francisco superintendent Moulder seemed to cast Mamie's citizenship into question by writing, "[Tape] demands admittance . . . for his daughter, who he *alleges* is native born."[74] Later, Superintendent Welcker stated that any Chinese who asserted California citizenship likely did so with "perjured witnesses." Welcker further explained, "[I] should not be surprised to see gray-haired Chinamen apply for admission to our schools, and with plenty of witnesses to swear that they had been born in California, and less than seventeen years ago."[75] The fact that Mamie was born in San Francisco, California, carried little weight in the eyes of school officials. She was Chinese—not American. In what a San Francisco newspaper called "an Exhaustive Communication," Welcker argued, "It would be the strongest inducement to Chinese immigrants to give them free education. The Chinese are extremely anxious to learn English." He said that these individuals would even pretend to be Christian to learn, thereby throwing their motives into question.[76]

When separate schools were initially suggested in January, Superintendent Welcker lamented, "Where is the money to come from! There are thousands of children in San Francisco for whom we cannot provide."[77] By March, the *Daily Alta California* reported, "The city can draw $10,000 for the support of the special schools for Chinese, which will be ample."[78] While the school was under construction, newspapers continued to make claims about the Chinese. In observing that the walls of the new Chinese school were covered with slang, a reporter wrote, "It is more than probable that the children will become familiar with it [slang] before they learn the rudiments of the English language."[79] This statement inferred two things asserting the students' "forever foreigner" status: (1) Chinese children did not speak English, and (2) they were more likely to learn substandard slang than even basic English. These Tape children and the Chinese children they represented, irrespective of citizenship, did not belong.

Despite the contention that the Tapes represented yellow peril and forever foreigners, the politics of respectability also meant that they represented an early version of "the model minority." While they were characterized by most as Mongolian monsters, family members were simultaneously called American. Joseph and Mary Tape were transformed from "Chew Diep" and "the Chinese girl" into American entrepreneurs and homeowners. Over the course of the court case, newspaper reports referred to Joseph as an "Americanized Chinaman" initially, and then reverted back to "a Chinese resident of California" and "Chinaman" shortly thereafter.[80] Journalists made similar observations about the Tape children. After Mamie's original petition to the court, a journalist described her as being "eight years of age, a native of California, in good health, [and] of good character and cleanly habits."[81] When the Chinese school first opened, the reporter on-site observed that the children spoke English well, declaring, "They are as conversant with the language as many white children of foreign birth or parentage."[82] This directly contradicted the assertion that Chinese children did not speak English. Furthermore, while the pupils were called "white," it was still a foreign form of Whiteness. Nonetheless, the journalist went on to observe, "Mamie Tape is, perhaps, the most intelligent member of the class."[83] When compared to the other children who were attired in "Chinese costume," the correspondent wrote that Mamie "was gorgeously attired in American clothes."[84] Another reporter observed, "Both children [Frank and Mamie Tape] are bright and talk English as well as most pupils at the public schools. They are dressed neatly in clothes like those worn by American children and have none of the Chinese peculiarities in regard to the manner of wearing their hair."[85]

There was no one, however, more adamant of Mamie's status as an American than Mary Tape. "My children don't dress like the other Chinese," she stated in a letter to the school board. "They look just as phunny [*sic*] amongst them as the Chinese dress in Chinese look amongst you Caucasians."[86] In describing "the other Chinese" as funny looking in their Chinese dress, Mary set herself apart from the general Chinese population. She further distanced herself when she wrote of her daughter, "Her playmates is [*sic*] all Caucasians ever since she could toddle around.... You better come and see for yourselves. See if the Tape's not same as other Caucasians, except in features."[87] At first glance, these statements could be (and have been) interpreted as embracing assimilation and used as evidence of worthiness. With assimilation comes denial, so to speak, that racism exists as a hindrance. "If *they* can do it," goes the model minority saying, "why can't *you*?"

However, when her remarks are placed in the context of her letter, it is clear that Mrs. Tape recognized that her treatment directly resulted from racism and discrimination on the part of prejudiced men. For example, after asserting that all of Mamie's friends were White, she also asked, "If she is good enough to play with them! [*sic*] Then is she not good enough to be in the same room and studie [*sic*] with them?" Later in her letter, Mary Tape asserted, "I will let the world see sir What [*sic*] justice there is When it is govern by the Race prejudice men." She even declared Mamie to be "more of a[n] American than" board members.[88]

Altogether, I contend that Mary Tape was not arguing to be recognized as white. Nor was she asserting that she achieved honorary Whiteness. In fact, she was very clearly pointing out the absurdity of racism that allowed children to play but not study together. She was not endorsing racial sameness, but she was advocating the recognition that Mamie's race should not preclude her from the same rights as Whites. Finally, Mary directly accused the White men she wrote to of racism, and she suggested that Mamie, a Chinese American child, represented more of the American ideal than they ever could. Just as the San Francisco Ladies' Protection and Relief Society fired the kitchen worker and laundress who refused to work with Mary when she was younger, Mary stood up for her daughter years later. In examining her letter within its historical context, I argue that Mrs. Tape's words and actions were a form of protest. Even in the face of legislative defeat, this mother still wanted the public to know that it was the White men on the school board, and not her own family members, who were un-Christian, foolish, and un-American.

Years later, the Tapes' middle-class status brought into question their description as forever foreigners and solidified their position as model minorities. In 1892, Leland Gamble of the San Francisco *Morning Call* visited the Tapes' home in a neighborhood at Washington and Stockton at the edge of Chinatown and made several observations regarding the family's wealth and Americanness. First, Gamble was surprised by Joseph Tape's ability to speak " good English," and declared it was the best he had "ever heard in [his] life."[89] When left alone for a moment in the home's parlor, Gamble wrote that "everything in the room bore the unmistakable signs of refinement."[90] He also described Mary Tape as "charming," "pretty," and "intelligent," noting that she spoke "the best of English."[91] He deemed Joseph Tape an accomplished businessman and sportsman who was "thoroughly American in every way possible."[92]

In Gamble's article, Mary Tape is quoted as saying, "Since that time [her marriage to Joseph] we have always lived as Americans, and our children have been brought up to consider themselves as such."[93] Once again, this declaration could be interpreted as embracing assimilation. However, as Mary explained, she and her family straddled the Chinese world and their upper-class existence. "[Our children's] education in the common branches has been gained at the Chinese public school on Clay Street and their other accomplishments by private tutors," she remarked.[94] With the means to hire private tutors, the Tapes conceivably had no reason to send their children to the Chinese school.

In demonstrating racial flexibility, the Tape family vacillated between status as yellow peril, forever foreigners, and model minorities, depending on the circumstance and the observer. They argued for citizenship, equality, and full recognition of their rights, insisting on their Americanness. Arguing that that insistence is a declaration of Whiteness is attempting to interpret history through modern definitions and experiences of race. Superintendent Welcker perceived the Tapes as a threat, newspapers characterized them as unassimilable foreigners, and journalist Leland Gamble declared them "thoroughly American."

While I am not certain how many readers of the *Morning Call* consistently read Gamble's column, it is clear that whoever read the story was introduced to an extraordinary family. While the *Tape v. Hurley* trial was not mentioned in Gamble's article, readers who were familiar with the Tapes had the task of reconciling the family the newspapers created with the one Gamble interviewed. To equate the Tapes with honorary Whiteness, selling out, or assimilation would be to disregard the fact that they put themselves and their families under the microscope of a society that detested their very existence. To declare them assimilated would also preclude the possibility that the Tapes, too, experienced a form of the double consciousness and twoness set forth by W. E. B. Du Bois. Perhaps they were balancing and reconciling their Chinese identities with their American identities, wholly aware that they were being observed and judged by Whites.

This discordant characterization of the family as yellow peril, forever foreigners, and model minorities was, I believe, a result of the inability to place the Tapes in any particular category due to their class. They could not represent yellow peril because instead of taking jobs, they were creating businesses. Furthermore, they, like many Whites, were homeowners. The Tapes could not be forever foreigners because they spoke English fluently and did not engage in traditional Chinese practices. Finally, they were not model minorities because, while impressive, Mary Tape's letter and the family's performance of respectability were not about demonstrating Asian Americans as White but challenging the very notion of American democracy and freedom.

In considering the second tenet of AsianCrit, transnational context, the presence of China in *Tape v. Hurley* was recognized repeatedly by newspapers, school officials, and jurists. The United States and its democracy were on display on the world stage. In Judge McGuire's opinion, he wrote, "It would be a sad commentary upon our institutions and our civilization if it should appear to the world that by our laws we *levied forced contributions*, in the shape of special taxes for school purposes . . . upon our Chinese residents, and then refused to let them share in the benefits."[95] The phrase "it should appear to the world" acknowledged the deleterious effects the Tapes' case could have internationally. At this point, the United States had recently celebrated its centennial, and the Fourteenth Amendment had only just passed in 1868. The *Tape* case captured the national struggle to reconcile messages of freedom and democracy with discriminatory, racist practices.

Superintendent Culver referred to a report by the U.S. Bureau of Labor and Statistics and warned the school board, "It is difficult to overrate the effect and influence of the Chinese upon our industrial condition of our State. At a rough estimate we have about 104,000 of them here at present—eighty per cent of that number directly competing with white labor, and the remaining twenty per cent engaged in trading with China."[96] In line with both CRT and AsianCrit, it is clear the Chinese represented a threat to domestic labor and international trade. Culver further attempted to calculate how much money had been paid to the Chinese in the form of wages and reports, estimating the sum at a little over $27 million. "What do you think of that showing[?]" he asked his audience during a speech. He continued, "There is no work except at starvation prices; but there is $20,280,000 per year paid to this thrice detested race.... Think of it—the prosperity, the homes, the business that amount of money would produce if spent here instead of being shipped to China."[97]

Even the Tapes' connection to the Chinese consulate did not escape Gamble's adoration. The reporter wrote that Joseph Tape acted as an interpreter for the "Imperial Consulate in China," possessed a "monopoly of transporting Chinese," and supplied wholesale Chinese merchants in Chinatown.[98] In today's world, Tape would be revered for keeping Chinese business within Chinese hands. Gamble also seized the opportunity to ascertain whether the Tapes intended to return to China. The Tapes answered, "We may some day [*sic*] if we feel that we can afford the trip, but it will only be as tourists visiting a foreign country. California is our home."[99]

Traditional CRT does not capture this Chinese American experience. Black plaintiffs could not avail themselves of the services of a consulate. They did not have the force of an entire country's economy at stake in their legal cases. They were neither accused of pretending to be Christian in order to learn English, nor subject to immigration laws that limited their entry into the United States and made it increasingly difficult for them to stay. Apart from racist calls for them to "go back to Africa," African Americans were not seriously asked whether they were going to visit or return to an unidentifiable country of origin. The Tape family represented the yellow peril, forever foreigners, and model minorities. Yet their model minority presentation did not shield them from some forms of discrimination, as perhaps it would today, even temporarily. The *Tape* case reveals the temporal nature of the model minority myth. With no population against whom the Chinese could be constructed, it served no purpose. Furthermore, as forever foreigners, the Tapes were inexorably tied to a country of origin regardless of their birthplace. A double-edged sword, being from a foreign country invited exclusion on the one hand but protection on the other, as it was subject to the checks and balances that come with a global economy. To assert their citizenship rights and belonging, the Tapes were deeply committed to the principle that, as an American, Mamie deserved the same treatment as her White friends with whom she "toddled around."

MAMIE TAPE: "AS WELL AS . . . AN AMERICAN GIRL"

As described, the Tapes were a thoroughly Americanized Chinese family. They possessed "American" names, lived outside of Chinatown, and spoke English fluently. By 1895 Berkeley had became home to the Tapes, and they seemed more at ease among wealthier Whites than their Chinese customers. It was there, in Berkeley, that the Tapes became "archetypal members of the first Chinese American middle class," and it was there where they lived a life marked by an impressive upper-class life replete with "touring cars, hunting dogs . . . and society weddings."[100] Their success, however, could not shield them from being subject to, judged by, or safe from the controlling images of pagans, prostitutes, and poor creatures.

Nonetheless, a review of twelve newspaper articles from the *Daily Alta California* regarding the *Tape* case makes it clear that even the Americanized Tapes could not escape the controlling image casting Mamie and her brother Frank as heathens.[101] The state superintendent of public instruction accused the Tapes of pretending to be Christian in order to be bilingual.[102] At a meeting of the board of education, James H. Culver declared, "Those brave men who signed that immortal declaration [of independence] . . . Never thought their descendants would permit heathen temples with idolatrous worship to be reared beside our churches dedicated to the living God, or that the barbarous dim of gongs or invocation of gods of wood should rise and mingle with the sweet church bell."[103] Such pagan imagery painted the Tapes as non-Christian, non–English speaking, and ultimately not worthy of the valuable benefits of citizenship. Their "gods of wood" were no match for the ethereal beauty of church bells and cherubic angels.

After having her family's Christianity questioned in newspapers, Mary Tape retaliated by publicly challenging the school board's Christianity in her letter. She wrote, "Dear sirs . . . Didn't God make us all!!! . . . I suppose you all goes to churches on Sunday!"[104] The issue, however, was that she questioned the board members' faith but did not confirm her own. Thus her letter could be publicly perceived as the ranting of an angry, uneducated mother. Furthermore, the missive came too late. She wrote it after the school board had decided to create a separate Chinese school. Throughout the *Tape v. Hurley* ordeal, reporters obsessively followed and described the Tapes without mentioning their strong ties to their local Presbyterian church or connection to the San Francisco Ladies' Protection and Relief Society.[105] Consequently, this aspect of the Tape family's life was never captured or reported in the local newspaper.

The Tape family also failed to escape the vitriol normally reserved for criminal elements like prostitutes or poor creatures. According to Culver, Mamie was among the "Mongolian monsters" representing a deadly threat to White society and civilization.[106] The state superintendent explained that the admission of Chinese children would "drive many of the Caucasian children out of the schools."[107] In a speech to the school board, he asked whether White children should be ignored "for the Chinese who ... [thrust] themselves [into our society]."[108] Finally, school superintendent Moulder proclaimed that "he was not ashamed to avow his belief in the existence of a natural feeling of dislike to the people of the Chinese race."[109] The school officials made it clear that Mamie Tape was not one of their own children. Instead, she was a "monster" and a disastrous threat to White civilization who would always be subject to a "natural feeling" of disdain.

It is clear that the Tapes were mischaracterized by the board and consequently the newspapers. In fact, on Mamie's first day in the new Chinese school, recall that a reporter described her "American" attire in tremendous detail, noting the color of her stockings and even the size of a feather in her hat.[110] The Tapes' status and "difference" might have been useful to their case if this description had been reported before the school board's decision, or when the school first refused Mamie admission. Joseph and Mary were the recipients of similar treatment.

For *Tape*, the *Daily Alta California* published two accounts that followed the fighting father narrative. In the very first article about the case, the newspaper reported, "The first application was made by Joseph Tape, a Chinese resident of California for eighteen years, who has a daughter aged 10."[111] In this initial piece, the author used Joseph's full name and did not refer to him as a Chinaman. The readers were also told that Joseph had lived in California for eighteen years. This fact at least signaled that he was not a recent immigrant. Most importantly, at age ten, his daughter was very young. What father wouldn't fight for his ten-year-old daughter?

Joseph Tape appeared in the newspaper again a month and a half later. This article described *Tape v. Hurley* as "the case of Joseph Tape, a Chinaman who has sued the board to compel them to admit his daughter."[112] While the account still used Joseph's full name, this time it referred to him as "a Chinaman." His residency was not mentioned. Finally, instead of making an application, Joseph "sued" and "compelled"—the language is much more forceful than formal. Nevertheless, he was still acting on behalf of his daughter.

While there were not many instances of Joseph and Mamie named together, Joseph Tape appeared the most in the newspaper coverage, interchangeably referred to as "an Americanized Chinaman" or simply a "Chinaman." The *Daily Alta California* also reported on his connections with the Chinese consulate and his ardent attempts to gain admission for Mamie in spite of the diversions and trickery deployed by the school board.

Mary Tape inserted herself into the narrative when she wrote her fiery letter to the board after the opening of the Chinese school. Therein, she tenaciously defended her daughter and simultaneously attacked the board's integrity, Christianity, fiscal responsibility, and overall humanity. Had that letter been the only thing the public learned about Mary Tape, it would have been a mere glimpse into this remarkable mother. While she was referred to as simply a "Chinese Mother," later reporting and research reveals that she was a mother, an entrepreneur, a professional telegrapher, and a photographer. She was cast first as an indignant mother and ultimately an impressive matriarch.

In 1892, reporter Leland Gamble visited the Tape family home to investigate the "fairy tale" of "a young Chinese woman who devoted most of her spare time to photography."[113] This story might have been considered a "fairy tale" for two very significant reasons: First, very few female photographers existed in the late 1800s. Also, the sheer equipment and materials necessary to master photography limited its enjoyment limited to those who could afford it.[114] Frances Benjamin Johnston, one of the most well-known "lady photographers" in the late nineteenth and early twentieth century, explained that being a woman photographer involved "personality, mental poise, physical strength, staying qualities, technical training, unrestricted patience, and endless attention to detail."[115] The details of this interview elevated Mary Tape, who had publicly scorned the school board only a few years prior, to the same status as Johnston and other noted women photographers.

In the late 1800s, it was unheard of for women, much less a Chinese woman, to be in photography.[116] Of his meeting with Joseph Tape, Gamble wrote, "On being asked if the story was true that his wife understood photography, he answered with a laugh and said ... 'Yes, sir, and a good many other things too.'"[117] Joseph invited the journalist into his home, described as "a cozy little parlor furnished with the best of taste ... an upright piano, on the top of which rested a French horn and a zither ... a combination library and specimen case [with] a goodly array of books ... [and] some beautiful specimens of California birds [which] had all been shot by the master of the house."[118] Gamble portrayed Mrs. Tape in the following manner: "Mrs. Tape ... is dressed in a gown of soft clinging silk or some Indian stuff which set off her figure to good effect. Her hair was arranged in the latest American fashion and was as black and glossy as ever graced the head of an Andalusian beauty. Her face was comely, one might even say pretty, because it had so much intelligence and was set off by a fine mouth behind which were a set of pearly teeth."[119]

Eager to see Mary Tape's photographs, the correspondent was escorted into a room while Mary retrieved them. As he waited for Mary, Gamble observed a full set of encyclopedias, copies of Shakespeare, birds preserved by a professional taxidermist, gold and silver galena, seashells the family had accumulated from their world travel, and a telegraph used to communicate between the home and the business, all markers of wealth and achievement. He remarked, "I saw that with proper instruction before they [the Tapes] had become imbued with national traits they were as susceptible of civilization as any nation in the world."[120]

Once Mary returned with the photographs, Gamble professed himself "fully prepared to see some exquisite work in photography" and declared, "My expectations were more than realized."[121] Observing that her photographs were on par with professionals', Gamble sorted through a pile of portraits and was amazed that they were "all done by a native-born Chinese woman."[122] Mary laughed and told him that those were the picked-over photographs. She explained, "Oh, these are nothing. . . . My friends usually beg everything good and leave me the rest."[123] More than a devotee of a simple hobby, Mary displayed expertise as she described her process and education to the astonished journalist. "I not only take my own pictures but prepare my own plates and make my own prints," she said. "You will no doubt wonder how I came to understand so much about the business, and I can tell you that everything I know has come from reading different authorities on the subjects and then studying the methods to see which was the best." As proof of her statement, Gamble selected a few photographs to reproduce in the newspaper. It is also clear from the article that Joseph was proud of Mary. He shared the diplomas she earned from the mechanics' institute, as well as her paintings. Gamble described one of these paintings as "an excellent still-life painting of fruit which made his mouth water."[124] His astonished admiration for Mary Tape was evident throughout the article.

Mary, in all her splendor and wealth, would never be confused with a prostitute or pagan. Those controlling images of Chinese women held no control over Gamble's perception of her and the picture he drew for his audience of her family, home, and life. Instead, Mary Tape's class elevated her to an intelligent, gifted, and even pretty woman, wife, and mother. This Chinese family had been rescued from the "national traits" that had beset other Chinese in San Francisco. The Tapes had traveled to beaches across the world and collected seashells. They had money to pay a professional taxidermist to preserve the birds Joseph had successfully felled. They had obtained galena, a crystalline lead mineral. Their galena, however, was suffused with gold and silver. The Tapes probably had more money than the White journalist they invited into their home.

Despite all these achievements, Mary Tape was still given the moniker be-stowed on her during her early years in the orphanage. The title of the Gamble article was "What a Chinese Girl Did." Despite revealing very little of her life as Mary McGladery, Mary Tape was still, in the eyes of this journalist and perhaps the public, a "Chinese girl."

A fascinating family, the Tapes were definitely worthy of newspapers' report-ing. In fact, I suggest the Gamble article could have helped them, but it came seven years too late. If the public had learned of them through this account, the Tapes would have been inundated with accolades for their Americanization. For exam-ple, upon learning from Mary Tape that, "Mamie is quite proficient in piano," Gamble wrote:

> I expressed a desire to hear the young lady play and imagine my surprise when with-out any of the backwardness and diffidence of American girls of the same age she took her seat at the piano and began to finger the keys . . . to play the "Mocking-bird" and brought out its notes as well as I have ever heard them brought out by an American girl. . . . I was sitting in a room with a family of full-blooded Chinese listening to a Chinese girl playing an old-time favorite on an American piano and talking to me with as much spirit as any girl of my own race.[125]

In this article, regal Mamie Tape stood in stark contrast to the earlier descrip-tions of Chinese prostitutes. She was regal compared with them. Mamie, because she dressed like an American girl and played piano better than an American girl, was far from a poor creature. Gamble's account was almost a tribute to the Tape family. He made it clear to his San Francisco readers that this Chinese family was different. In fact, he even confessed, "When I saw around me the father, the mother and their accomplished children I *changed my opinion* in regard to the race in general.[126]

What if this article had appeared at the same time the Tape family filed suit? Could they have been presented in such a way to contradict controlling images? How many other opinions would have been changed? Would the public have been outraged at how the school board treated this assimilated family? Would Mamie have been considered worthy of an American education? The Tapes' faith and Americanized identity, as well as Mamie's impressive piano skills, did not reach the public until it was too late. Would this information have been of any benefit at all? Though Mamie won the legal battle, the Tapes lost the race war. The Tape family, their attorney, and the Chinese consulate could not capture the American imagination and position themselves as sympathetic symbols in the pursuit of the American Dream.

CHAPTER 4

Piper v. Big Pine—
the Forgotten

My generation is now the door to memory. That is why I am remembering.

—JOY HARJO, poet, Muscogee Nation

The photographer desperately tries to get all the students to look in the same direction and sit still, if only for a moment. The boys seem tired of sitting in the hot sun, perhaps fidgeting with their shirts and ties in hope of some relief. The White kids look comfortable and almost confident, especially Albert, the boy in the front row. He sits there relaxed, as if he has had his picture taken before. For the others, the tan-skinned reminders of a promise forcefully fulfilled, it is their first time.

The White boys' hair is cut and combed close to their heads. The Paiute boys have hair that is thick and looks shaggy, especially Jeff and Ike. They both look like they do not want to be there. The White boys have their fancy bow ties and neckties . . . except one. Maybe that is why he was put in the back? One of the Paiute boys has a tie, but he doesn't appear to know how to tie it; it sits lopsided, looking like two tails hanging side by side. Another boy didn't bother at all, opting for a crisp white shirt. Still another boy has donned a suit, a full dark suit in this heat!! His parents must have spent a lot of money for it—I think they knew this day was special. Only one of the White boys, Hank, is wearing a suit, and he didn't even bother buttoning it up. Instead, he stands there, hands in his pockets, looking like a future elected official.

The other girls are all dressed up in pretty white dresses. Only one of them, Banta, looks like her dress was made at home. Amid all the bangs and pressed dresses of the White girls sits Alice, wearing a long-sleeved dress. Her hair is much darker than the other White girls', but her skin is as light as theirs. She almost looks like the actress Louise Brooks, as her hair is bobbed like pictures found in American Hairdresser *magazine.*

FIGURE 4.1.

Big Pine School integrated, 1925. *Top (L–R):* Weldon Bartels, Hank Houghton, Charlie Conners, Blanch Steward, Ken Steward, and Marvin Steward. *Middle (L–R):* Alice Piper, John Davito, Banta, Jeff Tibbe. *Bottom (L–R):* Ike Baker, Maxine Brown, Albert Cuddubac, Myrtle George, Ward Rogers. Courtesy of Big Pine Paiute Tribe of the Owens Valley and Big Pine Unified School District.

The Paiute children seem clustered together. Alice and John look like they are excited to be there. Their look is filled with the promise of a better education beyond baking, cleaning, sewing, and physical labor. They have the look of dreamers . . . of children who know their world is bigger than Big Pine. Banta, Jeff and Ike, on the other hand, look as if they were forced to be there, unwilling participants of a legal victory. Ike, especially, looks as if he is saying, "When can I go home?" This is the first picture of all the children together—a moment frozen in time whose effects touched every Native child in the state. It is a photograph that says, "We belong here too!"

Figure 4.1 captures the end result of the *Piper v. Big Pine* story. However, these students' journey to belonging began much earlier and wove a complicated tale pitting formal and informal modes of storytelling against each other. While the research on *Piper* is scant, what exists is informative. Only two scholars have written about the case, and they both identify it as the most influential one in Native American educational history.[1] While interdisciplinary scholar Nicole Blalock-Moore was able to secure newspaper accounts and some archival material regarding either the case or the political atmosphere of Owens Valley at the time, much of the story of Alice Piper has been told from an outsider's perspective rather than that of someone within the Big Pine Paiute Tribe of the Owens Valley. The story of the case from the Paiute point of view has largely been passed down through the oral tradition characteristic of Indigenous cultural practices.

Capturing the Paiute ethnohistory requires, in the words of Indigenous scholar Leo Killsback, an understanding that "time must be deconstructed, especially when discussing Indigenous peoples and their histories."[2] As a result, traditional methodologies must be decolonized as suggested by Linda Tuhiwai Smith. Smith contends that telling history from an Indigenous perspective requires an understanding that much of it is "*re*writing and *re*righting our position in history."[3] Indigenous communities, she explains, possess "a very powerful need to give testimony to and restore a spirit, to bring back into existence a world fragmented and dying."[4]

In an effort to *re*right the story, I rely on both traditional and decolonized methodologies. In this chapter, I first provide the story according to traditional methodologies (i.e., archival research, newspaper accounts, and secondary research). I identify this section as the research according to "the papers." Next, I deliver a fuller account of the *Piper* story as I learned it from "the people." This narrative includes not only past understandings of the case but also the contemporary efforts to ensure that future generations will always remember Alice Piper and her legal struggle for equality. Learning the stories from the papers and the people allows for a richer understanding of the parties involved, including both an outsider's perspective and an insider's understanding.

What the Papers Say . . .

The year was 1924 in Owens Valley of Big Pine, California, home to members of the Paiute and Shoshone Tribes. Two important historical events coincided with the *Piper* decision: a bitter struggle for water rights and the closure of Indian schools across the country. The fight over water rights had begun as early as the 1860s, when White settlers helped themselves to the Owens Valley Paiute irrigation system, thereby destroying the Paiute food supply.[5] In 1907, the state government designated Owens Valley as an area that would supply water to Los Angeles via an aqueduct set to be completed in 1913. Between 1905 and 1935, the Los Angeles Department of Water and Power purchased several acres of land from the Owens Valley Paiute farmers and ranchers.[6] The ultimate battle over water rights challenged the deceptive manner of obtaining signatures for the 1937 Land Exchange Act. This statute effectively stripped the Owens Valley Paiutes of their rights to land and its life-sustaining water. In fact, Owens Lake became a "dry lake bed" as a result of quenching the demand for water pulling from Los Angeles.[7]

As water was being drained from the community, children all over the country were returning to their homes after taking part in the failed system of Indian day and boarding schools. Indian day and boarding schools had begun shortly after the passage of the 1887 Dawes Act, introduced by Senator Henry Dawes. Also known as the "Indian Emancipation Act," the ordinance allowed the president of the United States to, at his discretion and *without the consent of tribal leadership*, deed 160 acres of reservation lands to the heads of Native American families. This land would be ineligible for sale for twenty-five years, and participants in the program would be granted U.S. citizenship. The act's stated goal was to "protect" Native Americans from theft so that they could farm their own land, "adopt civilized habits," and live side by side with their White neighbors, who also received 160 acres from the reservation "surplus." The *Congressional Record* explained what supporters of the measure anticipated: "With white settlers on every alternative section of Indian lands there will be a school-house built, with Indian children and white children together; there will be churches at which there will be an attendance of Indian and white people alike.... They [Indians] will readily learn the ways of civilization."[8] Despite its stated beginnings, the Dawes Act ultimately resulted in the loss of over ninety million acres of "Indian land," making Indigenous nations landless and impoverished.[9]

In the late nineteenth and early twentieth centuries, the federal government determined that the best way to ensure civilization was through education. With the goal of assimilation, the Dawes Act allocated funding to public schools that taught Indian children beside White children. The ranks of public schools, however, did not swell with Indian youths. Instead, America witnessed the tremendous growth of government-sponsored Indian boarding schools and trade schools purporting that the best path to civilization was removing children from the reservation.

According to Indigenous education scholar David Wallace Adams, over twenty-one thousand Native American children were removed from their homes. Even so, Indian commissioner Frances Ellington Leupp declared these tactics an abysmal failure by 1905. Shortly after this declaration, the population of Indigenous children in public schools increased dramatically (Table 4.1, Figure 4.2).[10]

We learned from the *Tape* case that separate Indian schools were already determined to be legal provided they were equal.[11] By 1912, the federal government begged California public schools to accept more Native American children.[12] These students weren't admitted until the 1920s, only after the government confirmed that public schools would receive more federal funding.

In Big Pine, the government-run Indian school was established in 1891.[13] As federal schools closed around the state, public school systems were required to

TABLE 4.1
Distribution of Indian Students by Institutional Type, 1900–1925

	1900	1905	1910	1915	1920	1925
GOVERNMENT SCHOOLS						
Off-reservation boarding	7,430	9,736	8,863	10,791	10,198	8,542
Reservation boarding	9,604	11,402	10,765	9,899	9,433	10,615
Day schools	5,090	4,399	7,152	7,270	5,765	4,604
SUBTOTAL	22,124	25,537	26,780	27,960	25,396	23,761
Public Schools	246	84	2,722	26,438	30,858	34,452
OTHER						
Mission, private, and state institutions	4,081	4,485	5,150	5,049	5,546	7,280
TOTAL	26,451	30,106	34,652	59,447	61,800	65,493

SOURCE: *Annual Report of the Commissioner of Indian Affairs (ARCLA),* 1900, 22; *ARCIA,* 1905, 50; *ARCIA,* 1910, 56; *ARCIA,* 1915, 51; *ARCIA,* 1920, 147; and *ARCIA,* 1925, 51. Drawn from Education for *Extinction: American Indians and the Boarding School Experience, 1875–1928,* 2nd ed., by David Wallace Adams, published by the University Press of Kansas, © 1995, 2020, www.kansaspress.ku.edu. Used by permission of the publisher.

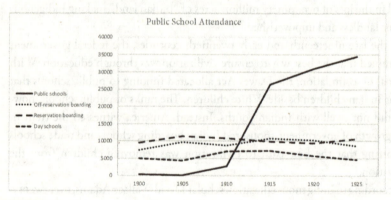

FIGURE 4.2.
Rise in public schools (1900–1925).

accept the displaced children due to compulsory attendance laws. By 1920, the population of students in California's government-run schools had dropped by 25 percent.[14] By 1920 a brand-new facility housing Big Pine's public high school was constructed, and Paiute parents, including Alice Piper's, expressed interest in enrolling their children. During the fund-raising efforts for the new high school, members of the Paiute community were very much a part of the process, and they were also "promised that their children would be able to come to school here."[15] In *Piper*, the judge described the public school system of California as "a product of the studied thought of the eminent educators of this and other States of the Union." The justice continued, "Each grade is preparatory to a higher grade, and, indeed, affords an entrance into schools of technology, agriculture, normal schools, and the University of California. The common schools are doorways opening into chambers of science, art, and the learned professions."[16] With such a promise of advancing education beyond the traditional trades taught at the government-run school, it was no wonder the Pipers sued for Alice's right to walk through the doorways afforded by California public schools. Yet the school board closed the door, citing Political Code §1662 requiring Indian children to attend a government-run school within a three-mile radius of their homes.

In December 1923, the Pipers, through their attorney J. W. Henderson, filed a writ of mandate for the California Supreme Court to review the administrative decision not to admit Alice to the all-White public school. Six other students joined the suit because they, too, were excluded from attending the local White school on the basis that they were Indian. Henderson delivered two arguments. First, he maintained that because the Pipers were citizens and lived away from the reservation, Alice was eligible to be admitted to the local school via the Dawes Act. Second, using the Fourteenth Amendment, he challenged the constitutionality of Political Code §1662 and its three-mile radius requirements, as well as the board's ability to create separate schools for Native American children so long as they were equal in every substantial respect. At that time, Big Pine had a government-run school for Native Americans, but Alice lived approximately thirty miles away in Fish Lake Valley and was therefore not required to attend.[17]

The board argued that the federal school was "in all respects . . . equal" to their public school, and was "better adapted to the education of members of the Indian race."[18] Board members also argued that there were plenty of private schools that Alice and her family could consider in lieu of the public school system. Furthermore, they claimed that admitting Alice and the other six children would increase the attendance of other Indian children, "who [could not] be cared for because of the economic or administrative problem which it [would] create."[19] Finally, because the board maintained that it would fight the matter to the California Supreme Court, the application for writ was made directly to the state supreme court and accepted.

The court held that even though Alice was a "descendant of the aboriginal race," the policy of the federal government had been "to promote the general welfare of the American Indian, even to the point of *exercising paternal care*."[20] Under the Dawes Act of 1887, the Pipers were considered citizens of both the United States and California because they maintained "a residence separate and apart from any tribe of Indians . . . and [had] adopted the habits of civilized life."[21]

Since they were citizens who lived apart from the Paiutes, and since the board had not established its own public Indian school, Alice was entitled to attend the all-White public school. In a letter dated June 4, 1924, Jess Hession, the district attorney from Independence, wrote the following to Mr. L. L. Goen, a clerk for the Big Pine School District:

> Dear Mr. Goen,
>
> I beg to advise that I am to day [sic] in receipt of a postal card from the Clerk of the Supreme Court, informing me that on the 2nd of this month the Court ordered the writ to issue as prayed for in the Alice Piper case. This means that the Court has taken the petitioner's view of the law in the case and is undoubtedly holding the state law unconstitutional so far as it attempts to make the Indians attend a government school. I will be in receipt of a copy of the opinion in a few days and will know than [sic] definitely what they have done. We gave them the best we had and apparently had them stuck for awhile [sic] anyway.
>
> Yours very truly,
>
> (signed) Jess Hession.[22]

The final sentence in the letter provides some insight into how desperately the school board did not want to admit Paiute children. The notion that attorneys "apparently had them [the Pipers] *stuck* for awhile anyway" provides evidence of using the court system to delay the process or at least delay the decision to admit Alice.

Coincidentally, the *Piper* decision was issued the same day that Congress passed the Indian Citizenship Act of 1924 declaring all Native Americans, regardless of tribal affiliations, U.S. citizens with the right to vote. While this event could be coincidental, the decision did come at a time when the country was experiencing large shifts in Native American policies. Enrollment in government-run schools in California had dropped by 25 percent by 1920, and the federal government was not reimbursing public schools that accepted Native American students.[23] This perfect storm of state policy, federal policy, structural changes in education, and the collective response of Indigenous communities made the *Piper* case so unique compared with the other four Native American cases discussed in chapter 2.

What the People Say . . .

I interviewed representatives from the Big Pine Paiute Tribe of the Owens Valley and a representative from the Big Pine Unified School District. Those individuals are listed in alphabetical order below:

> Danelle Gutierrez, tribal historic preservation officer
> Pamela Jones, superintendent of Big Pine Unified School District
> Sage Andrew Romero, outreach coordinator for the tribe

Together, they shared a story of a family who did not, as the *Piper v. Big Pine* opinion suggested, abandon their Paiute heritage. Instead, they fought for the dignity of their tribal legacy and the right to secure an education beyond trades.

According to Pamela Jones, the families participating in *Piper v. Big Pine* "did not necessarily want to be assimilated but they wanted to be a part of this new world they were building, and they wanted the best thing for their children."[24] Gaining access to the White public school required them to surrender their identities and communities. Yet for the Pipers and the families of the six other children involved in the case, it was a matter of gaining access that was deserved.[25] In fact, as Sage Romero shared, "These were the ones that were sticking to it. They were like telling them, 'We're not gonna move!' It's not like they were stepping from the people because they were stronger with their culture and their homeland." Indeed, Pike and Annie Piper's Office of Indian Affairs (OIA) records were signed six years *after* the case. In those papers, the Pipers affirm their Paiute identity and list the residence they maintained on tribal land.[26] They were absolutely members of their tribal nation (Figure 4.3).

FIGURE 4.3.
Big Pine Paiute community, date unknown. Alice Piper is the first person in the last row from the left. Pike Piper, her father, is the first man on the far left. Annie Piper is not pictured. Courtesy of Big Pine Paiute Tribe of the Owens Valley.

According to their OIA records, Pike and Annie Piper claimed membership in the Paiute Tribe of Inyo County, California. Pike Piper stated he had one-half degree of "Indian blood" because his mother, Sepsey, was full Paiute and his father was White. His mother's Indian name, typed phonetically, was "Te-va-ku-wa." When asked to list his father's name, Pike simply answered, "Do not know." It appears from the records that he knew his family lineage on his mother's side, including the identity of his maternal grandfather ("Co-ma-hah-nuh-gu") and grandmother ("Ya-pah-cu-ha"). Unfortunately, he knew nothing from his father's side. Pike, too, had an Indian name, "Maw-che," as dictated in the record.[27]

Annie Piper, according to her records, was full Paiute. Her maiden name was Stewart. Her parents, Mike and Peggy, were also known as "Wo-ho-ki-ke" and "Pow-now-we," respectively, and they were married according to "Indian Custom." Unlike Pike, Annie knew both her paternal and maternal grandparents, who were all members of the Paiute Tribe.

From the opinion of *Piper v. Big Pine*, it sounds as if Pike and Annie had separated themselves from tribal affiliations. The court record reflects that the couple had "adopted civilized habits," but it doesn't explain what those habits entailed other than choosing to live off the reservation and owning land unconnected to a tribe. However, the Pipers' OIA records and my informants demonstrate the family's clear connection to their Paiute Tribe. This begs the question of whether compliance with the Dawes Act was nothing more than a legal strategy to establish U.S. and California citizenship in order to win the case. To solidify the Pipers' connection to the land, Danelle Gutierrez explains a custom that solidifies the Pipers' connection to the land: "Traditionally . . . and even to this day, back then families in their birthing ceremonies would do it some place special that connects them to their area to their ground that locks you in . . . gives you your strength . . . and calls you back and what keeps you solid."[28]

What did Alice do after graduating from Big Pine? According to her father's OIA record, she was "attending high school at Los Angeles California."[29] Thanks to the information found in over two hundred pages of her federal employment record, her life after the case becomes more defined. She attended Polytechnic High School in Los Angeles. While she did not formally graduate, she did complete the twelfth grade in 1930.[30] For several years between 1931 and 1938, Alice worked a variety of jobs from arranging programs for young Indigenous girls with the YWCA to serving as an interpreter in Bishop, the next town over from Big Pine.

Her life changed in 1938 when she began working at Stewart Indian School. Like that of many Indian boarding schools, the history of Stewart is fraught with conflicting stories of acceptance and abuse.[31] The role Alice played in those stories is unclear. However, it seems she had a special connection with the school, because

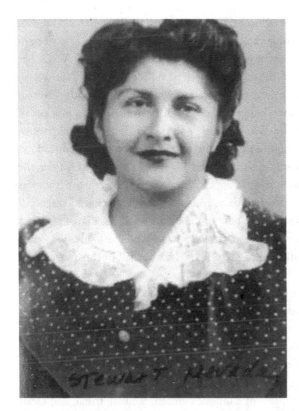

FIGURE 4.4.
Alice Piper's Stewart Indian School photograph, date unknown. Courtesy of an anonymous donor to the Big Pine Paiute Tribe of the Owens Valley.

she returned after leaving to get married in 1939 and resigning for unknown reasons in 1951.[32] According to her employee records, Alice served in various positions but spent most of her time working in the boys' dormitory (Figure 4.4). Her employee application notes indicate an affinity for the children under her care. She listed her job responsibilities as the following: "Organize and teach boys so that in each job he performs, skills are developed, Ideal habits are formed, attitude and appreciation are developed and related knowledge is acquired. Be available for counseling and advise any time. Encourage religious and athletic activities. Have mixed group house parties where they do the planning." This entry is a conflicting mixture of institutionalization, autonomy, and emotional support. On the one hand, what exactly are "ideal habits"? On the other, Alice recognized students' need for counseling and advice.[33]

In her employment application dated March 20, 1961, Alice wrote the following about working with the "special 5-year Navajo Boys": "Worked with regular high school boys and the special 5-year Navajo Boys. They (Special) were older Navajo—received training equivalent to graduation at 12th grade level. Worked and lived [in] cottage dormitory. The Navajos were non-English speaking group.

[They] understood enough English and interpreted for us (Leaders).... The Navajos were different group, older and set in tribal way." Miss Piper acknowledged that these pupils were a "different group" who were "set in tribal way." Was it her responsibility, then, to "reset" the boys and teach them "ideal habits?"[34]

According to a document prepared by Stewart Museum curators, the "Navajo Boys" consisted of young men between the ages of twelve and twenty, some of whom were among the World War II Navajo code talkers.[35] The federal government decided that the Navajo "deserved the opportunity to get an education," which was framed as a reward for their service.[36] Designed by Hugh O. Tyler, the Stewart Indian School's supervisor of vocational training, the Navajo program was a five-year curriculum where the first three years were dedicated to academic studies, and the last two years were split between academics and vocational training. The program began in 1947 with 147 Navajo students who required interpreters and entire dormitories dedicated to them. By 1958, over half of the Stewart students (613) were Navajo.

Alice's selection (self or otherwise) to be the matron for the Navajo students reveals an underlying confidence from the institution's leaders that she could manage these young men who did not readily surrender their language. Once again, this information represents the competing realities of Stewart, as do the oral histories about the school collected by the University of Reno.[37] Was Stewart a place that offered food, housing, and security? Or was it a place that represented the painful process of being stripped of a unique cultural, familial, tribal, and racial identity and having it replaced it with a monolithic, one-size-fits-all version of an American identity.

Research on Indian boarding schools is rife with individuals whose experiences were too traumatic to share. In other instances, the trauma may not be fully realized. Dr. Eulynda Toledo, founder of the Boarding School Healing Project, shares of her own experience, "I always knew somewhere in my being that I was hurt even though, at age five, I didn't understand the school's true mission of 'killing the Indian to save the man.'"[38] Engaging with the history of Stewart Indian School requires an understanding of the role of intergenerational trauma that is outside of my expertise.[39] Nevertheless, consistent with other Indian schools, the "curriculum" at Stewart was largely vocational and consistent with gendered roles. The men learned mechanics, carpentry, masonry, and farmwork, while the women learned home economics, music, and arts and crafts and trained to be nursing assistants.[40] Whether Alice Piper offered comfort or consternation, I do not know. What is known, however, is that she gave over twenty-five years of her life to the children that passed through Stewart, and it is my hope that she showed them love, guidance, and acceptance.

FIGURE 4.5.
Alice Piper's home at 971 Bowers. Author's photograph.

Sick with diabetes, Alice retired on June 29, 1968, at the age of sixty, stating, "There are many days that I do not feel like working."[41] Danelle Gutierrez suggested Alice Piper was *called back* to her home, as evidenced by the fact that she maintained a residence on the reservation until her death (Figure 4.5). Furthermore, Alice's parents were both interred in the burial site maintained by the tribe.[42] Unfortunately, her home fell into disrepair. However, to the left of the house are the remains of her greenhouse. According to Sage Andrew Romero, Alice was an avid gardener. Danelle explained that someone purchased the home with the intent to fix it up, but she was unsure of where those efforts stood.

The *Piper* story is incomplete without telling the story after the story. During our interview, Pamela Jones and Sage explained how they met at Big Pine's centennial celebration in 2009. There, Pamela suggested that the school needed something to commemorate Alice Piper. "I was thinking a plaque or *maybe* a head," she recalled.[43] But Sage dreamed bigger and suggested a life-sized statue.

Through fund-raising efforts, a challenging Kickstarter campaign, various conference presentations, visits to powwows, local radio advertisements, and collaboration with Native American actress Misty Upha and Native American rapper Lady Xplicit, Pamela and Sage earned enough funds to commission an artist in

FIGURE 4.6.
Alice Piper Memorial.
Author's photograph.

Utah. The sculptor created the statue from a sketch rendered by Robert Gutierrez, a local Paiute artist (Figure 4.6).[44]

The Alice Piper Memorial was unveiled on June 2, 2014, the ninetieth anniversary of the *Piper* decision, in a ceremony filled with celebration and tears for having accomplished such an amazing goal. Alice Piper's contribution to educational equality is forever commemorated in a plaque situated at the base of her statue. It says,

ALICE PIPER MEMORIAL

"Fighting for Education, a Paiute Student Breaks Down Barriers"

Alice Piper, the daughter of Pike and Annie Piper, was a 15-year-old Paiute
girl living in Big Pine, California in 1924. She, along with other Indian
students in Big Pine, wanted to attend Big Pine High School, but was denied

because state law prohibited Native Americans' attendance if an Indian School was nearby. Piper sued the school district claiming the state law establishing separate schools for Indian children was unconstitutional. The State Supreme Court ruled in her favor. Due to this historic action, the Big Pine School District and Alice Piper are memorialized as major players in the constitutional battle over the rights of Native Americans to attend public schools. The decision has been used as a precedent in other cases such as Brown v. Board of Education.

Piper v. Big Pine (1924) 193 CAL 664

HONORING EQUAL EDUCATION FOR ALL

While *Piper* was not cited as *legal* precedent in the *Brown* opinion or briefs filed on behalf of *Brown*, I argue that it set an important historical precedent, particularly in California. Though there are two stories to be told through the papers and the people, the significance of the story is the same: Native American education was transformed that day in the small town of Big Pine, California. As Sage passionately shares in one of several fund-raising videos for the memorial, "Alice Piper has been hidden away for too long and now is the time for us to bring her story out and honor her."[45]

TRIBALCRIT AND PIPER

To reveal the significance of this hidden story and honor the unique racial position of Native Americans, I specifically consider the following TribalCrit tenets: the liminal space Native Americans occupy, the problematic governmental policies built around assimilation, and the importance of obtaining autonomy and self-determination. Together with the two stories of *Piper*, these precepts provide a more layered understanding beyond questions of authenticity, acceptance of assimilation, and surrendered contentedness with being absent from the segregated-schooling narrative.

As it relates to occupying liminal spaces, the Piper family possessed both a racial and a political identity. In its opinion, the court referred to the Pipers as belonging to the "aboriginal race" and as "persons of the Indian race and blood."[46] The family also possessed a political identity, as established in the OIA records where they outlined their lineage. Recall that the Pipers not only summarized their blood quantum in these documents, but also recognized their Paiute names and revealed that they were married according to "Indian custom." The opinion and the OIA paperwork provide conflicting evidence regarding blood quantum, cultural practices, and federal requirements.

Within CRT, there is much discussion on the one-drop rule for African Americans and using customs and social relations to identify the "true race" of the racially ambiguous. For Native Americans, however, the one-drop rule is inapplicable. One drop, so to speak, would not be enough to be recognized by not only the tribe but also the government. This biologically determined method of identifying individuals who are Native by blood confounds sociological assertions that race is a social, not biological, construct. Even using the term "Indian race" is problematic because, as Gross explains, "making blood quantum... the *sine qua non* of tribal citizenship has helped to turn national identities into racial ones."[47] Alice Piper was not a member of the Paiute race. She was a member of the Paiute Nation. The traditional language of race within the race scholarship does not provide a space for the Pipers. The Pipers exemplify what Brayboy calls a "state of inbetweeness," as represented in the possession of both a racialized identity ("Indian blood") and a legal/political identity (Paiute).[48]

This in-betweenness is similar to the border identity outlined by Gloria Anzaldúa.[49] The difference, however, is that a border identity represents the social pressures that arise from living between two cultures: one Mexican and one American. The Pipers' liminal space was both socially constructed and subject to legal requirements. Furthermore, it was not an internal battle of authenticity. It involved more than "feeling" their race or split identities; it was very often the difference between rejection and recognition. TribalCrit provides the language and the analytic framework necessary to describe the racialized experiences of Native Americans.

Piper also represents the TribalCrit tenet of identifying and interrogating problematic government policies that require assimilation. In order to win their case, the Pipers had to meet certain requirements under the Dawes Act. In its opinion, the court recorded their compliance: "Neither the petitioner nor either of her parents has ever lived in tribal relations with any tribe of Indians or has never owed or acknowledged *allegiance* or *fealty* of any kind to any tribe or 'nation' of Indians or has ever lived upon a government Indian reservation or has at any time been a ward or dependent of the nation."[50] The requirement for the family to reject their nation of origin and pledge allegiance or fealty to the United States is akin to asking U.S. citizens to renounce their citizenship, cut all ties with their families, sell their homes, move to Mexico, learn Spanish, and pledge allegiance to the Mexican government. Such a suggestion would seem absurd, yet it was standard treatment of sovereign tribal nations within the United States.

The court further conceded that Alice's political and civil citizenship was not in dispute. They recognized the following: "She is a descendant of an aboriginal race whose ancient right to occupy the soil has the sanction of nature's code. Since the founding of this government its policy has been, so far as feasible, to promote the general welfare of the American Indian, even to the point of exercising paternal care, and whenever he has shown an inclination to accept the advantages which our civil and political institutions offer, to permit him to enjoy them on equal terms with ourselves."[51] This quote not only captures how Alice was raced but also how she was rendered mythical and characterized as bound to the earth. The words are almost romantic, ethereal. Nonetheless, despite the court's fascination with "nature's code," its justices claimed in a completely revisionist fashion that the policy of the federal government was to "promote the general welfare of the American Indian." To benefit from this government "paternal care," a Native American must, per the Dawes Act, "voluntarily [take] up . . . his residence separate and apart from any tribe of Indians therein, and [adopt] the habits of civilized life."[52] Alice Piper fulfilled what Paige Raibmon calls the "one drop of civilization" rule.[53]

According to my informants, the Pipers did none of those things required by the court. They remained Paiute through and through. Acquiescing publicly yet subverting the law privately was a legal strategy, and it reveals how lax the policing of assimilation was after the failure of Indian industrial schools. My interviewees posit that the federal Indian schools were no more than glorified trade schools designed to teach Native Americans skills that would ultimately serve Whites. As Sage explained, women were taught to be housekeepers, and men were taught to be groundskeepers.[54] That Alice's parents desired to enroll her in the White public school suggests that those skills were not part of the life they imagined for her. According to Pamela, the Piper family "didn't want to necessarily be assimilated but they wanted to be a part of this new world . . . They wanted the best thing for their children. They wanted access."[55]

This leads to the third TribalCrit tenet, which identifies Indigenous people's desire for autonomy, self-determination, and self-identification. I argue that the Piper family then and the Paiute Nation today engaged and are engaging in a powerful form of self-identification. Then, the Pipers rejected government policy and reconciled their liminal positions by maintaining their connection to the Paiute Tribe. Furthermore, photographs of the integrated school show that Alice was significantly lighter skinned than her Paiute classmates. Passing could have very well been a possibility for her. All evidence presented in her life choices, however, points to maintaining a strong connection to her community. She accepted a position as a matron for the Carson City Stewart Indian School. She lived on the reservation. She buried her parents in the tribal cemetery.

Today, the Paiute Tribe continues its efforts of self-determination and self-identification. In coordinating community efforts to erect a memorial to Alice and her role in the *Piper* case, the Paiutes of Owens Valley have "defined themselves and create what it means to be Indian."[56] They were not "ecology-loving, bead-wearing, feather-having, long-haired" men and women.[57] They were activists, organizers, and change agents. They did not settle for a plaque, as was initially suggested when discussing the memorial to Alice Piper. They wanted and earned a life-sized statute. As young Paiute student Alicia Peterson explains in one of the many videos created to promote the memorial, "The Alice Piper case isn't known very much anywhere. It's kinda sad. That's our own Native American history. We gotta get it out there and teach it to everybody."[58] According to the modern-day keepers of knowledge, *Piper* inspired the Paiute community to redefine and reconstruct the narrative of the case and attempt to insert it into the civil rights narrative. Race scholars should not diminish the contributions of *Piper* to the civil rights narrative simply because the plaintiffs won using the Dawes Act and not the Fourteenth Amendment. If anything, the case demonstrates the complex ways equality was achieved and how, to borrow a phrase from Audre Lorde, it is necessary to use the "colonizers' tools" against them in order to win.[59]

ALICE PIPER: "A PERSON OF GOOD HABITS AND CHARACTER"

When considering the role of controlling images in *Piper*, the evidence to ascertain how the court perceived Alice and her family is more circumstantial than direct. But for the opinion, a few photographs, and vague recollections from Big Pine informants, we know very little about Alice's childhood. We know that, at least for legal arguments, she and her family "severed" ties with their Paiute community. These contentions, however, were more ruse than truth. Also, in the opinion, both the attorneys for the Pipers and the school board admitted, "She [Alice] is now and at all times . . . [has] been a person of good habits and character, in good physical health, and . . . she is in need of and desirous of obtaining an education such as is obtainable in the public school of this state and . . . her parents are desirous that she should obtain such an education."[60] These "good habits and character" requirements were directly constructed against the same laws that denied children of "filthy or vicious habits" entry into the school. These behavior assessments were mostly assigned to children of color who wished to attend White schools.[61] As such, I suggest that this statement was included in the opinion to counter any notions that Alice and her family were still "uncivilized" or "savage." As was the case with Native populations, according to the federal government and its education policy, these children were more likely to assimilate, unlike their Black, Asian, and nonpassing Mexican counterparts.

Alice was also the lightest-skinned Paiute child in the integrated photo with her classmates. She might have been able to pass for White. Sporting a plain white dress and a hairstyle more contemporary than those of her blunt-browed female classmates, she seemed the very picture of assimilation. Alice represented what many of the creators of the Indian boarding schools attempted to capture in photographs.

As for Alice's parents, Pike and Annie, the newspaper accounts were unfortunately limited, generally discussing "Indian schools" without referring specifically to the Pipers. My informants explained that, generally speaking, more is known about Alice's father than her mother. Pike and Alice Piper appear in the community photograph, but Annie is nowhere to be found. In fact, none of the known relatives of the Pipers could produce a photograph of her. Recent articles on the *Piper* case published in the *Inyo Register* and on the Indian Country Today and Sierra Wave websites only mention Alice.[62] In the two academic treatments of *Piper*, Blalock-Moore only mentions the parents' Native and English names and does not go into detail, and Wollenberg, the first academic to write about the case, only mentions Pike Piper.

The reason for this lack of information may be as simple as the fact that only men were allowed to file lawsuits. However, California passed the Married Women's Property Act in 1850, which allowed wives to purchase property, file lawsuits, and manage family assets as the legal representative.[63] However, much of the Married Women's Property Act required deference to the husband, and a woman's rights were mostly triggered upon her husband's death. Still, the strength of the daddy-daughter narrative is indicative of a patriarchal society painting men as strong and women as silently supportive.

One thing we do know for sure is that education was deeply significant for the Piper family. After completing her course of study in Big Pine, Alice attended high school in Los Angeles and eventually served as a matron with the Stewart Indian School. She was far from "traditional"—her matron photo alone reveals a well-styled woman wearing lipstick and a simple polka-dot dress. Furthermore, in an anonymously donated collage of photographs, Alice appears in scenes from her life that could never be attributed to a "squaw princess." One image shows her at a traditional wedding at the age of twenty-five (Figure 4.7). In pictures with unidentified female friends and family members at various points in her life from childhood to adulthood (Figure 4.8), Alice and her companions are always dressed in contemporary "Anglo" attire. If only the donor of the photographs were known, I would have a better idea of the circumstances behind each picture. Instead, I am only left to piece together a life that, according to my informants, was well lived.

Alice obtained her education at Big Pine, continued it in Los Angeles, shared it with others in Carson City as a headmistress, and then returned home, where she lived a quiet life tending to her beloved garden. At a minimum, these photographs and stories are evidence that, in those captured moments, she was happy, loved,

FIGURE 4.7.
Wedding party photo, April
16, 1945. Alice is to the right
of the bride. Courtesy of
an anonymous donor to
the Big Pine Paiute Tribe
of the Owens Valley.

FIGURE 4.8.
Alice Piper with unidentified friend and solo, dates unknown.
Alice is on the right of the friend. Courtesy of an anonymous
donor to the Big Pine Paiute Tribe of the Owens Valley.

and connected to friends and family. Taken together, the *Piper* opinion, the photographs of her life, and her family recollections demonstrate that Alice was most certainly not a savage, a traditionally dressed squaw, or a sacrificial maiden as constructed by popular culture for the American imagination. Alice Piper's ability to be mobile, pursue education, and live independently both on and off the reservation situates her, like Mamie Tape, in a middling position where she could not be considered uncivilized, sexual, or poor.

CHAPTER 5

The Mendezes— the Understated

And now I see the present, and still, I am the campesino, I am the fat, political coyote in a country that has wiped out all my history, stifled all my pride . . . and placed a different weight of indignity upon my age-old burdened back. Inferiority is the new load. . . .

I shed tears of anguish as I see my children disappear behind the shroud of mediocrity, never to look back to remember me. I am Joaquín. I must fight and win this struggle for my sons, and they must know from me who I am.

And now the trumpet sounds, the music of the people stirs the revolution. Like a sleeping giant it slowly rears its head to the sound of tramping feet, clamoring voices. . . . And in all the fertile farmlands, the barren plains, the mountain villages, smoke-smeared cities, we start to MOVE.

—RODOLFO GONZALES, *Yo Soy Joaquín*

The date is July 5, 1945, one day after patriotic celebrations of America's independence. A woman sits on a bench in a courtroom listening to men in suits arguing back and forth. Thinking of her four children, she braces herself when she hears her attorney, David Marcus, say, "I call Mrs. Ochoa." She walks to the stand, hearing the echo of her footsteps bounce off the walls. The clerk asks her to raise her right hand and swear to tell the truth. She does so because that is all she wants . . . the truth. As she looks out to the courtroom, she sees White men and women on one side and the faces of her community members on the other. The clerk asks, "State your name please." She takes a breath and says clearly, "Manuela Ochoa."[1]

This testimony began the trial portion of *Mendez v. Westminster*, a wholly parent-led effort to break down the barriers between White and Mexican schools in California. The lawsuit occurred in the late 1940s as World War II was ending and soldiers were slowly returning from their service. Filed just before *Brown v. Board of Education*, this Fourteenth Amendment case stood on the precipice of dismantling segregated schooling across the United States. It did not become the groundbreaking case for this issue because of one legally insignificant but socially entrenched technicality. The *Mendez* case was about denying equal protection based on descent rather than race.[2] This small but critical difference sparked a milieu of misinformation about the case, the families involved, and its legal significance. If not for the efforts of Christopher Arriola, a district attorney in California, and Sylvia Mendez, the lead plaintiff in the case, *Mendez* might have wallowed in obscurity.[3] While *Mendez* has gained and is receiving more national attention, it is still an exceedingly understated lawsuit in the school desegregation movement.[4] In this chapter, I provide details that will contribute to a more complete picture of the Mendez family, their communities, and the missed opportunity to overturn *Plessy v. Ferguson*.

The Mendez Family

The Mendez story began in 1913 in the city of Chihuahua, Mexico, where the named plaintiff and organizer of the suit, Gonzalo Mendez, Sylvia Mendez's father, was born. Gonzalo and his family came to Westminster, California, in 1919.[5] There, he attended Westminster Main School until fifth grade, when he was transferred to Hoover Elementary, "the Mexican School." Once administrators became aware of his advanced English skills, Gonzalo was returned to the Westminster school. Unfortunately, he subsequently dropped out of school to help with the family finances—the sad fate of many Mexican and Mexican American children in the 1920s.[6] Nonetheless, Gonzalo was a diligent worker who learned the ins and outs of farm management, a skill that would help him later in life (Figure 5.1).

As for Sylvia Mendez's mother, Felícitas Gómez Martínez was born in Juncos, Puerto Rico, on February 5, 1916.[7] In 1926, her family was part of a large group of 1,500 Puerto Ricans recruited by the Arizona Cotton Growers (ACG) organization to move to Arizona with the promise of a two-dollar daily wage, drinking water, sanitary conditions, and homes with electricity.[8] The Puerto Rican labor force was supposed to be a workforce to rival the Mexican and Mexican American workers of California.

Upon their arrival in Arizona, the Puerto Ricans unfortunately met with the realities of conditions that were unacceptable to them but the norm for many

FIGURE 5.1.
Gonzalo Mendez, date/
age unknown. Used with
permission from the
Gonzalo Mendez family.
Cannot be reproduced
or copied without
written consent.

FIGURE 5.2.
Gonzalo and Felícitas Mendez. Used with permission from the Gonzalo Mendez
family. Cannot be reproduced or copied without written consent.

Mexican workers. The ACG's plan might have worked except for one critical detail: Puerto Ricans were U.S. citizens. To assert their rights as citizens, the Puerto Rican workforce "staged a minor rebellion[,] ... deserted the camps," and reduced the number of available laborers by 50 percent.[9] Though the Puerto Rican workers had the American Federation of Labor (AFL) and the Porto Rico Federation of Labor (PRFL) on their side, the governor of Arizona used the police force to arrest those that refused to work.[10] As a result, many Puerto Ricans, including Felícitas's family, moved to California.

The Gómez family eventually made their way to Westminster, California, and worked alongside the Mexican labor force. This was where Felícitas and Gonzalo met, married in 1935, and had three children in quick succession: Sylvia, Gonzalo Jr., and Gerónimo (Jerome) (Figure 5.2). Both Felícitas and Gonzalo exhibited an entrepreneurial spirit in that, after three years in the fields, they opened "the Arizona Café" in Santa Ana. According to Strum, "They prospered during the early years of World War II, accumulating sufficient funds to purchase three houses."[11] Managing a farm, however, was the ultimate dream for Gonzalo Mendez. That opportunity presented itself through a tragedy that was transformed into a triumph over racist U.S. policies.

In 1943, President Roosevelt signed Executive Order 9066 evacuating Japanese Americans into "relocation" (a.k.a. concentration) camps throughout the West and Southwest. According to Sylvia, her family was friends with the Munemitsus, a Japanese family who owned an asparagus farm just outside of Westminster.[12] Fearing their farm would be "repossessed" by the federal government and lost forever, the Munemitsus asked whether the Mendezes were willing to lease the farm until they returned. The Mendez family agreed, and the two families signed a lease. Along with his brother-in-law Frank Vidaurri, Gonzalo Mendez moved to Westminster and began "running the 40-acre Munemitsus asparagus farm, which employed fifteen workers . . . and as many as thirty braceros during the peak season."[13]

Shortly after moving to Westminster, in September 1944, Gonzalo's sister Soledad Vidaurri took her two daughters and their cousins Sylvia, Gonzalo Jr., and Jerome to enroll them in the school closest to their home. According to several accounts, the teacher in charge of registering the children pointed to the Vidaurri daughters and said, "We'll take them." She then pointed to the Mendez children and said, "But we won't take those."[14] The Vidaurri children were very light skinned, as their father was Mexican with French ancestry. Due to their non-Spanish name and fair skin tone, the school administrator believed them to be Belgians. The Mendez children, on the other hand were, as Felícitas once described them, *"igual de prietos que yo,"* which translates to "dark like me" (Figure

5.3).[15] Aunt Soledad recalled confronting the teacher: "I said no way! She [the teacher] told me I am going to report you. I said, you? You are not going to report me. I am going to report you!"[16] With that, she returned to the farm and relayed the incident to her brother.

Outraged by the slight, Gonzalo Mendez appealed in vain to various school officials. He argued that, as a taxpaying citizen, he should be allowed to send his children to Westminster. The school board refused, explaining that there was an equal Mexican school, Hoover Elementary, available for his children. Sylvia reported that Hoover was "near a ranch and at that time the ranchers electrified the fences that surrounded their property to keep their cattle from leaving." She further recalled, "I remember a girl touched that fence. The shock did not kill her, but she did not get up until adults came to help her."[17] These were the very schools Gonzalo himself attended when he was a child, schools he left in order to help his family. In a full-circle moment, he was now attempting to secure a future for his children that he had been denied so many years before.

With no other alternative available, Mendez considered legal recourse. One of his truck drivers told him about David Marcus, an attorney who successfully sued the city of San Bernardino for refusing to allow Mexicans and Mexican Americans use of the public pool.[18] In various parts of Orange County, public pools designated Mondays as "Mexican Days," a practice similar to ones in the Jim Crow South. Public officials ordered the pools drained every Monday evening in order to clean and prepare them for Whites to use for the remainder of the week.[19] San Bernardino, however, refused to have "Mexican Days" and barred all Mexicans from its public pool. David Marcus sued on behalf of Ignácio Lopez, an American citizen, University of California graduate, World War II veteran, and translator for the California Division of War Information. Marcus understood the symbolics of World War II service, and this knowledge informed his selection of plaintiffs and witnesses. Eight thousand residents of "Mexican and Latin descent and extraction" joined Lopez and won. Mendez reached out to Marcus and hired him to sue the school district (see appendix B). Together, they rallied the community and began a nearly four-year legal journey for public school integration.[20]

As Gonzalo and Marcus recruited the families, Felícitas made significant yet largely unknown contributions to the case; these included, but were not limited to, running the farm.[21] While Felícitas oversaw the farm, Gonzalo and Marcus recruited four more families representing four different school districts and five thousand Mexican American children to join the suit filed in federal district court. The following fathers and their children were among the petitioners:

- Mendez and his children Sylvia, Gonzalo, Jr. and Jerome
- William Guzmán and his son Billy
- Frank Palomino and his children Arthur and Sally
- Thomas Estrada and his children Clara, Roberto, Francisco, Sylvia, Daniel, and Evelina
- Lorenzo Ramirez and his sons Ignacio, Silverio, and José.[22]

Together, these plaintiffs challenged the constitutionality of segregated Mexican schools under the Fourteenth Amendment and alleged discrimination based on their Mexican descent. Westminster officials offered Gonzalo and Felícitas the compromise of admitting their children but no other Mexican children.[23] In a display of solidarity, the Mendezes refused. After the customary legal exchange of petitions, answers, briefs, and pretrial hearings, the trial finally began on July 5, 1945, when Manuela Ochoa was sworn in to offer her testimony. Over five days, the families' testimony opened a window into the social, cultural, and political challenges they encountered, the community support they displayed, and their shared commitment to their rights as citizens.

The School Administrators

Even though these families were situated just south of Los Angeles in the small, rural towns of Orange County, they were not immune to the social, cultural, and political influences of the big city. Two major events preceding the lawsuit placed education squarely in the political spotlight: the Sleepy Lagoon murder trial of 1942 and the Zoot Suit Riots of 1943. The 1942 Sleepy Lagoon murder trial involved the wrongful convictions of seventeen Mexican American youths for the murder of José Díaz, a man whose body was found in the vicinity of a party where large groups of young zoot-suiters were seen.[24] The convictions gave rise to rampant anti-Mexican sentiment that exploded into the Zoot Suit Riots. During these ten days in early June 1943, two hundred White servicemen raided various parts of Los Angeles and attacked zoot-suited men and women.[25] These two events dominated Los Angeles headlines, and Mexican American youths "became objects of scrutiny and concern for civic leaders, law enforcement, academics, journalists, and cultural commentators in general."[26]

Educational intervention was the order of the day, and White city and community leaders organized a bevy of conferences, committees, and workshops to investigate the roots of Mexican American juvenile delinquency. An editorial in the *Los Angeles Times* urged Governor Warren to investigate the riots and abandon the focus on race in favor of "eradicating the causes of gangsterism."[27] Experts at the tenth annual meeting of the Southern California Youth Conference suggested that trade schools might help curb "juvenile gang outbreaks."[28] Shortly before the 1943 school year, Los Angeles City and County schools held a workshop to discuss the racial animosity generated by the Zoot Suit Riots. According to one newspaper article, the seminar's purpose was to formulate "programs which [would] ground Los Angeles youngsters, including those of Mexican descent, in an all-American tradition."[29]

In addition to combating the stereotypes generated in the popular press, the *Mendez* families had to challenge the vicious characterizations of their children by the school administrators. Officials labeled the youths dirty and mentally inferior, then laid the blame for this biased treatment squarely at the feet of the children and families. Legal scholar Juan Perea calls the prevailing assumption within education "that Latino students cannot do difficult work and cannot be competitive with the Anglo counterparts" the *pobrecito* syndrome.[30] The word *pobrecito* translates to "poor thing." It is supposed to evoke complete sympathy and sadness for utterly helpless, hapless, and hopeless youths.

Reviewing the superintendents' testimony reveals that overcoming the *pobrecito* syndrome, along with all the accompanying stereotypes, was the *Mendez* families' greatest challenge. During the trial, the superintendents evaded questions or refused to answer them, or provided complicated explanations in response to simple inquiries. With their attorney repeatedly objecting to his line of questioning, the defense succeeded in frustrating Marcus. However, as the trial progressed, the superintendents transformed into a plaintiff attorney's dream when the judge began asking them to "illustrate" their points. The best thing Marcus could do was allow the school officials to speak freely and remain silent as the judge asked them very pointed questions.

The administrators' testimony demonstrated the attitudes Mexican parents encountered when they asked to move their children from one school to another. The schools' justifications for maintaining segregation fell into one of five categories:

- The language handicap brought on by growing up in a Spanish-speaking household
- Health and safety issues related to personal hygiene
- Neighborhood zoning
- Testing as evidence of "retarded" learning
- The need for Americanization.

James L. Kent, the superintendent of the Garden Grove school district, explained that the reasons for segregating Mexican children concerned language, hygiene, and the need for Americanization. He even dedicated his master's thesis to the subject.[31] Kent maintained that the school segregated all "non-English-speaking students."[32] He further claimed that Mexican children had a "bilingual handicap." This handicap apparently did not afflict bilingual Japanese or Filipino students who could attend the school, but Kent did not explain the distinction.[33] Despite the superintendent's contentions, all the parents under his jurisdiction testified in English and shared that their children spoke English as well.[34] Even so, Kent asserted that Mexican children's language deficiency made them "a year retarded in comparison with white children."[35] While he testified that he had records to prove this disparity, he neither produced them for trial nor submitted them into evidence. Marcus suggested that if the schools were integrated, Mexican children would benefit from special classes at the White school that would help them close their learning gap. Kent disagreed, explaining, "Our teachers would not be trained to work with Mexican children."[36]

In addition, the superintendent explained that hygiene was a problem for students seeking admission to White schools: "Mexican children have to be Americanized.... They must be taught ... cleanliness, and ... manners, which ordinarily do not come out of the home."[37] Kent found evidence of the youths' lack of cleanliness "in the care of their heads, lice, impetigo, tuberculosis; [and in their]

generally dirty hands, face, neck, ears."[38] Once again unable to produce health figures, he could only say that "a large portion" of the students in Hoover were so af-
flicted.[39] Kent testified that he believed that 75 percent of Mexican children were
inferior to the White race in "personal hygiene . . . scholastic ability . . . economic
outlook, their clothing and their ability to take part in the activities of school."[40]

It must have been difficult for the parents to hear their children described in an
almost inhuman manner. In a recording for *StoryCorps*, Sylvia Mendez recalled, "I
remember being in court every day. They would dress us up really nice and we'd be
there sitting very quietly."[41] Imagine the children sitting there quietly, listening to
the adults testify that they were dirty, lice ridden, and unmannered. If they won
the case, these youths would encounter this very same ideology at their schools.

It did not matter to Kent whether the children were dressed nicely and well be-
haved. He admitted that even exceptional students at Hoover could not transfer
to Lincoln, explaining, "There is the psychology of the thing. There is one thing in
putting one lone Mexican child in a group of 40 white children . . . by himself, [it]
would not be fair to him or to the other children."[42]

Frank Henderson, the superintendent for the Santa Ana school district, maintained that the schools were segregated because of the neighborhood zoning. The
fourteen schools under his jurisdiction were simply representative of the populations closest to them. The Mexican school was Mexican because the neighborhood was Mexican. Most of Henderson's answers were limited to "I don't remember the details" or "I don't recall." He maintained that the children were sent to the
Mexican school because their parents had never asked for permission to stay in the
White school, implying that their request would have been granted.[43]

Eventually Judge McCormick asked more pointed questions that criticized the
permission policy. In particular, he asked why the school granted African American children who lived in the Mexican school district permission to transfer without a formal request. Henderson answered with renewed clarity. "Let us illustrate
with little colored children," he began. "The little colored children who reside
in the Fremont [Mexican school] district are very few. . . . They are permitted to
transfer . . . to the school where they will find most of their own people."[44] Apparently, community solidarity was a priority for African American students but not
Mexican American students.

In his testimony, El Modeno superintendent Harold Hammarsten explained
that he relied exclusively on testing: "Our tests show that in spite of the fact that
these so-called Mexican children have the better opportunity because of their
American parentage . . . they are still in . . . the lower percentage . . . in grade placement, and mental ability and everything."[45] He argued that the curriculum was
equal, and that any intellectual shortfall on the part of Mexican students was

largely due to their "language handicap." Hammarsten's argument appeared convincing until he mentioned one exceptional class in the Mexican school that even outperformed the students at Roosevelt, the White school.[46]

The exceptional class remark caught Judge McCormick's attention. If these pupils were so outstanding, the judge asked, "why couldn't they be transferred to Roosevelt[?]"[47] After fumbling and attempting to backpedal, Hammarsten finally offered the following explanation: "The advantage to this system [segregation] is that the children that are high mentally amongst the Mexican group become the leaders in that group and form the nucleus. . . . They are the ones that push the programs in that classroom, and it is a distinct advantage to have those children in the Mexican school. . . . If you took those out of the Mexican school, it would leave the lower class again by themselves, and there would be no initiative for those that are left."[48] In short, exceptional Mexican student leaders remained segregated for their own good and the good of their classmates.

Richard Harris, the superintendent of Westminster, attempted to sever the Westminster district from the case because the school board had voted to end segregation. For the families, this would have been an incredible victory. However, Marcus asked an important question: When did the board intend to integrate the school? After evading a direct answer, Harris explained that the schools would be integrated once the district secured the necessary funding.[49] Without an assurance that segregation of Mexican children would end in the fall of 1946, Harris was required to testify.

Like his colleagues before him, Harris argued that the district segregated Mexican children because of a "language handicap" and "inferior test results."[50] He, too, encountered the most trouble when he attempted to explain the purpose of segregation. According to Harris, the Mexican children needed to learn "American culture as seen through English words."[51]

Asked to explain the difference between growing up in a Spanish-speaking home and an English-speaking home, Harris delivered a problematic history lesson: "In an English-speaking home . . . there are certain cultural backgrounds which undoubtedly were formed . . . and came in earlier days from England. Out of those come Mother Goose rhymes. Out of those come stories. Out of those stories of our American heroes, stories of our American frontier, rhymes and rhythms."[52] After the judge asked for clarification, Harris admitted his expectations for integrated education: "They [students] would probably fall about as they are, in my estimation. They will be in separate rooms."[53] Later, the superintendent shared that he believed 60 percent of the Mexican children spoke English, and that they were not inferior in any way.[54] Why, then, could they not be allowed to attend the school of their choice? Harris answered, "Because [their] conception of symbols and words of the English language . . . is still not up to the children of Anglo-Saxon descent."[55]

Not all educators were proponents of segregation. Many directly challenged the stereotypical justifications for the practice. One year before the *Mendez* trial, the *Los Angeles Times* ran an article entitled "Problems of School Child of Latin Lineage Studied."[56] The 1944 piece identified Marie Hughes as "a specialist in education of minor groups in Los Angeles County schools," and it quoted her extensively regarding her opinion of segregated learning environments.[57] Sharing her thoughts at a social work conference, Hughes declared, "I honestly don't know how thoroughly we can impress the American-born child of Mexican parentage with our good intentions toward him, when he has to submit to restricted seating in the school cafeteria, or goes past the well-equipped playground of the school reserved for children of American parentage to his own small and meager school facilities or face similar discriminations."[58]

As an ardent advocate for Mexican American children, Mrs. Hughes was a frequent speaker and presenter at local health, youth, education, and social conferences held in the Los Angeles area. She believed segregation compounded the challenges some students faced: "Adjustments in school are difficult enough for the Mexican-American child; he should not have them made more difficult by such embittering and unexplainable experiences."[59] Unfortunately for the superintendents, Hughes became one of the plaintiff's leading experts, representing one of the many supporters for the *Mendez* families.

The Community: Testimony from Families

While most of the newspaper coverage of *Mendez* focused exclusively on "the five fathers" who were the named plaintiffs, this case was a community effort.[60] It involved numerous attorneys, civil rights organizations, and, most importantly, families who were committed to enacting change. In total, seven mothers, six fathers, two sisters, and one brother took the stand to give compelling testimony on behalf of the children, speaking against the racist arguments of the school districts, and in opposition to the criminalization of Mexican American youths by the mainstream White media.

The parents and children took the stand ahead of the superintendents, and their testimony contrasted sharply with the school officials' declarations of language handicaps, low intelligence, and questionable personal hygiene. While some witnesses shared very little and spent limited time on the stand, others offered clear, passionate, and spirited statements.[61] Their testimony revealed their commitment to full citizenship, equal rights and treatment for their children, and community organizing.

While the jurists struggled to identify Mexican Americans with nonracial language, the plaintiffs maintained a fierce hold on their identity as American citizens. According to Gross, this battle between "formal citizenship and nominal legal whiteness played a more complex role in their [Mexican Americans'] exclusion from full social and political citizenship."[62] On the one hand, the U.S. Census largely classified Mexicans as White in the 1940s, so the families could not allege racial discrimination under the law. On the other hand, the plaintiffs were prepared to offer substantial evidence of the uneven treatment between Mexican schools and White or racially mixed schools.

The court and the attorneys settled on the phrase "persons of Mexican descent," but that phrase's use remained highly inconsistent throughout the trial. Attorneys for the school district referred to the plaintiffs as follows: the Mexican race,[63] "Spaniard or a Mexican,"[64] Caucasian,[65] non–English speaking, Spanish speaking, and even Mexican speaking.[66] References to Mexican students even contained evidence of the influence of scientific racism and genetic determinism. Kent explained the difference between the "Mexican race" and the "White race" in this way: "Your Mexican child is advanced. . . . He matures physically much faster than your white child, and he is able to do more in games. Therefore, he goes more on physical prowess than he does mental ability."[67]

At one point during the trial, Kent admitted that he did not consider the Mexicans to be "of the White race," an admission that could have devastated the defense's case.[68] During the pretrial hearing, defense attorneys argued that since Mexicans were White, there was no racial discrimination in barring them from White schools, and the court should dismiss the case. After Kent's admission, the schools' attorney quickly requested a recess. Upon returning, Kent testified that he was "merely talking of color when [he] said white."[69] Marcus asked him, "At this time you believe that a Mexican is of the Caucasian race?" Kent replied in the affirmative, and then Marcus piercingly asked, "When did you determine that, during the recess?"[70]

The court, the school officials, and their attorney were inconsistent in their identifications throughout the trial. The families, however, unfailingly asserted their identity as American citizens. Mrs. Ochoa, the first witness to testify, set the tone for the trial when she declared, "I am of Mexican descent, although I was born here, and I am an American citizen."[71] Frank Palomino, one of the named plaintiffs and a married father of two, said that his ultimate goal was simply to "raise them [his children] as a good American, if given a chance."[72] Felícitas Mendez, while not on the stand very long, delivered one of the more powerful and oft-quoted statements of the trial. Sitting there, perhaps even looking at her daughter's and sons' faces, she shared, "We always tell our children they are Americans, and I feel I am American myself, and so is my husband."[73]

Chicano scholars such as David Gutiérrez and Vicki Ruiz characterize this embrace of an American identity as a rejection of a Mexican identity, an attempt to assimilate or "pass" as White.[74] The League of United Latin American Citizens (LULAC), an organization often criticized for promoting its legal "whiteness," coordinated fund-raising efforts to pay for legal fees.[75] The Mendezes' association with this middle-class Mexican American civil rights group could support an argument that the family's patriotism was a form of passing.

However, Mrs. Ochoa, a married mother of four who had lived within the Garden Grove school district for over twenty years, directly contradicts that characterization. She lived closer to the racially mixed Lincoln school, but the school officials directed her to Hoover Elementary, the Mexican school that was over a mile away from her home.[76] When Kent refused her request to transfer her children, she asked why Mexican children who lived closer to Hoover were able to attend Lincoln.[77] According to Mrs. Ochoa, Kent said "they were probably of Spanish ancestry"[78] and suggested she register as Spanish. Had she simply registered her children as Spanish, she could have given them access to the privilege of attending the "better" school. Instead, she replied, "My children cannot be registered as Spanish, because their father is Mexican."[79] When presented with the opportunity to deny her children's Mexican identity and pass, Mrs. Ochoa did not.

The *Mendez* families also demonstrated their united commitment to securing equal rights for their children by attacking the stereotypical, discriminatory characterizations schools cited as reasons for segregation. Families' strongest reactions were against the allegations that Mexicans were "too dirty." Nearly every superintendent argued that Mexican children were dirty, diseased, or even both, indicating the stereotype's pervasiveness in the school system.

Felícitas Fuentes, a mother of two who had lived in the area for over twelve years, gave a strong response to her children's accusers. She testified that a Fremont school official wanted to know

> "why the Mexican people are so dirty."[80] She shrewdly responded, "why [are] the Oklahoma people . . . so dirty and filthy."[81] Because one of her sons, Joe, was in the U.S. Navy, "working in the post office somewhere in the Philippines,"[82] she also asked the school official,
>
> "If our Mexican people were so dirty . . . why [don't] they have all of our boys, that are fighting overseas, and . . . bring them back and let us have them home."[83]

Fuentes's challenge reveals the contradictory nature of asking mothers—indeed an entire community—to sacrifice their sons without the promise of honoring that service with basic human rights. Like proponents of the "Double Victory" campaign created in African American newspapers, Mexican Americans had hoped that that securing a victory abroad would secure "first-class citizenship" at home.[84]

Throughout the trial, the plaintiffs evoked images of the Mexican American youths serving in World War II. In his opening brief, Marcus wrote, "Of what avail are the thousands upon thousands of lives of Mexican-Americans who sacrificed their all for their country in this great 'War of Freedom' if freedom of education is denied them?"[85]

The hypocrisy of fighting against fascism and racial hatred abroad while racial prejudice in the form of legalized segregation existed in America was not lost on the community. In her book on the *Mendez* case, Strum quotes a former paratrooper who shared, "We didn't like it when we came home and found out we'd risked our lives . . . but our children wouldn't be getting as good an education as the white student."[86] The patriotic, sacrificial Mexican American soldier became a powerful symbol deployed throughout the trial to combat stereotypical characterizations of Mexicans. When school officials alleged dirt and disease, the families demanded dignity.

Juan Muñoz, a married father of four who had lived in the area for over twenty years, supplied riveting testimony as he recounted his confrontation with a school official: "He said the Mexicans were too dirty to go to that school [Lincoln]. . . . Naturally, well, I had an answer to him. I said, 'Do you judge everybody alike?' He says, 'For one Mexican the whole town has to take it.' I says, 'But that is not right . . . I am fighting for my children's rights.'"[87] On behalf of his daughter, Mr. Muñoz pled for her school to change the way it asked students to report to the nurse's office for tuberculosis testing. Instead of making announcements over the loudspeaker, he suggested that teachers help facilitate a more discreet way of testing the children. As he explained, "The other pupils go by and they stare at them. . . . My gosh, not all Mexicans are dirty."[88]

The families involved in the case did not hesitate to name the behavior of the school district as discriminatory. Felícitas Mendez testified, "We thought that they [the pupils] shouldn't be segregated like that, they shouldn't be treated the way they are."[89] Frank Palomino explained why he opted to send one child to a private parochial school instead of the Mexican school: "The other way they are segregating them, discriminating, I will say."[90] Once again, a parent in the *Mendez* lawsuit made it clear that these acts were rooted in discrimination.

Mrs. Fuentes proved to be a formidable witness as she faced the school's attorney. He asked whether she thought the White school was small. Her reply likely made him regret he even asked the question. "I think it is big enough for my child," she said, "and for the children that are claiming their rights."[91] Like Mrs. Fuentes, John Marval, a married father of three, gave equally spirited and confrontational testimony.[92] The principal instructed Mr. Marval to transfer his child from Franklin to Fremont. Mr. Marval recalled that he told the school official, "I will send him to the Fremont School with this condition, that you send all your white children from the white families to the Fremont school. . . . I own property . . . and I have got a business here, and I don't see why my child can't have the same opportunity the rest of them have. . . . I am fighting for my child."[93]

Lorenzo Ramirez also gave compelling testimony on behalf of his three sons. He had lived in the area since 1922 and attended Roosevelt school when it was not segregated. "I wanted my boys to be educated at the Roosevelt school because their father had his education there," he explained, "and to give them the opportunity, the same chance to go where the rest of the boys will go."[94] He demonstrated that, at some point in history, the school had adopted a policy of discriminatory segregation. This policy denied children an equal education and parents the ability to build a legacy of learning.

Mr. Ramirez's testimony also carried themes of racial solidarity. He proclaimed, "The days will come when the Japanese, Filipinos, and Negroes would be together again."[95] According to Mr. Ramirez, Hammarsten replied, "I tell you why a Negro is supposed to have better rights. Because he was brought here during slavery days, and that was just the truth, and that is the reason I think they should have better rights."[96] Hammarsten's statement was likely not a wholehearted endorsement regarding the ills of slavery and the joys of Black/White harmony. It was, however, a useful trope to effectively separate racial groups deploying a divide-and-conquer strategy. Yet Mr. Ramirez's reply evoked images of unity and sacrifice as he sermonized, "Thanks the Lord, we live in a country that everybody was equal. . . . I wanted my kids . . . to go and march through up until the end of the war like the boys be marching right along."[97]

Not all witnesses were as gripping and certain as Mrs. Fuentes, Mr. Marval, and Mr. Ramirez. William Guzmán, married father of three, was incredibly nervous on the stand, stumbling and unsure whether he remembered everything that happened. He explained that he was "too excited."[98] Eventually, Marcus told him, "Now, look, Guzmán, don't get excited, and just think of these things before you answer. Don't become confused."[99] The intensity of the trial and pressure to do well is palpable throughout his testimony.

It is generally good practice for attorneys to invest a great deal of time preparing their witnesses for trial. However, throughout these proceedings, the judge had to instruct many of the witnesses in answering the questions. Testifying is a painstakingly slow and methodical process that often requires simple "yes" or "no" answers before witnesses can get to the crux of their testimony. Marcus might not have properly prepared his clients. As a result, their testimony was subject to countless objections from the defense. For example, the school's attorney characterized nearly every individual's statements as "incompetent, irrelevant, and immaterial."[100] Imagine trying to speak your truth and being told your truth is useless, unimportant, and meaningless. This no doubt had the potential to be a great source of anxiety for the witnesses, making their appearance in court that much more meaningful.

Ultimately, the school attorney severely limited the testimony of only four witnesses. The first, Mrs. Nieves Peña, was a married mother of four who was called to testify that her children were clean and that she spoke English.[101] The second was Robert Pérez, a seventeen-year-old who had attended segregated schools since 1941. He was there to demonstrate a pattern of segregation practiced by the school. Unfortunately, the court only wanted to hear testimony about "situations that exist[ed] in these schools at the ... time."[102] The third witness was Mrs. Virginia Guzmán, the wife of William Guzmán. While she fared much better than her husband did, her purpose was to identify the "non-Mexican" neighbors in her district who were permitted to stay in the White school.[103] Finally, Felícitas Mendez would have had more time on the stand, but Marcus stipulated that she was simply going to say the same things that her husband, Gonzalo, shared. While her time was severely limited, hers is still one of the most quoted testimonies in articles about the case.[104]

Understanding the challenge of taking the stand makes the appearance of fourteen-year-old Carol Torres that much more gripping.[105] Her testimony revealed the strategic and organized nature of the community's effort to organize the lawsuit. Miss Torres stated that the students in Lincoln Elementary, the Mexican school, called a meeting with the principal to ask him why he separated them when there were children of Mexican descent attending Roosevelt, the predominantly White school.[106] Hinting at possible classism, Miss Torres declared, "[The] pupils of Mexican descent that went over to Roosevelt School considered themselves superior to us, and sometimes they wouldn't even talk to us."[107]

Marcus asked her why she never asked the administrators for permission to transfer. Her response was perfection: "I guess that we just felt hurt because they wouldn't admit all of them [her fellow classmates], and it didn't seem right. ... We all wanted to be together."[108] Her testimony illustrates how invested the youths had become in the movement to change policy and practices. They called a meeting, questioned authority, and demonstrated solidarity. They were foreshadowing the kind of student activism that would eventually shake Los Angeles twenty years later during the Chicano Student Walkouts.

Mabel Mendez, a married mother of five children, member of the PTA, and twenty-two-year resident of Santa Ana, also organized parents.[109] She was part of a group of twenty-five families who received a letter from the school board requiring them to withdraw their children from the White school and reenroll them in the Mexican school. She and twenty-five other parents attended the local school board meeting to demand an explanation for the letter and to challenge the policy.[110] While the board promised an investigation, she testified that she had not heard anything else from its members.

Gonzalo Mendez, the man credited with organizing the families, outlined how the community members rallied to have their voices heard. Mendez testified that he, along with four or five mothers and fathers, called a meeting with Ray Atkinson, the superintendent over the entire Orange County School District.[111] His account shows the strategic nature of the parents' visit. Mendez explained that two mothers discussed how their sons were fighting abroad only to return to an unfair system of segregation.[112]

The petitioners gave Atkinson a letter signed by thirty-eight parents. Read into the record, the letter stated:

> Dear Sir:
>
> We, the undersigned, parents, of whom about one-half are American born, respectfully call your attention to the fact that . . . the segregation of American children of Mexican descent is being made at Westminster, in that the American children of non-Mexican descent are made to attend Westminster grammar school on W. Seventeenth Street at Westminster, and the American children of Mexican extraction are made to attend Hoover School on Olive and Maple Street. Children from one district are made to attend the school in the other district and we believe that this situation is not conducive to the best interests of the children nor friendliness either among the children or their parents involved, nor the eventual thorough Americanization of our children. It would appear that there is racial discrimination and we do not believe that there is any necessity for it and would respectfully request that you make an investigation of this matter and bring about an adjustment, doing away with the segregation above referred to. Some of our children are soldiers in the war, all are American born and it does not appear fair nor just that our children should be segregated as a class.
>
> Respectfully submitted.[113]

The claims of citizenship, combat sacrifice, and social justice peppered throughout the document are unambiguous. The mothers of these World War II vets made clear the hypocrisy of a country that was willing to let their children die in war but not sit together in a school cafeteria. Most importantly, at no point in the letter did the parents claim Whiteness. Instead, they specifically used the phrase "racial discrimination" to describe their plight, which contradicts the accusations of assimilation and passing usually associated with this particular generation of Mexican Americans. Mr. Mendez informed the judge that he and the other parents "were forming a club in Westminster and trying to do [their] best to send

[the] children clean to school."[114] While this admission seemed troubling, Mendez also asserted that he and other parents had formed a "Father's Association," "interviewed a lawyer," and were working with the Latin American League of Voters.[115] This group of parents was organized and determined to stop the practice of segregation in order to "create a better democratic way of living."[116] *Mendez* was a pivotal trial for this community.

An incident demonstrating the effect this trial had on the local community happened at the beginning of day three. Marcus seemed almost frenetic as he engaged with the school's attorney and Judge McCormick. It was almost as if he was searching for something. Finally, he explained the problem to the court: "Your Honor, I have been seriously handicapped here. Over the weekend, I had my automobile stolen, and my brief case including all of the papers in this case, the entire file, was in it, along with a suit case [*sic*] of clothes."[117]

Whether the theft was connected to the case is unclear. However, the first few days of testimony were certainly going in the families' favor. Marcus had strong witnesses, even to the extent that the judge personally acknowledged their intelligence. During the Mabel Mendez testimony, Judge McCormick corrected Marcus and told him, "Why don't you put a question to her instead of making a statement? She can answer the questions. She is very intelligent."[118] During the Carol Torres testimony, he corrected Marcus again by saying, "Don't lead her. You don't have to lead this girl. She is a very intelligent witness."[119] Finally, during Felícitas Mendez's testimony, he said, "I have heard sufficiently from her to form my own estimate of her qualifications. She seems to have a pretty good knowledge of the vernacular, beyond the commonplace vernacular."[120]

This observation from the judge aggravated the school districts' case. After all, their main argument was that growing up in a Spanish-speaking home resulted in mentally inferior children. Marcus had an admission from three of the four superintendents of their inherent bias against Mexicans. Even the judge was compelled to ask questions that resulted in less than favorable responses for the defense. There were numerous reasons for someone who did not want to see the schools integrate to steal the attorney's car and make it that much more challenging for the families and their case.

In a final show of community support, Marcus called local education experts Dr. Ralph L. Beals, chair of the Department of Anthropology and Sociology at the University of California, and Mrs. Marie M. Hughes, a doctoral candidate at Stanford University. Together, they delivered the final devastating blow to the defense, which arguably secured victory for the plaintiffs. Judge McCormick referenced their testimony heavily in his judicial opinion. Dr. Beals testified, "The disadvantages of segregation, it would seem to me, would come primarily from the reinforcing of stereotypes of inferiority-superiority."[121] Mrs. Hughes told the court, "It is not in the best interest of the children in America to work and play together and go to school together under segregated conditions. . . . Segregation, by its very nature, is a reminder constantly of inferiority, of not being wanted, of not being part of the community."[122]

With those words, Mrs. Hughes not only validated the families' experiences but also acknowledged their place in America and the Orange County School District. This was a declaration that they, indeed, were not inferior! Their families and lives and language and culture should be wanted and welcomed.

Finally, this community was their community too! The *Mendez* families were not visitors to a home subject to the owner's rules. This was their home, and these were their lives, their children, and their schools. Collectively, their testimony turned the tide of educational inequality toward justice.

On the Precipice of Change . . .

"Ruling Gives Mexican Children Equal Rights," read the front-page headline in the *Los Angeles Times* after Judge McCormick issued his opinion.[123] *La Prensa*, a Spanish newspaper in San Antonio, Texas, quoted the section of McCormick's opinion that stated, "Segregation . . . fosters antagonism in the children and suggests inferiority among them where none exists."[124] African American newspapers also celebrated the *Mendez* ruling, including the *Afro-American* in Baltimore, the *New England Journal and Guide* in Virginia, and the *Phylon* in Atlanta, and the *Chicago Defender* announced the appellate victory.[125]

The historical significance of the case was not lost on scholars and journalists of the time. Famed journalist Carey McWilliams declared, "The Westminster case is a perfect one for testing the constitutionality of segregated schools."[126] Lester H. Phillips of the Black journal *Phylon* wrote, "This case must be ranked among the vanguard of those making a frontal attack upon the 'equal but separate' canon of interpretation of the equal protection clause."[127]

The impact of *Mendez* was lost on the families who filed suit. The ruling was not the result of grand-scale community organizing and mobilizing. While they did not generate multipage manifestos, circulate impressive magazines, assemble huge conferences, or author intellectual essays on the identities of Mexican Americans in Los Angeles, these families asserted their rights to first-class citizenship, organized on behalf of their children, and literally took the stand against inequality, discrimination, and injustice. McWilliams observed the following: "The suit was not 'rigged,' 'inspired,' or 'promoted' by any cause committee. It was put forth because rank-and-file citizens of Mexican descent in Southern California realized that they had long since 'had enough.'"[128] These citizens consisted of mothers, fathers, sisters, and brothers who organized and overcame overwhelming social, cultural, and political challenges to effect a significant legal change.

I designate the *Mendez* case "the understated" because it almost made it to the Supreme Court. After the McGuire decision, the school districts appealed the case to the Ninth Circuit. The Ninth Circuit issued a unanimous ruling: "By enforcing the segregation of school children of Mexican descent against their will and contrary to the laws of California, the respondents have violated federal law by denying them the equal protection of the laws."[129]

After the Ninth Circuit decision, the school districts voted not to appeal the case to the Supreme Court. Instead, the governor of California, Earl Warren, successfully lobbied the state legislature to integrate all California public schools, declaring Chinese, Mexican, and Indian schools unconstitutional. As history would have it, Warren was eventually nominated by President Eisenhower to serve as chief justice of the Supreme Court. His first case? *Brown v. Board of Education*, where he famously lobbied his fellow jurists to vote unanimously to overturn *Plessy v. Ferguson* and find that that "separate is inherently unequal."

In his article, California superior court Judge the Honorable Frederick P. Aguirre masterfully compares the California attorney general's amicus brief in *Mendez* to Warren's opinion in *Brown*. The correspondences are uncanny and riveting, and they provide the strongest and most undeniable legal connections between *Mendez* and *Brown*.[130] Both cases involved the Fourteenth Amendment. The difference is that Marcus had to argue that discrimination was based on descent, while *Brown* could directly address race. But for this legal difference without a distinction, *Mendez* could have been legally useful to the NAACP's valiant efforts.

What makes *Mendez* even more remarkable is the array of multiracial organizations that filed amicus briefs on their behalf. Briefs were submitted at the appellate level from the Japanese American Citizens League (JACL),[131] the American Jewish Congress (AJC), the American Civil Liberties Union (ACLU), the National Lawyers Guild (NLG), and, perhaps most powerfully, the National Association for the Advancement of Colored People (NAACP). While Thurgood Marshall was said to have limited contact with the *Mendez* case, Robert Carter referred to it as a "trial run for *Brown*."[132]

Subsequent interviews with Robert Carter revealed that he also met with Marcus to discuss his legal strategy, particularly the use of experts. Carter is said to have used the "skeletal structure" of *Mendez* for *Brown*.[133] Even though Marcus made it clear that the case was not about race, the NAACP knew that it held tremendous potential for *Brown*. However, because *Mendez* was not about race, *Brown* could only limit its use to a footnote in a brief filed in *Brown*.

LATCRIT AND *MENDEZ*

When it comes to race, however, *Mendez* provides the most evidence of racial flexibility that worked both for and against the family. From Puerto Rico to pre-trial arguments, the *Mendez* case is full of confusion and contradictions regarding where to "place" the Mendez family on the racial hierarchy. To analyze the lawsuit, I consider the LatCrit tenet of Latino/a essentialism that challenges a singular definition of Latinos' racialization. A review of the case reveals that Mexicans' and Mexican Americans' racial identity resembles a moving abacus bead more than a cloak or wedge within the Black/White binary.

In her story alone, Felícitas Mendez was racialized by four different groups: the growers, her adopted Mexican community, the schools, and Felícitas herself. The growers who recruited her family for their labor either did not know or did not understand that Puerto Ricans were considered citizens of the United States. Regardless, the growers believed they could compete with Mexicans by subjecting Puerto Ricans to the same pay and working conditions. Unlike the Mexican workers, the Puerto Rican workers could organize against and ultimately leave the farms in Arizona. They had the benefit of choice. This was not an option available to Mexican workers, largely due to a threat of deportation. But Puerto Ricans' departure was not wholly easy. Agricultural workers who broke their contracts were gathered into concentration camps and referred to as both Puerto Rican and Negro.[134]

Second, Felícitas was racialized in her adopted Mexican community in California, where she became the cultural minority. Prior to her marriage to Gonzalo, she was married to a "Mexican boy" who was deported. When asked whether she wanted to go to Mexico, she replied, "I didn't want to go, because I did not know the Mexican way of living."[135] Once married to Gonzalo, she adopted the identity of her Mexican husband. Research on early immigrant marriages indicates that wives commonly left their own cultures to adopt their husbands'.[136] In one journey, according to education specialist Jennifer McCormick and sociologist César Ayala, Felícitas and her family were considered "mulattos" in Puerto Rico, "black" in Arizona, and Mexican in California.[137] This is in line with Latino/a essentialism that struggles with how and where to categorize Latiné communities.

Third and fourth, school officials racialized Sylvia Mendez by skin tone just as Felícitas Mendez racialized herself. When Aunt Soledad brought her daughters and their Mendez cousins to enroll in the White school, the school official racially sorted the children. Recall that the Vidaurri children were very light skinned and could pass for White. The Mendez children, on the other hand, were, according to their mother, "*prieto*" like her.[138] Sylvia could also have been described as "India" or Indigenous looking. Had Aunt Soledad gone to the school by herself, her children would have been accepted. Instead, she rejected the acceptance and returned home. Her behavior on behalf of the whole family, I argue, is a direct refusal to be covered by, and benefit from, the Caucasian Cloak.

This post–World War II generation of Mexicans and Mexican Americans is often referred to as White passing or assimilated.[139] I contend that the families actions throughout the *Mendez* lawsuit tell a different story. Take, for example, the letter the parents sent to the Westminster school board. They very clearly named the actions of the school officials as racial discrimination. The letter did not say, "We are White; therefore, we should be treated as such." Instead, the parents condemned discrimination with powerful imagery of their sons' World War II service, exposing the country's hypocrisy in deeming their children good enough to die in war, but not good enough to sit next to Whites in a classroom. The letter's writers were not declaring Whiteness. They were expecting equality.

Nowhere was Latino/a essentialism more apparent than in the pretrial record. As previously explicated, David Marcus had to deploy a descent-based discrimination strategy. Naturally, it would be in the schools' best interest to have the case dismissed on the grounds that Mexicans are White and therefore not subject to racial discrimination. The attorney for the schools, Mr. Holden, tried to put forth these arguments and failed. In the following exchange, take note how often the attorney and jurist confuse themselves and each another. To provide clarity, I will italicize my comments, narration, and remarks and separate them in brackets. This excerpt is taken from the pretrial transcript recorded on June 26, 1945:

[*From the very beginning, they are trying to "avoid" raced language.*]

MR. HOLDEN: They have 14 elementary schools in the city, and they divide the city into eight territories and one school serves each territory. It happens that there are three school [*sic*] that serves Mexican descendants almost 100 per cent. There are three schools that serve white or—well, white isn't, of course, the proper term to use here, but it has been used in the pleadings.

MR. MARCUS: No, it hasn't, counsel.

MR. HOLDEN: Let's divide them into English speaking and Spanish speaking just for the purposes of talking here. . . .

[*Later, the judge asks a question.*]

THE COURT: Has the Board of Education . . . enacted any memorial in writing with respect to the classification of schools as to the student personnel relative to the linguistic qualities of the student who would attend those schools?

[*The court is asking whether the schools have a test for determining language proficiency.*]

MR. HOLDEN: They have not.

[*No longer able to rely on dividing the students via language, both attorneys attempt another route.*]

MR. MARCUS: They have established certain arbitrary lines, which curve and
    bend and twist to include only those children of Mexican descent. There are
    children that are attending the school where Mexican children attend that
    have to go through various lines where only American children attend.
THE COURT: Wait just a moment. "Only American children attend." What do
    you mean by "American children?"
MR. MARCUS: Well, we will say of Anglo-Saxon descent.
THE COURT: You mean the children of Mexican lineage, do you not?
MR. MARCUS: That is correct, your Honor, but I was using the language adopted
    by counsel in his answer.
THE COURT: On what page?

[*Later, Mr. Holden stipulates the following:*]

MR. HOLDEN: I will stipulate to this: That in that district there are probably
    between 5 and 10 pupils who are not of the Mexican descent, but are, we will
    say, English speaking pupils, and they are permitted to go to another school.

[*Later, language gets conflated with race and with descent in one interaction.*]

MR. HOLDEN: Don't we mean that it is people of Mexican descent who speak
    Spanish at home and in the communities where they reside?
MR. MARCUS: I can't agree with the fact that . . .^

[*Holden interrupts and the court corrects him.*]

MR. MARCUS: . . . . that a child three or four years of age is not proficient in the
    English language. I am willing to say this, however, that they have the same
    proficiency with respect to speaking the English language as, we will say—
    what was the word your Honor suggested?
THE COURT: English speaking people.
MR. MARCUS: You see, I run into that difficulty again, your honor because these
    children do speak English.

[*Later, Mr. Holden refers to the children as "Mexican speaking pupils" and Whites
as "non-Spanish speaking pupils."*]

THE COURT: [*To Marcus*] You contend, I believe, that those [policies] are based
    upon race or ancestry or heredity or ethnic or anthropological features?

MR. MARCUS: That is correct.... We may make this statement to the Court, that we do not contend that there is such a thing as the Mexican race. That will eliminate the question of race. We do, however, contend [the schools' practice] is based upon the fact that they are of Mexican or Latin descent.

[*This is the crux of Mr. Marcus's argument. It is often interpreted to mean that he and his plaintiffs reject being called a race. This is clearly a misreading of the text and a misunderstanding of legal nuance. Later, Mr. Holden lays out his argument, but it is not nearly as eloquent. He continues to stumble over how to identify children of Mexican descent.*]

MR. HOLDEN: The purpose of the segregation is simply this. They live in communities that talk Spanish. When they come to school, they do not understand one word of English, [*It is almost as if he has realized that he has opened the door for Dr. Marcus to prove the students speak English fluently.*] ... that is, most of them don't. There are exceptions, and the petitioners in this case, I will admit the petitioners in this case, the named petitioners, probably are able to speak fairly good English, but they also go into these schools, and they are not, in the lower grades, able to complete or to carry the work that these students who are familiar with the English language are able to do so. [*You can almost sense his growing frustration.*] We have a five-year-old—this is confusing me, too, because I don't want to say white people, because Mexicans are white, but say the non-Mexican.[140]

In this short pretrial interaction, the attorneys racialized Mexican children as "of Mexican descent," "Spanish speaking vs. English speaking," "Mexican children vs. American children," and "Anglo Saxon descent vs. Mexican lineage." Finally, they stated, "Mexicans are white."[141] They never truly resolved the question of what to "call" Mexican children. During the trial, the judge, the attorneys, and the witnesses used several descriptors to define and identify Mexicans. What follows is a small sample from just one day's testimony:

- "Mr. Kent said, 'On the other hand, if your children were registered as Spanish, they could attend the Lincoln [White] school.' I said, 'My children cannot be registered as Spanish, because their father is Mexican.'"[142]
- "[The school official] said the Mexicans were too dirty to go to [the White] school."[143]
- "[The school official] says, 'the Japanese and Filipino race was classified higher, a higher race than Mexicans.'"[144]
- "We mean that Mexican children have to be Americanized much more highly than our so-called American children.... They must be taught manners. They must be taught cleanliness ... [habits] which ordinarily do not come out of the home."[145]

- "If we put them with our white children, they naturally cannot go at the same rate of speed."[146]
- "Putting one lone Mexican child in a group of 40 white children merely because he has come up to the level of the other white children … is not fair to him."[147]
- "Your Mexican child is advanced, that is, he matures physically much faster than your white child."[148]

In one day, Mr. Marcus was able to elicit testimony from the parents and the school officials that was both powerful and tragic. Throughout the trial, the parents and children, in perfect English, consistently delivered one message: "I am an American." Even when advised that her child would be admitted if she declared a Spanish background, which presumably was considered European and therefore White, Mrs. Ochoa refused to do so.

The school official, James Kent, provided ample evidence of an anti-Mexican bias based on the stereotypes of being dirty, diseased, and dumb. I should note that when describing a child who "matures physically faster than your white child," Mr. Kent was clearly referring to a boy conjuring all the stereotypes associated with overpowering Mexican men, whose only strength is physical, not mental.

Finally, in the racial hierarchy of this school system, Mexicans seemingly ranked below Black, Filipino, and Japanese students. When asked to explain why, Mr. Kent did not mince words when he told a parent, "The Japanese and Filipino race are classified as higher." I surmise that Filipinos were placed higher because they were American allies in World War II. This classification of Japanese students, however, perplexes me, considering that the case took place soon after the end of Japanese American concentration camps. Nevertheless, the categorization represents another "flip" in the racial hierarchy, with Mexicans, not African Americans or Asian Americans, at the bottom. This flip further supports what Lipsitz asserts in *The Possessive Investment of Whiteness*: "Even though there has always been racism in American history, it has not always been the same racism. Political and cultural struggles over power shape the contours and dimensions of racism in any era."[149]

POLITICS OF RESPECTABILITY MEETS THE PIANO

When it comes to the role of controlling images, the Mendez family, like the Tapes, possessed a solidly middle-class position as "temporary owners" of the Munemitsus asparagus farm and owners of a café. A review of the court transcripts and interviews suggests that the Mendez family and Marcus strategically positioned the plaintiff families before and during the trial. First, Sylvia Mendez could never be mistaken for a spicy *mamacita* or a traitorous, unpatriotic *pachuca*. In examining a photograph of her taken during the trial, she was a stereotype-defying

FIGURE 5.4.
Sylvia Mendez, age nine,
1947. Used with permission
from the Gonzalo
Mendez family. Cannot
be reproduced or copied
without written consent.

symbol of angelic purity in her white dress (see Figure 5.4). Furthermore, her status as a little girl made her too young to be sexualized. Sylvia projected an image that is more saint than spitfire. But as they were called "dirt farmers" and "mentally handicapped," the Mendez family was still very much subject to controlling images, particularly that of the mentally inferior.

There is no better evidence of the strength of the mentally inferior controlling image than what was recorded in the *Mendez* transcripts. Because it was applied to both boys and girls, the image itself is not inherently gendered. In response to why the Mexican American children were separated from White children, Harold Hammarsten, a superintendent, said, "We keep them separate and apart because during the first two or three years the teachers that have those children . . . are better able to get those children to progress more rapidly, when they are with their own group."[150] When the judge asked him what would happen if the Mexican children and the White children went to the same school, Hammarsten referred to nonexistent tests that revealed nonexistent results of lower mental abilities that were never truly measured.[151]

Mr. Holden, another superintendent, who admitted that 60 percent of the children in the Mexican school spoke English fluently, was asked why those students were not "afforded the same opportunities or the same privileges" as White students. He replied, "It is the degree of sufficiency . . . which is still not up to the children of Anglo-Saxon descent."[152] In Holden's opinion, children who spoke Spanish in the home were forever damaged: "'I think this retardation of children . . . who speak the Spanish language in their homes,' Holden testified, '. . . well I think that the retardation continues. I would say that there is a degree to which it handicaps the child.'"[153] Because of Mexican pupils' perceived mental inferiority, recall that school administrators also accused them of being unfamiliar with cleanliness and hygiene. Superintendent James Kent testified to their lack of cleanliness and propensity to contract lice. Though Kent kept no formal records, the Mexican children of his district were considered diseased and dirty health risks. In his mind, segregation was the only solution. According to district officials, mentally inferior Mexican children were "retarded" in their learning, "handicapped" by their language, and lacking in personal hygiene.

The plaintiffs' biggest obstacle to overcome was the pervasive image of the mentally inferior Mexican child who was unworthy of and would not benefit from White schools. As a result, the Mendez family and Marcus made sure that the students could never be judged mentally inferior. Similar to the *Lopez* case, Marcus employed a "we are no different from you" strategy. This approach was not a proclamation of Whiteness, but rather a demand for recognition as American citizens worthy of the same rights, treatment, and opportunities afforded White citizens. In their first letter to the school board the families clearly alleged, "It would appear that there is racial discrimination" and proudly referenced their sons' military service.[154]

This was especially important since many Mexican American men were serving valiantly during World War II. Recall that Marcus selected World War II veteran Ignácio Lopez as the lead plaintiff in the segregated pool case. In 1975 Felícitas Mendez affirmed the importance of this strategy when she recalled, "The young boys . . . went and fought [in the war], and they came back with that feeling, that if they were good enough to fight for their country they were good enough to do everything else here."[155]

From the battlefields to the classrooms, this message of being "good enough" resonates strongly with Sylvia to this day. In a recording created for National Public Radio's *StoryCorps*, Sylvia recalled how once she began attending the integrated Westminster school, a White boy came up to her and said, "What are you doing here? You don't belong in this school. They shouldn't have Mexicans here." She returned home crying and told her mother that she no longer wanted to attend

Westminster. According to Sylvia, Felícitas replied, "Don't you realize that this is what we fought for? Of course, you are going to stay in that school and prove that you are just as good as he is."[156]

In photographs, young Sylvia was a picture of cleanliness and respectability. During the trial she was dressed nicely and sitting quietly, the exact opposite of a dirty, mentally inferior Mexican. The image of Felícitas Mendez dressing her child for the trial evokes images of how Mary Tape must also have dressed her child for her first day at the Chinese school. The mothers' children were on display in the court and in the media. In their innocence, the youths might not have even realized that their little bodies were carriers of a message they did not author or control. As Sylvia Mendez often shares in her speeches and interviews, she thought the case was about letting her play on a "beautiful playground."[157]

In yet another similarity with Mamie Tape, the piano played an interesting role in Sylvia Mendez's life. Sylvia was photographed sitting in front of a piano, and this image signaled her intelligence in mastering a refined instrument. Seated with her fingers over the keys, the little racialized nine-year-old wearing a pressed dress and pigtails was anything but mentally inferior. According to Sylvia, who hated playing piano, her father had her take piano lessons to become assimilated to "American" culture.[158] In a private conversation, she affirmed that the aforementioned photograph was purposely taken at the time of the *Mendez* trial. It was a staged, well-constructed picture with a clear message of worthiness. In a recent article regarding the timeless influence of a piano, Mary MacVean writes, "The piano has been the center of many American homes for generations, not only a proclamation of love of music but also often a statement about striving for success. 'In a very traditional sense, the piano did stand for something. It was a symbol of mobility, moving up,' especially among immigrant families, said Joe Lamond, president of the International Music Products Association."[159] Upon inspection, the piano was made by Ivers and Pond and had a likely value of $600 to $1,000.[160] Assuming the Mendezes owned the instrument, this fact further supports their middle-class standing symbolically and financially. Though Mamie and Sylvia were not immigrants to the country, the piano asserts their family's American success.

Sylvia Mendez was not a *mamacita* or a *malinche*, nor was she mentally inferior. Like Mamie Tape, she was simply the eldest daughter in a middle-class family that was trying to, as Felícitas Mendez testified, "do the right thing and just asking for the right thing, to put [their] childrens [sic] together with the rest of the childrens [sic]."[161] Unlike Mamie Tape, Sylvia Mendez won her legal battle at both the district court and federal circuit court levels. This suggests that while historically oppressed groups were shut down by systems of inequality that generated oppressive, caricatured controlling images, the one small area of agency these groups possessed was the selection and strategic framing of their litigants. I argue that these young girls held a position in which they were too young to be sexualized and too accomplished to be significantly diminished.

Mendez followed a similar narrative when it came to Gonzalo, and because of the trial transcripts, there are many more instances of fatherhood on display. The *Orange Daily News* reported, "The suit was filed in Los Angeles federal court... on behalf of students of Mexican or Latin descent in Santa Ana... by Gonzalo Mendez, father of a student at Westminster."[162] The Spanish newspaper *La Prensa* named all five fathers, writing,

> *La demanda fué presentada a nombre de cinco padres de familia.... Esos cinco señores son Gonzalo Mendez, William Guzmán, Frank Palomino, Thomas Estrada y Lorenzo Ramirez, suyos hijos han sido objecto de discriminación.*

> The demand was presented on behalf of five family men. Those five men are Gonzalo Mendez, William Guzmán, Frank Palomino, Thomas Estrada y Lorenzo Ramirez, whose children were objects of discrimination.[163]

Even African American newspapers on the other side of the country, such as the *Norfolk Journal Guide* and the *Baltimore Afro-American*, reported on the case.[164] The *Baltimore Afro-American* noted that the petition was "filed by *five Mexican fathers* charging racial discrimination against their children."[165] While these papers incorrectly reported that the case was based in racial discrimination, they also mentioned the fathers but never talked about the mothers.[166]

During the *Mendez* trial, four of the five fathers testified. Frank Palomino was the first to do so, and he explained to the court that he paid tuition to send his children to private school rather than the Mexican school.[167] Unfortunately, Mr. Palomino also testified that he did not ask to go back to Garden Grove again after being rejected. The judge asked him, "How did you happen to choose the Fremont School [Mexican school] to send your boy to?" Mr. Palomino admitted that he sent his son there to be with his cousins. "In other words," Judge McCormick replied, "it was your choice to send the boy to that school."[168] Admitting that he had initially chosen to send his children to the Mexican school took away the argument that the Palominos were forced to do so.

Mr. Guzmán testified on the second day of the trial but, as previously discussed, was terribly nervous. While it is not clear whether Marcus sufficiently prepped his clients, testifying in court can be a stressful and overwhelming experience. Recall that at one point, David Marcus urged Mr. Guzmán to relax to avoid confusion. It did not help.

Father of seven Lorenzo Ramirez, whose spirited testimony regarding race was

outlined in the previous chapter, offered even more insight into the racial dynamics of the case. He explained that Japanese, Filipino, and African American children were admitted to the White school while Mexican Americans were relegated
to Mexican schools. In this particular instance, African and Asian Americans had
"better standing" than Mexican American youths. Nonetheless, rather than distance himself from African Americans, Mr. Ramirez put forth themes of equality
and justice, marching alongside African Americans. Where Mr. Hammarsten had
tried to divide Blacks and Mexicans racially, Mr. Ramirez pushed back against any
suggestion related to the racial hierarchy.

Mr. Mendez, as the lead plaintiff, spent the most time on the stand. He was
definitely more confident than the other fathers who testified. He identified himself as the leader of the group of parents and relayed the conversation the parents
had at his ranch with Mr. Harris, the superintendent of Westminster: "Mrs. Pena
related her story, saying she had two sons in the army and saying she thought it
[school admissions] wasn't . . . very democratic . . . on the basis that her sons were
out there fighting for all of us, and the rest of her [family] was out here being segregated as a class."[169] Mr. Mendez related another conversation from another mother
whose sons were fighting in the "European theater"; she, too, did not think it fair
to segregate the children. Normally such testimony regarding what others have
said would be considered hearsay, and the school officials tried to challenge it,
with the defense counsel saying, "I wouldn't object to one or two statements, but
when he [Mendez] takes in the whole country[, I protest]."[170] The judge, however,
responded, "There is no jury to be prejudiced by any such statements. . . . He has
mentioned four Mexican folk who went there together with himself. . . . Go ahead
with the conversation you had with Mr. Harris."[171] It is clear from the transcripts
that the attorney for the school districts was very frustrated.

He had reason to be, as Mr. Mendez was not only invoking motherhood and
military service in World War II, but also offering the most detailed descriptions
of his children's experience in the Mexican school. After being told that the school
board failed to obtain the necessary votes for a new health room and bigger cafeteria in the White school, Mr. Mendez testified,

> Yes, Mr. Harris, but that wouldn't benefit us at all, as to your having a nice cafete-
> ria . . . and a health room, while we over there in our Hoover School have nothing but
> a small building, and without any trees, or benches for my children to come and have
> their lunch at noon. To the contrary, at noon, when they go out to eat their lunch,
> they have to sit down on the ground or on the stairs, and the teachers do not even ask
> our children to go in the room and eat their lunches. . . . They do not care about our
> children.[172]

Explaining that he did most of the talking for the group, Mr. Mendez also went on to relay Mr. Harris's "protests" against Mexican children: "One of the main protests ... was that all the Mexican people lived in nothing but shacks, and [were] unsanitary, and that was not sufficient[ly] hygienic as to go to the Main school. 'How could we send our children, when they were so dirty?' That we should elevate our standard of living up to the standard of living of their race, meaning the Anglo-Saxon race."[173] Mr. Mendez then argued that Japanese families were allowed to attend the White school. Even though his house was just like their homes, his children were denied entry and theirs were accepted. Mr. Harris dismissed his observation. Mr. Mendez went on to testify, "The main point was we wanted to see if we could come to some agreement where we could unite the two schools together. And we said that we have created ... prejudice between the Anglo-Saxons and the Mexicans, because some of them would not want their children to be seated near *a Mexican boy*, on account that some were a little bit dirty."[174]

The following day, the judge began to question Mr. Mendez about his farm business. Mr. Mendez testified that he oversaw 40 acres of his own asparagus farm and was a foreman for another farmer's 22 acres of asparagus, 100 acres of chili peppers, and nursery of avocados and oranges. In all, he managed over 150 acres, supervised over 100 employees, negotiated market prices, and "kept the books." The judge continued to question Mr. Mendez and ask him about his family. He asked whether Mrs. Mendez spoke English, and Mr. Mendez affirmed this fact but explained that she had an accent. The judge replied, "Well, of course, that would be natural. That would not only apply to the Mexican people. Any person of Latin or Slavic or Teutonic origin, or perhaps of other origin, would naturally have some. It might be an accent or a brogue. It might even be in our own country where someone would have an accent because he comes from the south or from New England."[175] The judge made it clear that an accent was not troublesome so long as Mrs. Mendez could express herself in English. At this point in the trial, the school officials were arguing that the Mexican families did not speak English and were poor, unkempt, and inferior overall. By the time Mr. Mendez was dismissed from the stand, I imagine the defendants were not quite as confident as they had been in the beginning of the trial.

In a short amount of time, Mr. Mendez established his leadership, referenced themes of democracy and justice, demonstrated that he managed a large business, and, most importantly, contradicted every stereotype put forth by the school systems' attorney. Mrs. Mendez was next to testify, but Mr. Mendez had done such a great job describing the parents' experience that the defense stipulated that his wife would give substantially similar testimony. This might have been done in an effort to get her off the stand as quickly as possible. Marcus explained that he simply wanted the judge to hear Mrs. Mendez speak in English, to which the judge replied, "She seems to have a pretty good knowledge of the vernacular beyond commonplace vernacular, and as it should be spoken."[176]

Over the five days of the trial, several community members testified on behalf of the Mexican families. All the witnesses were married. All lived close to the White school and spoke English. Some were parents of valiant and respectable World War II soldiers. Though more women than men testified, the only names ever published were of the five fathers.

Finally, even when *Mendez* is reported in modern news accounts, Gonzalo is the most mentioned member of the Mendez family. A 2004 article states, "If somebody else had written U.S. history books over the past half-century, Sylvia Mendez would be as familiar to us today as Oliver Brown, the plaintiff in *Brown v. Board of Education*."[177] Later in the article, the author explains how, "infuriated, her [Sylvia's] father, Gonzalo Mendez, looked up a firebrand lawyer, David Marcus." Another contemporary account describes Gonzalo as "an immigrant who was born in Chihuahua, with a strong and willful temperament." The account continues, "Never one to give up, he got together four Mexican families and in 1945 they sued the city of Los Angeles."[178]

Felícitas Mendez was equally impressive yet conspicuously absent from narratives of the case. Again, she was never mentioned or named in the news coverage. Furthermore, while she was allowed to testify, her time was cut short. When Mr. Marcus stipulated that she would testify to the same points Gonzalo shared on the stand, Gonzalo's testimony became her testimony even though she had her own story to tell. This silence and absence from the historical record obscured Felícitas's exceptional contributions to the proceedings. Far from a trashy *malinche* or provocative *mamacita*, she would become an organizer, entrepreneur, and determined promoter of the *Mendez* story.

As Gonzalo and Marcus rounded up the five thousand families for the case, Felícitas ran the farm's day-to-day operations for over a year. She was captured in a photograph working a tractor (see Figure 5.5). According to the Mendez family, "She not only ran the farm well, but it became more prosperous than ever" under her supervision.[179] Her contributions on the farm are also represented in a children's book written and illustrated by Duncan Tonatiuh. In the book, he describes how she took care of the children, the farm, and the workers, and even "started an irrigation system."

In addition to running the farm, Felícitas also created the *Asociación de Padres y Niños México-Americanos* (Association of Mexican American Parents and Children), which organized the parents and children represented in the case. Beyond

FIGURE 5.5.
Felícitas Mendez on the family tractor, mid-1940s. Used with permission from the
Gonzalo Mendez family. Cannot be reproduced or copied without written consent.

even this remarkable leadership, the Mendezes' generosity shone through when
they arranged transportation to and from the courthouse for the families, reim-
bursed their resultant loss of pay so they could attend the trial, and, of course, covered all legal fees. Perhaps Felícitas's early childhood experience with Puerto Rican
organizing was reflected in her service to her beloved adopted Mexican community. The *Asociación* held 151 meetings with parents in the community, "which
both provided moral support for the effort and signaled to school officials that the
Mexican community was behind the fight."[180]

What Felícitas should most be remembered for, however, was the promise
she garnered from her daughter prior to her death in 1998. In her many appear-
ances and interviews, Sylvia Mendez shares a story about how her mother often
lamented that no one knew the family's story. "People have forgotten. They don't
remember what we did." Felícitas obtained a promise from her notoriously shy
daughter to tell the story of *Mendez v. Westminster*. Since then, Sylvia has dutifully
accepted hundreds of speaking requests. Each time she tells the story of *Mendez*,
she honors her parents and donates the honorarium she receives to the City of
Westminster's efforts to erect a memorial to the famous case. Yet even in initial
drafts of the memorial depict only Gonzalo Mendez. It is only at Sylvia Mendez's

insistence that her mother will be added to the final plans. Felícitas Mendez will be missed no more.

Different Cases, Similar Stories

Three cases, three plaintiffs, three sets of families, and three different time periods all tell a similar story of seeking justice through the courts when it was denied by those in power. Still, even as powerful as the stories of the *Tape*, *Piper*, and *Mendez* cases are, when it comes to the civil rights narrative in the United States, they remain the omitted, the forgotten, and the understated. Each lawsuit provides insight into how education was transformed from the dream of a common school created for children of all races to commonplace schools marked by the extreme racial prejudice of the times, including Chinese exclusion, the failure of Indian boarding and day schools, and the Zoot Suit Riots. Across time, each group was characterized as filthy, uncivilized, mentally inferior, and unwanted. While all the cases were legally "victorious," they still fell short of *Brown*. *Tape* solidified separate schools in California, *Piper* questioned but did not end the practice, and *Mendez* dismantled desegregation, but only in California and eventually Arizona.

This, however, is where most researchers end their analysis and discussion, with the families and the facts of the individual cases. Taking comparative Critical Race Theory and controlling images into consideration, I extend the research by critically examining and comparing the *Tape*, *Piper*, and *Mendez* civil rights narratives to demonstrate that the cases' fight for justice complicated race, involved class politics, deployed deeply gendered images, and strategically used age.

These young plaintiffs and their families inhabited a respectable position within the controlling images of their time. They were neither Black nor White, poor nor rich, disastrous nor desirable. While they would never "achieve whiteness" and were distanced, intentionally or not, from Blackness, they possessed a flexibility that represented a balance between extremes. Ultimately, I suggest that considering the role of race in the school desegregation movement by itself provides an incomplete picture of this civil rights narrative.

These cases, while focused on issues of race, citizenship, and descent, were also decisively shaped by gender, class, and age. As representations of immorality, unworthiness, and poverty, the controlling images were contradicted by the plaintiffs through the politics of respectability. The families were racialized middle-class imitations of traditional nuclear White families. Joseph Tape, Pike Piper, and Gonzalo Mendez were fathers who stood up on behalf of their daughters and used their resources to maintain a long legal battle for educational equality. Mary Tape and Felícitas Mendez worked powerfully, yet without recognition, behind the scenes. Mamie Tape, Alice Piper, and Sylvia Mendez were the pretty little plaintiffs whose middle-class lives set them apart from the controlling images of their time. By blending controlling images and the politics of respectability, we can theorize whether activists, organizers, and lawyers can exercise what little agency they possess to resist the images "controlling" the American hegemonic and racist imagination. If court cases are ultimately performances, as asserted by CRT scholars, then the fathers were on the stage while the mothers worked behind the curtain. The daughters, however, were the stars.

CONCLUSION

The fruits of the African American battle for civil rights
are positions of power held by African Americans in the
public and private sectors. And now we find ourselves in
the position of defending that power against other people
pushing for inclusion. Though we pride ourselves on our
leadership role in civil rights, paradoxically, we guard the
success jealously. "We're the ones who marched in the streets
and got our heads busted. Where were they? But now they
want to get in on the benefits."

—BRENDA PAYTON, columnist for the *Oakland Tribune*

We need to stop playing Privilege or Oppression Olympics
because we'll never get anywhere until we find more effective
ways of talking through difference. We should be able to
say, "This is my truth," and have that truth stand without a
hundred clamoring voices shouting, giving the impression
that multiple truths cannot coexist.

—ROXANE GAY, author of *Bad Feminist*

In the epigraphs above, the authors capture the tension that underlying social justice projects that propose inclusivity. Such tension can arise when examining the
iconic role of *Brown* and asking what histories may be hidden in its shadow. In
attempting to construct a more inclusive narrative of school desegregation, this
project is not meant to diminish the importance of this groundbreaking Supreme
Court case. It is also not a pronouncement of "We matter too!" or "You're not the
only ones!" as was suggested by a White colleague when I described this research
to her. Most importantly, it is not a project that ranks the experiences of differ-

ent racial groups and awards the gold, silver, and bronze medal for oppression accordingly. It is, as Roxane Gay suggests, an exercise in multiple truths that reveal the complicated yet connected narratives of Chinese American, Native American, and Mexican American families who initiated legal challenges against separate and unequal education.

The goals of this book are twofold. First, this work provides examples of how these disparate racial groups engaged in the legal battle for racial equality in education to advance the conversation on race. Second, *The Bricks before "Brown"* analyzes how race, class, gender, and age were constructed similarly and separately in each case and across time. In doing so, this research adds the legal and historical contributions of three families in an effort to enhance the significance of *Brown*. It also contributes to civil rights scholarship by expanding the analysis of school desegregation beyond questions of race to further discussions about the role of gender, class, and age. There are reasons why Rosa Parks was portrayed as a tired seventy-five-year-old seamstress her entire life even though she had been a forty-two-year-old secretary of the NAACP who investigated rape cases in the South. Gender, class, and age are important to consider as well.

In the first chapter, I also build very deliberate scaffolding in order to delve into the complexities of how Latiné, Indigenous, and Asian American plaintiffs and families were racialized during their respective legal efforts. I define and recognize the Black Foundationalist research and scholarship that laid the groundwork for such discussions. Much of the work by Black scholars exposes the deeply entrenched, systemic racial inequality endemic in the United States. Their investigations have paved the way for non-Black scholars like me to come forward, recognize the work accomplished within the Black/White binary, and move beyond the binary to include Latiné, Asian, and Native American perspectives both problematic and provocative—provocative because of their rejection of Whiteness, yet problematic because of assimilation and anti-Blackness.

Overall, I discuss how race was legally, historically, and socially constructed in very different ways among Asian Americans, Native Americans, and Mexican Americans. In so doing, I expanded traditional CRT analysis to include the specific issues addressed by LatCrit, AsianCrit, and TribalCrit, including, but not limited to, immigration, language, citizenship, and tribal sovereignty. Identifying these issues demonstrates how the experiences of Asian, Native American, and Latiné communities differ from one another and from African American communities, yet are still rooted in the intersectional, revisionist, and interrogative foundation of CRT. Specifically, I describe how Whiteness has been used as a racial wedge or protective cloak for Latinés; how Asians are characterized as the yellow peril, forever foreigners, or model minorities; and how Native Americans occupy a complicated, liminal space between a racial and political identity in the United States. Most importantly, I describe how Asians, Native Americans, and Latinés all occupy a vague, flexible position within the U.S. racial hierarchy that simultaneously benefits and punishes them individually and collectively for failing to be completely defined by either Blackness or Whiteness.

Finally, I analyze the role of gender, class, and age in the narratives surrounding the fathers, mothers, and children. Criminal and sexual controlling images did not define the roles these individuals played in this legal drama. Fathers, particularly Joseph Tape and Gonzalo Mendez, were featured prominently in school desegregation narratives. The mothers, on the other hand, were considerably absent from the story line despite their critical contributions. Mamie Tape, Alice Piper, and Sylvia Mendez represented "pretty little plaintiffs" that were too young to be declared criminals or sexual objects and too resourced to be considered pathetic, inferior, or poor. Their middle-class respectability and their youth made them ideal candidates because they portrayed a racial innocence that mimicked the purity of little White girls, who were the American ideal.

Entering the new analytical territory of comparative critical race studies requires breaking a few rules. First, I treated disciplinary boundaries as if they were lines in the sand. Second, I blended theories to fit the research rather than forc-ing the research to fit a singular theory. Finally, I saw connections between the stories while simultaneously recognizing and honoring the differences. In doing this, however, I knew that I would not make any one scholar satisfied with the end result. Historians would want more archival research. Legal scholars would want more legal analysis. Sociologists would want a cleaner presentation of social science. I am also certain that each case would have received different treatment in the hands of Latiné, Asian American, and Indigenous studies scholars. Nevertheless, my approach does not preclude these specialists from making their specific, focused, and necessary contributions. I contend that this book would have been incomplete if any one of the cases were removed or replaced.

Therefore, to tell a complete story, I combined CRT and its branches with controlling images and the politics of respectability, and borrowed heavily from law, history, and sociology. The result is a nuanced study of the school desegregation movement in the United States rooted in an intersectional, interdisciplinary, and inclusive paradigm. This work challenges the traditional Black/White racial narrative of segregated schooling, presents visual and legal evidence of its existence outside of the South, and dislodges it from its traditional 1950s timeline.

In chapter 2, my legal research generates a visual blueprint of the legal battle for educational equality. Beginning in 1849, with a little girl named Sarah Roberts and her father, Benjamin, plaintiffs filed legal cases and fought them in courts around the country, across time, and among different racial divisions.[1] Nearly all the cases were filed by Black families before and after *Plessy* for over one hundred years until a little girl named Linda and her father, Oliver, with the support of the NAACP, legally dismantled the separate but equal doctrine. Out of the cases I identified, only a handful have been the subjects of full monographs.[2] Even fewer books that use a comparative/historical approach.[3] These cases reveal that school desegregation has been studied separately and unequally across time and across racial groups. This explains the scant literature on Asian American, Native American, and Latiné school desegregation cases.

Identifying 105 bricks before *Brown* requires an even deeper legal analysis than I provide in this book. Specialized legal scholars and historians have been able to tell the unique circumstances of Oklahoma,[4] Virginia,[5] and the North.[6] The state of Kansas alone, with its ten cases that began in 1881 and ended in 1949, could fill eleven books—one book on each case and then another that discusses them all together. What was so special or unique about Kansas? This was a rabbit hole that I could not explore for fear of never finishing my dissertation and graduating.

With more archival and secondary research, I could have ascertained the gender, name, and age of each lead plaintiff in all the proceedings. It would be interesting to find out whether gender and age did, in fact, make a difference in the outcomes. How many pretty little plaintiffs existed across time? How many suits were brought by fathers, and how many by mothers? Again, these are questions that are beyond the scope of this book. However, in gathering all the cases, I am creating a digital version of the *Bricks before "Brown"* maps (B[3] map) for future scholars to explore and K–12 social studies teachers to incorporate into their curriculum.

The 105 cases reveal that segregated schooling arose almost as soon as the common school was created and set a damaging precedent for *Plessy* that took another fifty-eight years to dismantle. The maps also indicate where and when segregated schooling was legally challenged throughout the country. Most importantly, this chapter includes specific case histories of four lawsuits filed by Chinese Americans in the West and South, five actions filed by Native Americans in the West and South, and two cases filed by Mexican Americans in the West and Southwest. As a result, this research contributes to the literature by demonstrating that the road to *Brown* was multiracial, nonlinear, lengthy, and all connected with the mortar of inequality.

After laying out the legal landscape, I introduce the stories of the Tapes', Pipers', and Mendezes' experiences with racism, education, and discrimination. The Tapes endured hardship, humiliation, and rejection to win their case but were ultimately "outwitted" by the school board of San Francisco. Their legal efforts provide a disturbingly clear example of how individual acts of racism are and can be transformed into systemic racism over a relatively short period of time. Separate public Chinese schools in California did not exist in 1883. Two years later, however, they were created, and they were funded and maintained until 1947.

The Tapes also demonstrated how substantial wealth and limited social standing could not shield them from racism. Using the AsianCrit tenets of Asianization and transnational context, I show how it did not matter how Americanized the family had become. It did not matter that Mamie and her siblings were American citizens by birth. It did not matter how many connections they had made with their White Presbyterian church. The Tapes would bounce from foreignness to model minority status depending on the lens through which they were criticized and observed. Mamie and Mary separated themselves from the controlling images of the day so that they were not mischaracterized as pagans, prostitutes, or poor creatures. They were Christian. They were wealthy. They were well educated. However, because they were Chinese, legal justice could not necessarily translate to social justice.

In piecing together *Piper v. Big Pine*, two different stories emerge providing a compelling example of the need to decolonize traditional archival methodologies. Had I relied solely on traditional "four corners of the document" analysis, the Pipers would have been portrayed as an assimilated family who, as wards of the United States, happily traded their culture for second-class citizenship. Instead, relying on TribalCrit tenets of liminality, assimilation, and autonomy, I show how the their people, the Big Pine Paiute Tribe of the Owens Valley, transformed their nearly silenced whispers into a community-run effort whose echoes will continue to resonate over time. The subversive story of Alice Piper will continue to pass through generations as a reminder of how a courageous family skirted unjust laws to benefit their Paiute Nation.

The story of Alice Piper is not yet complete. At the beginning of this research project, Alice was a fuzzy face in a crowd that I enhanced with technology. Thanks to the generosity of the Big Pine Paiute Tribe of the Owens Valley and the Big Pine School District, she transformed into a beautiful young lady with family, friends, and dreams. With the recent discovery of her employment records with the Stewart Indian School, the next step in researching her life is to find former students who are willing to discuss their experiences with her. I am not certain what I will learn about Alice Piper. Did she contribute to the generational trauma that flows from the collective memories of students harmed by Indian schooling? Did she provide solace in a system that demanded assimilation? Was she a silently complicit casualty of a system she could not escape or change? Regardless of what I may find, I will share all the pieces of her story with the tribe because this is their story. As tribal historian Danelle Gutierrez told me, Alice is meant to return home.

Finally, in chapter 5, I gather secondary materials, original archival data, and current interviews to tell the influential yet understated story of the Mendez family and the five thousand plaintiffs that transformed California from a legally segregated to an integrated state. Theirs is a story where their collective, authentic community voices were captured using traditional tools for preserving history. In analyzing the case with the LatCrit tenet of Latino/a essentialism, I examine how the plaintiffs were able to tell their own story in their own words, building a narrative based on racial pride and a rejection of Whiteness. An astute attorney hired by a singularly focused father and supported by a resourceful mother authored one of the most understated stories of desegregation.

The *Mendez* story is an example of a Black-Brown alliance that changed history. It is a poignant tale of using legal Whiteness to protect Japanese American dreams. It is a story of a multiracial coalition of civil rights organizations. More than anything else, however, it is a story of families—families who stood up, put on their best outfits, strode into a courtroom, and endured questioning from bloated litigators in order to tell their truth. Fathers defended their children. Mothers took pride in their sons' service in World War II. Young sons and daughters knew they were not the dirty, diseased, and mentally inferior children administrators judged them to be.

Mendez was a true community effort led by five families. If it were possible to name a case the *Mendez, Guzmán, Palomino, Estrada*, and *Ramirez* case, then all of the plaintiffs would be equally remembered. Still, their demands for equality and citizenship are forever sealed in the historical record. This scholarly treatment of their testimony is merely the result of a trained lawyer and sociologist using her imagination to "hear" the transcripts in her mind.

These families were not simply Chinese Americans, Native Americans, and Mexican Americans. They were also accomplished, resourced families that maintained unquestionably respectable middle-class lifestyles marked by landownership, entrepreneurial spirits, financial generosity, and sophisticated hobbies. While their class did not protect them from discrimination, it did allow the families to exercise their agency without the fear of financial retaliation. They could not lose their jobs because they were the bosses. Most importantly, they could bankroll a lengthy litigation process, meeting a resourced school district face-to-face in the courts.

This research journey carried me through several parts of California and some parts of Nevada. With each visit, and with each gentle, careful turn of a page of archival records, these families became more alive to me. Never will I forget finally finding Mary Tape in the minutes of the San Francisco Ladies' Protection and Relief Society after spending several hours sifting through thousands of records. Never will I forget the chills I felt the first time I saw Alice Piper all grown up. I will always remember having to pull myself away from reading the transcripts and imagining Sylvia Mendez and her brothers sitting in the courtroom, hearing these school administrators testify that they were not good enough for White schools. I share their stories so they will cease to be the omitted, forgotten, and understated contributions to school desegregation efforts in the United States. I share their stories for the Latiné, Indigenous, and Asian American students who yearn to see representations of themselves in struggles, not on sidelines. I share to push the conversation on interracial coalition building from platitudes to practical examples that can inspire and anchor such efforts.

Once again, remove any one of these cases, and the collective stories change. When my Latiné and Asian American students asked, "Didn't we do anything?" I remember telling them, "Yes and no," because they might be inspired in some cases and ashamed in others. They had to be ready for both responses. In order to have deeper conversations about race and difference in the United States, we need to embrace the connections while anticipating the chaos. It means honoring the differences among racial groups without asserting unnuanced equivalencies.

Template for Inclusive, Intersectional, and Interdisciplinary Research

In describing the legal journey of *Tape*, *Piper*, and *Mendez*, as well as the ways in which race, class, gender, and age were constructed across the cases, I have generated a more inclusive, intersectional, and interdisciplinary narrative of school desegregation efforts in the United States. More than overlooked stories of school desegregation, however, I offer a template for conducting research that connects social justice efforts and racial projects represented across marginalized groups. Placing phenomena side by side is not an assertion of equality. Rather, it is an interrogation of oppression and how it manifests in one group versus another. It is also an invitation to consider events, organizations, leaders, and the like that can add to coalition-building efforts.

In this instance, once the cases are placed side by side, inclusive of *Brown*, the connections and differences between them become more compelling (Table C.1). *Piper*, for example, is set apart because of the liminal position of the Indigenous plaintiffs. The convoluted characterization of race by defendants, judges, and attorneys reflects how and why meaningful coalitions between and among groups

TABLE C.1
Comparative table of *Tape, Piper, Mendez,* and *Brown*

	Tape	Piper	Mendez	Brown
Year	1885	1924	1947	1954
Legal Claim	Fourteenth Amendment	Dawes Act	Fourteenth Amendment	Fourteenth Amendment
Race	"Every intelligent person knows that the Fourteenth Amendment was intended for persons of African descent."	Even though Alice Piper was of the "aboriginal race," the federal government was supposed to "exercise paternal care."	Segregation was based on Mexican descent (racialized); there were no claims for whiteness.	Segregation was based solely on race.
Gender/Age	The lead plaintiffs were all little girls when younger boys were readily available. Fighting fathers (the same daddy-daughter narrative). Missing mothers (women whose contributions were overshadowed by the fathers).			
Controlling Images	Pagans Prostitutes Poor creatures	Squaw Savage Sacrificial maiden	Mamacitas Malinches Mentally inferior	Pregnant teens Perpetually poor pickaninnies
Class	Drayman/consulate Translator/businessman	Owned land separate and apart from the rez	Tenant farmer Owner	Railway employee Assistant pastor
Middle-Class Respectability	"My eldest daughter Mamie is quite proficient in the piano."		Staged photograph of Sylvia at a piano	"When I'm out of college, I'd like to teach voice and piano—private lessons."

are difficult to identify. Yet what they all have in common is the thread and horror of White supremacy woven throughout the cases.

The gendered roles the fathers, mothers, and daughters played were nearly identical as they progressed across time. Similar to Mary Tape, Annie Piper, and Felícitas Mendez, even Leola Brown, the mother of Linda Brown, was not interviewed about her involvement in *Brown* until long after the trial took place. All of the young girls had to overcome stigmatizing controlling images of their time. For Linda Brown, her childlike innocence had to overcome characterizations African Americans constructed by Gunnar Myrdal's *An American Dilemma*, which painted an image of the Black family as marred by poverty and pregnancy. Moreover, Linda had to separate herself from the popular-culture characteristics of the disheveled, dirty, largely naked pickaninny.[7] Like Mamie Tape, Alice Piper, and Sylvia Mendez, Linda also held a middling position between competing sets of controlling images. She overcame it largely because of her middle-classness. Her father was not only an assistant pastor, a respected role in Black communities. He was also a railroad employee, which was a union-protected profession. Therefore, like Joseph and Gonzalo, Oliver Brown maintained solid job security in a time when most plaintiffs were threatened with unemployment, poverty, and even death.

Perhaps among the most fascinating evidence of the these plaintiffs' collective middle-class identities is the presence of the piano in the lives of at least three of the families. Whether a permanent fixture in the household or a part of a staged photograph with a reluctant student, this very "American" instrument had symbolism behind it that cannot be lost in examining these cases. In interviews with newspapers, even Linda Brown hinted that she would play/teach piano when she graduated from school.[8] These young women were not playing the Chinese harp, maracas, and banjo, respectively. They were associated with pianos, an instrument representing class, intelligence, and, most of all, the acquisition of cultural capital.[9]

Critical Connections

When I first proposed this project, I was advised by several trusted, knowledgeable scholars to select one case for study and apply an intersectional analysis to it. As one colleague explained to me, "You realize that this represents three dissertations in one?" However, this endeavor was not simply an exercise in the intellectual for me. It was, at its core, a social justice project dedicated to establishing the "critical connections" Patricia Hill Collins alludes to in *Black Feminist Thought*.

A singular focus would only slightly disrupt what Ronald Takaki calls "the Master Narrative of American History" marked by historical inaccuracies, the implied Whiteness of an American identity, and the othering of those deemed "different, inferior, and unassimilable."[10] American history, I was taught, is ultimately about *who* gets to tell the *story*. Therefore, the "master narrative" has been and continues to be redefined one story at a time by adding the various racial classifications, gender disparities, and class inequalities experienced by historically marginalized populations in the United States. The master narrative has been challenged, for example, by Danielle McGuire's research on Rosa Parks's role in investigating rape cases, Leslie Bow's account of Asian Americans in the South, Laura Gómez's sociohistorical construction of a "Mexican race" in New Mexico, and Linda Peavy and Ursula Smith's rich description of a Native American girls' basketball team in Montana.

Singular stories, while valuable, miss an opportunity to confront the master narrative using a multipronged interdisciplinary approach that connects and compares the raced, gendered, classed, and aged stories offered by Chinese Americans, Native Americans, Mexican Americans, *and* African Americans in the United States. American history, therefore, is not defined by one master narrative but instead comprises multiple parallel and sometimes interconnected narratives. Together, these bricks represent significant milestones on the path to educational equality.

Over the span of nearly seventy years, four different families representing four different racial experiences each added a chapter to a dreadfully familiar story. Each attempted to assert rights as citizens of the United States. Each used personal resources to fight for the dignity of relatives and communities. Finally, each tells a story describing a path to justice that was not designed for individual travel. The bricks of this path were constructed by collective efforts and etched with the multiple names and stories of overlooked, forgotten, or disconnected individuals and families who can and must proclaim that *they, too, are America*.

APPENDIX A

The Parties of *Tape v. Hurley*

The Tape Family	San Francisco School District, Spring Valley Primary School
Frederick A. Bee, *Chinese Consulate*	William Weckler, *Superintendent of Schools*
William F. Gibson, *Lead Attorney* Sheldon G. Kellogg, *Co-counsel*	Andrew Jackson Moulder, *Superintendent of Public Instruction*
Joseph Tape, *Named Plaintiff*	*Members of the School Board* Isidor Danielwitz Dr. Charles Cleveland* H. G. Platt R. J. Bowie* J. M. Foard* Earnest Brand Charles E. Travers Jesse A. Melcher Dr. J. M. Eaton J. H. Culver Unidentified Director *In favor of integrated schools
Mamie Tape, *Plaintiff*	
	Jeannie Hurley, *Principal*

APPENDIX B

Mendez v. Westminster and Witness Charts

Orange County School System
Ray Atkinson
County Superintendent

El Modino Harold Hammarsten *Superintendent*	**Garden Grove** James L. Kent *Superintendent*	**Westminster** Richard F. Harris *Superintendent*	**Santa Ana** Frank A. Henderson *Superintendent*
Roosevelt Elementary (White)	Lincoln Elementary (White)	Westminster Elementary (White)	Franklin Elementary (White)
Lincoln Elementary (Mexican)	Hoover Elementary (Mexican)	Hoover Elementary (Mexican)	Fremont Elementary (Mexican)

Witnesses	*Witnesses*	*Witnesses*	*Witnesses*
Carol Torres Robert Perez Lorenzo Ramirez Nieves Peña	Manuela Ochoa Frank Palomino Jane Sianez Juan Muñoz Isabel Ayala	Gonzalo Mendez Felícitas Mendez	Felícitas Fuentes William Guzmán Virginia Guzmán Mabel Mendez John Marval

APPENDIX C

Methodology

In addition to archival research, this dissertation is rooted in legal research to identify and select the 105 school desegregation cases preceding *Brown*. I collected my data for the inventory of these cases through an iterative process using the database LexisNexis Legal. This interface allows me to research state and federal lawsuits using Boolean search terms or names of specific cases. In order to be included in my data, the cases needed to meet the following criteria:

1) Filed on behalf of Black, Asian, Latiné, or Native American plaintiffs
2) Named a school or its representatives
3) Made Fourteenth Amendment equal protection claim
4) Filed before the *Brown* decision in 1954.

My initial goal was to identify all of the cases decided in state and federal courts involving the keywords "Fourteenth Amendment," "schools," and "education" and preceding the *Brown* decision. This general search yielded over three thousand results. My initial reading of these suits indicated that many of them did not fit within the scope of my research question. Narrowing the search to "Fourteenth Amendment" and "school" and "equal protection" generated a list of 1,477 more relevant cases.

I scrolled through each case, reading both the summaries generated by Lexis-Nexis and the opinions themselves. Because I used the search term "equal protection," the results included every criminal and civil case involving equal protection, whether they concerned unequal pricing on milk or racial exclusion on juries. The education cases were fairly easy to find, particularly since most of the case titles involved a form of the phrase "board of education." In the end, I identified sixty-one cases in all.

After this first search, I identified limitations of my search terms. In particular, as I reviewed the facts of each case, I noticed that the opinions were citing cases that were not included in my original findings. Furthermore, I noticed that proceedings of which I had direct knowledge did not appear (e.g., *Tape v. Hurley*). In order to "find" these missing cases, I used the "Shepardize" function on each of the sixty-one cases from my initial search. Shepardizing, as it is called, is a service that provides a summary of the legal history of a given case as well as any cases, law reviews, journal articles, or amicus briefs where it appears. Each time I found more results, I "Shepardized" those until I could no longer find any new cases. Four rounds of Shepardizing revealed forty-three more lawsuits. I am fairly certain I have captured every case related to school desegregation filed in state supreme and federal appellate courts in the LexisNexis database because cases began to cite one another.[1]

I coded the following social characteristics and facts from each lawsuit: name of the case; year it was decided; race, gender, and age of the plaintiff; where it was argued (state or federal court); state; school (i.e., elementary, high, college, etc.); and result (win/loss). I was able to ascertain the race of the plaintiffs in each action, but it was not as easy to determine their gender and age. Some of the cases listed the names and ages of the plaintiffs, but most did not. Further archival research is necessary. Fortunately, many archives are accessible online. I have found that state archives will be the best place to find the details of each case. One final issue was that some cases referred to the school as a "common school" instead of a part of a specifically graded school system (high school, elementary, etc.). Common schools were open to children between six and twenty-one years of age, making the coding of both the school and the students' ages challenging. Nonetheless, education scholars generally consider the common school to be the equivalent of elementary school.[2] As a result, I coded all common schools as elementary.

While I had decided that 1954 would be my end date, I had yet to determine my start date. Initially, I had considered using 1868, the year the Fourteenth Amendment was ratified. However, three cases that came before the passage of the Fourteenth Amendment were cited repeatedly by subsequent cases.[3] Because they were referenced by so many subsequent lawsuits, I decided to keep them as well for two reasons. First, they represent the very first cases decided by a state supreme courts regarding educational inequality. Second, their dates line up with important historical conditions—namely, the growth of common schools, the end of slavery, and the beginning of civil rights challenges to the Fourteenth Amendment.

Along the way, I had to make a few important research decisions regarding which cases to exclude. For example, in a few instances the legal strategy involved suing school districts as taxpayers to demonstrate that tax funds were not being equally distributed.[4] These cases involved adult plaintiffs and tax laws that were not relevant to the cases writ large. These cases were not brought on behalf of any one student or any groups of students, but by taxpayers in general.[5] With no identifiable lead plaintiff or plaintiffs, it was difficult to ascertain age, race, school type, and the like. Finally, in one case a plaintiff successfully argued that his children were White and were therefore eligible to attend the local White school.[6] Had, as in other cases, the result found that the children were "negro" or "colored" or possessed "red blood," I would have included it in the total.

This computerized system of research is not foolproof. For example, some other well-known civil rights cases such "the Little Rock Nine" and Hunter-Holmes lawsuit against the University of Georgia were neither included in my search nor cited by the identified cases. But this is also because they were decided after 1954. There were also three cases involving Mexican American plaintiffs that did not appear in the search results.[7] They were not included because they were either not appealed to their state or federal court system, or they were filed on behalf of taxpayers and not a student.

The other shortcoming to this type of research is the fact that it only captures cases filed and successfully appealed through the court system. Countless actions were never filed, were filed but never adjudicated, or were decided but never published.[8] Fortunately, the 105 identified cases provide a representative sample of case law involving the legal history of the struggle for educational equality from the local district courts, through the state courts, and ultimately to the Supreme Court, allowing me to examine any relevant patterns related to race and gender.

APPENDIX D

Archival Visits

California State Archives, Sacramento, May 11, 2015, to May 14, 2015

Because Earl Warren served as governor of California during the *Mendez* case and subsequently lobbied the state legislature and signed legislation to integrate the schools, I had hoped to find documents at the California State Archives related to the case. I even searched the materials that documented Warren's interactions with the attorney general because the AG filed an amicus brief in support of *Mendez*. Unfortunately, after a week of searching through letters, memos, minutes, and reports, I could not find a single document related to the lawsuit.

Stanford Special Collections, Stanford, California, January 19, 2016

This collection holds Christopher Arriola's original research on *Mendez*. Arriola is an attorney who authored the first article about *Mendez*, "Knocking on the Schoolhouse Door." In addition to his own extensive collection of notes, newspaper articles, and legal documents, Stanford holds the interviews Arriola conducted with former students from the schools represented in the case.

Bancroft Library, University of California, Berkeley, January 21, 2016

This was another exploratory visit to examine the library's Chinese in California Collection and Native American Collection. While the Chinese in California collection has excellent materials that capture the experiences of Chinese in San Francisco in the late 1800s, I found was nothing specific identifying Tape.

The Native American Collection has a publication that I spent over a year trying to find: *Western Story Magazine*. This weekly magazine dedicated to "Big, Clean Stories of Outdoor Life" is archived in a collection dedicated to Max Brand, a popular writer of Western stories. He published heavily in *Western Story*. While his collection does not have a sequential run of the magazines, it offers enough editions published between 1920 and 1925 to create a strong sample for content analysis for a later project.

Bancroft Library, University of California, Berkeley, May 9, 2016, May 12, 2016, and May 16, 2016

This was a return visit to scan stories related to Native Americans in *Western Story Magazine*. Over the course of several days, I digitally scanned fifty editions of the magazine dating from 1920 to 1924. They contain approximately 880 stories about Native Americans or involving Native American characters.

California Historical Society, San Francisco, May 18, 2016, and May 20, 2016

The California Historical Society (CHS) houses materials related to the San Francisco Ladies' Protection and Relief Society. Mary Tape became a ward of the society five months after she arrived in San Francisco. In her 1892 interview with the city's *Morning Call* newspaper, she disclosed that she had lived there for approximately five years beginning at age eleven. Looking for Mary Tape illustrates the reality that archival research on people of color often requires searching the archives of a White person or organization.

Working backward using Mamie Tape's age at the time of the case, I surmised she lived in San Francisco between 1871 and 1876. Just to be safe, I looked at orphan case histories, financial records, and meeting minutes dating from 1870 to 1880. On my third day at the archives, I finally found mention of her in the minutes of the San Francisco Ladies' Protection and Relief Society. It was an excellent find considering that little is known about her life prior to her marriage to Joseph Tape.

National Archives, Riverside, California, Online

The National Archives holds several digital copies of briefs filed in *Mendez v. Westminster*. Archivists generously provided me a CD disc containing briefs, pretrial transcripts, and full transcripts of the trial. It amounted to over seven hundred pages of archival materials.

California Digital Newspaper Collection (CDNC), Online

The CDNC is a free online digital archive of California newspapers that allows for simple keyword searches and advanced searches for particular issues. Critical to this project, it contained editions of San Francisco–based newspaper the *Daily Alta California* dating from 1849 to 1891 that were critical to the project. I conducted searches in the collection using the following words and phrases: "Joseph Tape," "Mamie Tape," "Mary Tape," and "Chinese school." This yielded several articles. After reading them, I searched for more material by using the phrase "Judge McGuire," Culver, Welcker, and "the Chinese Problem." This resulted in several more articles about the case that did not mention any of the family members but contained invaluable material about school board meetings, letters from the state superintendent, and articles printed in other newspapers such as the *Sausalito News* and *Sacramento Daily*.

NOTES

INTRODUCTION

1. Throughout this book, I use "Latiné" as a gender-neutral way to refer to people of Latin American heritage. Although the term "Latinx" has been popularized, it does not reflect the grammatical constructions of Spanish, the often preferred language among Latinés. "Latiné" is similar to the Spanish language's gender-neutral term for student (*estudiante*). Also, I capitalize the term "Indigenous" as a sign of respect. The Native American Journalists Association (https://najanewsroom.com/) explains that the capitalized "Indigenous" denotes a human being having tribal membership or citizenship, versus the lowercase "indigenous" representing a plant or animal. "Reporting and Indigenous Terminology," Native American Journalists Association News Room, 2018, https://najanewsroom.com/wp-content/uploads/2018/11/NAJA _Reporting_and_Indigenous_Terminology_Guide.pdf I also use "Native American" throughout the manuscript. The only time I use "Indian" is in historical context, such as references to Indian schools.

2. Jacqueline Houtman, Walter Naegle, and Michael G. Long, *Trouble Maker for Justice: The Story of Bayard Rustin, the Man behind the March on Washington* (San Francisco: City Light Books, 2019); Danielle McGuire, *At the Dark End of the Street: Black Women, Rape, and Resistance; A New History of the Civil Rights Movement, from Rosa Parks to the Rise of Black Power* (New York: Vintage Books, 2010); Juan F. Perea, "An Essay on the Iconic Status of the Civil Rights Movement and Its Unintended Consequences," *Virginia Journal of Social Policy and the Law* 18, no. 1 (2010): 44–58; Jo Ann Robinson, *Montgomery Bus Boycott and the Women Who Started It* (Knoxville: University of Tennessee Press, 1987).

3. McGuire, *At the Dark End*; Evelyn Brooks Higginbotham, *Righteous Discontent: The Women's Movement in the Black Baptist Church, 1880–1920* (Cambridge, Mass.: Harvard University Press, 1993).

4. Adrienne Berard, *Water Tossing Boulders: How a Family of Chinese Immigrants Led the First Fight to Desegregate Schools in the Jim Crow South* (Boston: Beacon, 2016); Nicole Blalock-

Moore, "*Piper v. Big Pine School District of Inyo County*: Indigenous Schooling and Resistance in the Early Twentieth Century," *Southern California Quarterly* 94, no. 3 (2012): 346–377; Mark Brilliant, *The Color of America Has Changed: How Racial Diversity Shaped Civil Rights Reform in California, 1941–1978* (Oxford: Oxford University Press, 2010); Stephanie Hinnershitz, *A Different Shade of Justice: Asian American Civil Rights in the South* (Chapel Hill: University of North Carolina Press, 2017); Loni Ding, *Mamie Tape and the Fight for Equality in Education, 1885–1995* [short documentary] (San Francisco: Center for Asian American Media, 2000); Joyce Kuo, "Excluded, Segregated, and Forgotten: A Historical View of the Discrimination of Chinese Americans in Public Schools," *Asian American Law Journal* 5, no. 7 (1998): 181–212; Mae Ngai, *The Lucky Ones: One Family and the Extraordinary Invention of Chinese America* (Princeton, N.J.: Princeton University Press, 2010); Juan Perea, "Buscando América: Why Integration and Equal Protection Fail to Protect Latinos," *Harvard Law Review* 117, no. 5 (2004): 1420–1469; Philippa Strum, *"Mendez v. Westminster": School Desegregation and Mexican-American Rights* (Lawrence: University Press of Kansas, 2010).

5. Jacquelyn Dowd Hall, "The Long Civil Rights Movement and the Political Uses of the Past," *Journal of American History* 91, no. 4 (2005): 1233–1263; Judith Stein, "Why American Historians Embrace the 'Long Civil Rights Movement,'" *American Communist History* 11, no. 1 (2012): 55–58.

6. Rudine Sims Bishop, "Mirrors, Windows, and Sliding Glass Doors," *Perspectives: Choosing and Using Books for the Classroom* 6, no. 3 (1990).

7. *Tape v. Hurley*, 66 Cal. 473 (1885); *McMillan v. School Committee of District No. 4*, 107 N.C. 609 (1890); *Wong Him v. Callahan*, 119 F. 381 (1902); *Crawford v. School District No. 7*, 68 Ore. 388 (1913); *Moreau v. Grandich*, 114 Miss. 560 (1917); *Piper v. Big Pine*, 193 Cal. 664 (1924); *Bond v. Tij Fung*, 148 Miss. 462 (1927); *Gong Lum v. Rice*, 275 U.S. 78 (1927); *Peters v. Pauma*, 91 Cal. App. 792 (1927); *Mendez v. Westminster*, 161 F.2d 774 (1947); *Gonzales v. Sheely*, 96 F. Supp. 1004 (1951).

8. "The Chinese Question: An Exhaustive Communication," *Daily Alta California* (San Francisco), January 15, 1885, 8.

CHAPTER 1. Laying the Foundation

Epigraph is from Ariela J. Gross, *What Blood Won't Tell: A History of Race on Trial in America* (Cambridge, Mass.: Harvard University Press, 2008), 9.

1. W. E. B. Du Bois, *W. E. B. Du Bois: A Reader*, ed. by David Levering Lewis (New York City: Holt Paperbacks, 1995); Paulo Freire, *Pedagogy of the Oppressed, 50th Edition* (New York: Bloomsbury Academic, 2018); Akasha (Gloria T.) Hull, Patricia Bell-Scott, and Barbara Smith, eds., *All the Women Are White, All the Blacks Are Men, but Some of Us Are Brave* (New York City: Feminist Press at CUNY, 1993).

2. Aldon D. Morris, *The Origins of the Civil Rights Movement: Black Communities Organizing for Change* (New York: Free Press, 1984); Manning Marable, *Race, Reform, and Rebellion: The Second Reconstruction and Beyond in Black America, 1945–2006*, 3rd ed. (Oxford: University of Mississippi Press, 2007); Barbara Ransby, *Ella Baker and the Black Freedom Movement: A Radical Democratic Vision* (Chapel Hill: University of North Carolina Press, 2003); Bettye

Collier-Thomas and V. P. Franklin, *Sisters in the Struggle: African American Women in the Civil Rights–Black Power Movement* (New York: New York University Press, 2001).

3. While I could not possibly cite every scholar, excellent monographs of the foundational work of Black sociologists are Aldon D. Morris, *The Scholar Denied: W. E. B. Du Bois and the Birth of Modern Sociology* (Oakland: University of California Press, 2017); Earl Wright II, *Jim Crow Sociology: The Black and Southern Roots of American Sociology* (Chicago: University of Chicago Press, 2020).

4. Ibram H. Rogers, *The Black Campus Movement: Black Students and Racial Reconstitution of Higher Education, 1965–1972* (New York: Palgrave Macmillan, 2012); Fabio Rojas, *From Black Power to Black Studies: How a Radical Social Movement Became an Academic Discipline* (Baltimore: Johns Hopkins University Press, 2007).

5. Stephanie Hinnershitz, *Race, Religion, and Civil Rights: Asian Students on the West Coast, 1900–1968* (New Brunswick, N.J.: Rutgers University Press, 2015); Raymond V. Padilla, *Chicano Studies Revisited: Still in Search of the Campus and the Community* (El Paso, Tex.: Chicano Studies Program, University of Texas at El Paso, 1987); Cathy J. Schlund-Vials, ed., *Flashpoints for Asian American Studies* (New York: Fordham University Press, 2018); Bradley G. Shreve, *Red Power Rising: The National Indian Youth Council and the Origins of Native Activism* (Norman: University of Oklahoma Press, 2011); D. J. Silverman, "Living with the Past: Thoughts on Community Collaboration and Difficult History in Native American and Indigenous Studies," *American Historical Review* 125, no. 2 (2020): 519–527; Michael Soldatenko, *Chicano Studies: The Genesis of a Discipline* (Phoenix: University of Arizona Press, 2009).

6. The few scholars that have engaged in this type of work inspired my own. They include Mark Brilliant's *The Color of America Has Changed: How Racial Diversity Shaped Civil Rights Reform in California, 1941–1978* (Oxford: Oxford University Press, 2010); Peggy Pascoe, *What Comes Naturally: Miscegenation Law and the Making of Race in America* (Oxford: Oxford University Press, 2010); Laura Pulido, *Black, Brown, Yellow and Left: Radical Activism in Los Angeles* (Berkeley: University of California Press, 2006); Ronald Takaki, *A Different Mirror: A History of Multicultural America* (New York: Back Bay Books, 2008).

7. Gloria Anzaldúa, ed., *Making Face, Making Soul / Haciendo Caras: Creative and Critical Perspectives by Feminists of Color* (San Francisco, Calif.: Aunt Lute Books, 1990); Cherríe Moraga and Gloria Anzaldúa, eds., *This Bridge Called My Back: Writings by Radical Women of Color*, 4th ed. (Albany: State University of New York Press, 2015).

8. The Black/White binary is also referred to as the Black/White paradigm.

9. Eduardo Luna, "How the Black/White Paradigm Renders Mexicans/Mexican Americans and Discrimination against Them Invisible," *Berkeley La Raza Law Journal* 14, no. 2 (2003): 232; Jeanne M. Powers, "On Separate Paths: The Mexican American and African American Legal Campaigns Against School Segregation," *American Journal of Education* 121, no. 1 (2014): 29–55; Nick Corona Vaca, "Who's the Leader of the Civil Rights Band? Latinos' Role in *Brown v. Board of Education*," in *The Presumed Alliance: The Unspoken Conflict Between Latinos and Blacks and What It Means for America* (New York: Rayo, 2004).

10. Derrick J. Bell, "Serving Two Masters: Integration Ideals and Client Interests in School Desegregation Litigation," *Yale Law Journal* 85, no. 4 (1976): 470–516; Derrick J. Bell, "*Brown v. Board of Education* and the Interest-Convergence Dilemma," *Harvard Law Review* 93, no.

3 (1980): 518–534; Roy L. Brooks, "*Brown v. Board of Education* Fifty Years Later: A Critical Race Theory Perspective," *Howard Law Journal* 47, no. 3 (2004): 581–626; Barbara J. Love, "*Brown* Plus 50 Counter-Storytelling: A Critical Race Theory Analysis of the 'Majoritarian Achievement Gap' Story," *Equity* 37, no. 3 (2004): 227–246.

11. Sohyun An, "AsianCrit Perspective on Social Studies," *Journal of Social Science Research* 41, no. 2 (2017): 131–139; Bryan McKinley Jones Brayboy, "Toward a Tribal Critical Race Theory in Education," *Urban Review* 37, no. 5 (2014): 425–446; Jean Stefancic, "Latino and Latina Critical Race Theory: An Annotated Bibliography," *California Law Review* 85, no. 5 (1997): 423–498.

12. Richard Delgado and Jean Stefancic, *Critical Race Theory: An Introduction* (New York: New York University Press, 2012).

13. Robert Chang, "Toward an Asian American Legal Scholarship: Critical Race Theory, Post-structuralism, and Narrative Space," *California Law Review* 81, no. 5 (1993): 1248.

14. Linda Martín Alcoff, "Latino/as, Asian Americans, and the Black-White Binary," *Journal of Ethics* 7 (2003): 5–27; Delgado and Stefancic, *Critical Race Theory*; Gross, *What Blood Won't Tell*; Ian Haney López, "Race, Ethnicity, Erasure: The Salience of Race to LatCrit Theory," *California Law Review*, 85, no. 5 (1997): 1143–1211; Juan F. Perea, "The Black/White Binary Paradigm of Race: The 'Normal Science' of American Racial Thought," *California Law Review* 85, no. 5 (1997): 1213–1258.

15. Eileen O'Brien, *The Racial Middle: Latinos and Asian Americans Living beyond the Racial Divide* (New York: New York University Press, 2008).

16. Jennifer Ann Ho, *Racial Ambiguity in Asian American Culture* (New Brunswick, N.J.: Rutgers University Press, 2015).

17. Eduardo Bonilla-Silva, *Racism without Racists: Color-Blind Racism and the Persistence of Racial Inequality in America* (Lanham, Md.: Rowman and Littlefield, 2014); Mia Tuan, *Forever Foreigners or Honorary Whites? The Asian Ethnic Experience Today* (New Brunswick, N.J.: Rutgers University Press, 2005).

18. Gross, *What Blood Won't Tell*.

19. Wendy D. Roth, *Race Migrations: Latinos and the Cultural Transformations of Race* (Stanford, Calif.: Stanford University Press, 2012).

20. Leslie Bow, *Partly Colored: Asian Americans and the Racial Anomaly in the Segregated South* (New York: New York University Press, 2010).

21. Edna Bonacich, "Class Approaches to Ethnicity and Race," *Critical Sociology* 10, no. 2 (1980):9–23.

22. Linda M. Burton, Eduardo Bonilla-Silva, Victor Ray, Rose Bucklew, and Elizabeth Hordge Freeman, "Critical Race Theories, Colorism, and the Decade's Research on Families of Color," *Journal of Marriage and Family* 72, no. 3 (2010): 440–459.

23. Michael Omi and Howard Winant, *Racial Formation in the United States: From the 1960s to the 1990s* (New York: Routledge, 1994), 154.

24. Jake Silverstein, "Why We Published the 1619 Project," *New York Times Magazine*, December 20, 2019, https://www.nytimes.com/interactive/2019/12/20/magazine/1619-intro .html; Nikole Hannah-Jones, Mary Elliott, Jazmine Hughes, Jake Silverstein, "The 1619 Project," *New York Times Magazine*, August 18, 2019, 4–5.

25. W. E. B. Du Bois, "Conservation of Races," in *W. E. B. Du Bois: A Reader*, ed. David Levering Lewis (New York: Henry Holt, 1995),24. For a more in-depth discussion of Du Bois connections with CRT, see Devin Avshalom-Smith, "Toward a Philosophy of Race: W. E. B. Du Bois and Critical Race," *1619: Journal of African American Studies* 1, no. 1 (2019), accessed January 15, 2020, https://www2.ccsu.edu/afamjournal/?article=419.

26. Patricia H. Collins, *Black Feminist Thought* (New York: Routledge Classics, 2009), at 41.

27. Neely Fuller Jr., *The United-Independent Compensatory Code/System/Concept: A Contemporary Counter-Racist Code-Revised Edition* (n.p.: NfJ Productions, 1984).

28. Gross, *What Blood Won't Tell*, 255.

29. Perea, "Black/White Binary Paradigm of Race," 1213.

30. Delgado and Stefancic, *Critical Race Theory*.

31. Kimberlé Crenshaw, "Mapping the Margins: Intersectionality, Identity Politics, and Violence against Women of Color," *Stanford Law Review* 43, no. 6 (1991): 1249–1299; Kimberlé Crenshaw, Neil Gotanda, Gary Peller, and Kendall Thomas, *Critical Race Theory: The Key Writings That Formed the Movement* (New York: New Press, 1995).

32. Bell, "*Brown v. Board of Education*."

33. Delgado and Stefancic, *Critical Race Theory*, 23.

34. Bell, "*Brown v. Board of Education*," 523.

35. Mary L. Dudziak, *Cold War Civil Rights: Race and the Image of American Democracy* (Princeton, N.J.: Princeton University Press, 2000); Azza Salama Layton, *International Politics and Civil Rights Policies in the United States, 1941–1960* (Cambridge: Cambridge University Press, 2000).

36. Delgado and Stefancic, *Critical Race Theory*, 24.

37. Brayboy, "Tribal Critical Race Theory," 425–446; Devin W. Carbado and Daria Roithmayr, "Critical Race Theory Meets Social Science," *Annual Review of Law and Social Science* 10 (2014): 149–167; An, "AsianCrit Perspective," 131–139; Stefancic, "Latino and Latina Critical Race Theory," 423–498.

38. Perea, "Black/White Binary Paradigm."

39. Robert R. Alvarez, "Jim and José Crow: Conversations on the Black/Brown Dialogue," *Journal of Asian and African Studies* 51, no. 3 (2016): 346–357.

40. Haney López, "Race, Ethnicity, Erasure."

41. Ibid., 1145.

42. Ibid., 1160.

43. Ibid.

44. Rubén Donato and Jarrod S. Hanson, "Legally White, Socially Mexican: The Politics of De Jure and De Facto School Segregation in the American Southwest," *Harvard Educational Review*, 82, no. 2 (2012): 202–225).

45. The "Good Neighbor Policy" of Texas "proclaimed Mexican Americans valued state citizens, as well as "members of the Caucasian race" against whom no discrimination was warranted." From Haney López, "Race, Ethnicity, Erasure," 1171.

46. While this project focuses on LatCrit theory, civil rights, and school desegregation, a ten- and fifteen-year review of LatCrit theory, writ large, is provided by Keith Aoki and Kevin R. Johnson, "An Assessment of LatCrit Theory Ten Years After," *Indiana Law Journal* 83, no. 4

(2008): 1151–1195; Steven W. Bender and Francisco Valdes, "At and Beyond Fifteen: Mapping LatCrit Theory, Community, and Praxis," *University of Miami Race and Social Justice Law Review* 1 (2011): 177–237.

47. Lilia Fernandez, "Telling Stories about School: Using Critical Race and Latino Critical Theories to Document Latina/Latino Education and Resistance," *Qualitative Inquiry* 8, no. 1 (2002): 45–65; Perea, "Black/White Paradigm"; Haney López, "Race, Ethnicity, Erasure."

48. Carlos Blanton, "George I. Sánchez, Ideology, and Whiteness in the Making of the Mexican American Civil Rights Movement, 1930–1960," *Journal of Southern History* 72, no. 3 (2006): 569–604; Michael Calderon-Zaks, "Debated Whiteness amid World Events: Mexican and Mexican American Subjectivity and the U.S. Relationship with the Americas, 1924–1936," *Mexican Studies* 27, no. 2 (2011): 325–359; Thomas Guglielmo, "Fighting for Caucasian Rights: Mexicans, Mexican Americans, and the Transnational Struggle for Civil Rights in World War II Texas," *Journal of American History* 92, no. 4 (2006): 1212–1237.

49. Maritza I. Reyes, "Opening Borders: African Americans and Latinos through the Lens of Immigration," *Harvard Latino Review* 17 (2014): 1–64. Mary Romero, "Racial Profiling and Immigration Law Enforcement: Rounding Up the Usual Suspects in the Latino Community," *Critical Sociology* 32, nos. 2–3 (2006): 447–473; Victor C. Romero, "The Child Citizenship Act and the Family Reunification Act: Valuing the Citizen Child as Well as the Citizen Parent (Latinas/os and the Americas: Centering North-South Frameworks in LatCrit Theory)," *Florida Law Review* 55, no. 1 (2003): 489–509.

50. Paula D. McClain et al., "Racial Distancing in a Southern City: Latino Immigrants' Views of Black Americans," *Journal of Politics* 68, no. 3 (2006): 571–584.

51. Frances R. Aparicio, "Not Fully Boricuas: Puerto Rican Intralatino/as in Chicago," *Centro Journal* 28, no. 2 (2016): 154–178.

52. Tanya Kateri Hernandez, "An Exploration of the Efficacy of Class-Based Approaches to Racial Justice: The Cuban Context (Rotating Centers, Expanding Frontiers: LatCrit Theory and Marginal Intersections)," *U.C. Davis Law Review* 33, no. 4 (2000): 1135–1171; Gloria Sandrino-Glasser, "LatCrit Theory, Critical Legal Education, and Board Diversity Reflections of an Afro-Cuban Law Professor," *Rutgers Race and Law Review* 8, no. 2 (2006): 199–258.

53. Luna, "Black/White Paradigm."

54. Luna, "Black/White Paradigm," 225 and 233.

55. Juan Perea, "Buscando América: Why Integration and Equal Protection Fail to Protect Latinos," *Harvard Law Review* 117, no. 5 (2004): 1420–1469.

56. Ibid., 1425.

57. Donato and Hanson, "Legally White, Socially Mexican."

58. Jeanne M. Powers and Lirio Patton, "Between *Mendez* and *Brown*: *Gonzales v. Sheely* (1951) and the Legal Campaign against Segregation," *Law and Social Inquiry* 33, no. 1 (2008): 127–171; Jeanne M. Powers, "Forgotten History: Mexican American School Segregation in Arizona from 1900–1951," *Equity and Excellence in Education* 41, no. 4 (2008): 467–481.

59. José M. Alamillo, *Making Lemonade out of Lemons: Mexican American Labor and Leisure in a California Town, 1880–1890* (Urbana: University of Illinois Press, 2006); Michael E. Madrid, "The Unheralded History of the Lemon Grove Desegregation Case," *Multicultural Education* 15, no. 3 (2008): 15–19.

60. Bonilla-Silva, *Racism without Racists*.

61. Omi and Winant, *Racial Formation*.

62. Joe R. Feagin, *The White Racial Frame: Centuries of Racial Framing and Counterframing* (New York: Routledge, 2010).

63. Delgado and Stefancic, *Critical Race Theory*, 77.

64. Ariela Gross, "The Caucasian Cloak: Mexican Americans and the Politics of Whiteness in the Twentieth-Century Southwest," *Georgetown Law Journal* 95, no. 2 (January 2007): 337–392.

65. Mario García, *Mexican Americans: Leadership, Ideology & Identity, 1930–1960* (New Haven, Conn.: Yale University Press, 1989), 270 and 273.

66. Ibid., 37.

67. Neil Foley, "Becoming Hispanic: Mexican Americans and Whiteness," in *White Privilege: Essential Readings on the Other Side of Racism*, ed. Paula S. Rothenberg (New York: Worth, 2012), 60.

68. For a more detailed racial history of Mexicans in the United States, please read Laura E. Gómez, *Manifest Destinies: The Making of the Mexican American Race* (New York: New York University Press, 2007).

69. Calderón-Zaks, "Debated Whiteness"; Neil Foley, "Partly Colored or Other White: Mexican Americans and Their Problem with the Color Line," in *Beyond Black and White: Race, Ethnicity and Gender in the U.S. South and Southwest*, ed. Stephanie Cole and Alison M. Parker (College Station: University of Texas, 2004); Vicki Ruiz, "Morena/o, Blanca/o, y Café con Leche: Racial Constructions in Chicana/o Historiography," *Mexican Studies* 20, no. 2 (2004): 343–360.

70. Laura E. Gómez, "Off-White in an Age of White Supremacy: Mexican Elites and the Rights of Indians and Blacks in Nineteenth-Century New Mexico," *Chicano Latino Law Review* 25, no. 10 (2005): 9–60.

71. Ibid., 11.

72. Blanton, "George I. Sánchez"; Foley, "Becoming Hispanic"; Foley, "Partly Colored"; Daniel Aaron Rochmes, "Blinded by the White: Latino School Desegregation and the Insidious Allure of Whiteness," *Texas Hispanic Journal of Law and Policy* 13 (2007): 7–22; Steven H. Wilson, "Brown over 'Other White': Mexican Americans' Legal Arguments and Litigation Strategy in School Desegregation Lawsuits," *Law and History Review* 21, no. 1 (2003): 145–194.

73. Rochmes, "Blinded by the White," 21.

74. Perea, "Buscando América," 1442. *Pobrecito* means "poor thing." It is a word designed to evoke sympathy.

75. David García, Tara J. Yosso, and Frank P. Barajas, "'A Few of the Brightest, Cleanest Mexican Children': School Segregation as a Form of Mundane Racism in Oxnard, California, 1900–1940," *Harvard Educational Review* 82, no. 1 (2012): 11–12.

76. This is not to argue that such work does not exist, just that it is not as prevalent. I would be remiss if I did not recognize Gerald Horne, *Facing the Rising Sun: African Americans, Japan, and the Rise of Afro-Asian Solidarity* (New York: New York University Press, 2018); Paul Ortiz, *An African American and Latinx History of the United States* (Boston: Beacon, 2018); Scott Kurashige, *The Shifting Grounds of Race: Black and Japanese Americans in the Making of Mul-*

tiethnic Los Angeles (Princeton, N.J.: Princeton University Press, 2008); Ann Pollitt Phoebe, *African American and Cherokee Nurses in Appalachia: A History, 1900–1965* (Jefferson, N.C.: McFarland, 2016).

77. Blanton, "George I. Sánchez"; Garcia, Yosso, and Barajas, "A Few of the Brightest, Cleanest."

78. Foley, "Becoming Hispanic"; Rochmes, "Blinded by the White"; Vicki Ruiz, "South by Southwest: Mexican Americans and Segregated Schooling, 1900–1950," *OAH Magazine of History* 15, no. 2 (2001): 23–27.

79. Robert S. Chang, "Migrations, Citizens, and Latina/os: The Sojourner's Truth and Order Stories," *Florida Law Review* 55, no. 1 (2003): 479–488; John Hayakawa Török, "The Story of 'Towards Asian American Jurisprudence' and Its Implications for Latinas/os in American Law Schools," *Berkeley La Raza Law Journal* 13 (2002): 271–310.

80. Angelo N. Ancheta, *Race, Rights, and the Asian American Experience* (New Brunswick, N.J.: Rutgers University Press, 1998); Chang, "Migrations, Citizens, and Latina/os"; Mari J. Matsuda, "Looking to the Bottom: Critical Legal Studies and Reparations," *Harvard Civil Rights–Civil Liberties Law Review* 22 (1997): 323–399.

81. The author recognizes that various languages exist in Latin America, such as Portuguese, French, and a plethora of Indigenous languages.

82. Ancheta, *Race, Rights*.

83. Ibid., 45.

84. "Coolie" is a derogatory term used to describe unskilled Chinese laborers. Charles J. McClain, *In Search of Equality: The Chinese Struggle against Discrimination in Nineteenth-Century America* (Berkeley: University of California Press, 1994), 26.

85. Ibid., 30; Ronald Takaki, *Strangers from a Different Shore: A History of Asian Americans*, updated and rev. ed. (New York: Back Bay Books, 1998).

86. Elmer Clarence Sandmeyer, *The Anti-Chinese Movement in California* (Urbana: University of Illinois Press, 1973).

87. For a more detailed history of the lives of nineteenth-century Chinese, consider Wendy Rouse Jorae, *The Children of Chinatown: Growing Up Chinese American in San Francisco, 1850–1920* (Chapel Hill: University of North Carolina Press, 2009); McClain, *In Search of Equality*; Judy Yung, *Unbound Feet: A Social History of Chinese Women in San Francisco* (Berkeley: University of California Press, 1995); Takaki, *Strangers from a Different Shore*.

88. Sohyun An, "Asian Americans in American History: An AsianCrit Perspective on Asian American Inclusion in the State U.S. History Curriculum Standards, Theory, and Research in Social Education," *Theory and Research in Social Education* 44, no. 2 (2016).

89. An, "Asian Americans in American History," 262.

90. Chang, "Toward an Asian American Legal Scholarship," 1267.

91. Adrienne Berard, *Water Tossing Boulders: How a Family of Chinese Immigrants Led the First Fight to Desegregate Schools in the Jim Crow South* (Boston: Beacon, 2016); Leslie Bow, *Partly Colored: Asian Americans and the Racial Anomaly in the Segregated South* (New York: New York University Press, 2010); Joyce Kuo, "Excluded, Segregated, and Forgotten: A Historical View of the Discrimination of Chinese Americans in Public Schools," *Asian American Law Journal* 5, no. 7 (1998): 181–212; McClain, *In Search of Equality*; Ellen D. Wu, *The Color of*

Success: Asian Americans and the Origins of the Model Minority (Princeton, N.J.: Princeton University Press, 2014).

92. Rosalind S. Chou and Joe R. Feagin, *The Myth of the Model Minority: Asian Americans Facing Racism* (Boulder, Colo.: Paradigm, 2015); Tomás R. Jiménez and Adam L. Horowitz, "When White Is Just Alright: How Immigrants Redefine Achievement and Reconfigure the Ethnoracial Hierarchy," *American Sociological Review* 78, no. 5 (2013): 849–871; Jennifer Lee and Min Zhou, *The Asian American Achievement Paradox* (New York: Russell Sage Foundation, 2015).

93. Pascoe, *What Comes Naturally*.

94. Mari Matsuda, "We Will Not Be Used: Are Asian Americans the Racial Bourgeoisie?," in *Asian American Studies Now*, ed. Thomas Chen and Jean Yu-Wen Shen Wu (New Brunswick, N.J.: Rutgers University Press, 2010), 559.

95. Robert S. Chang and Neil Gotunda, "Afterward: The Race Question in LatCrit Theory and Asian American Jurisprudence," *Nevada Law Journal* 7 (2007): 1012–1029; Janine Young Kim, "Are Asians Black? Asian-American Civil Rights Agenda and the Contemporary Significance of the Black/White Paradigm," in *Contemporary Asian America: A Multidisciplinary Reader*, ed. Min Zhou and J. V. Gatewood, 2nd ed. (New York: New York University Press, 2007); Lee and Zhou, *Asian American Achievement Paradox*; Jeannbin Lee Shiao, "The Meaning of Honorary Whiteness for Asian Americans: Boundary Expansion for Something Else?," *Comparative Sociology* 16 (2017): 788–813.

96. Delgado and Stefancic, *Critical Race Theory*, 9.

97. Wei John Kuo Tchen and Dylan Yeats, *Yellow Peril! An Archive of Anti-Asian Fear*. (Brooklyn, N.Y.: Verso, 2014).

98. Madeline Y. Hsu, *The Good Immigrants: How the Yellow Peril Became the Model Minority* (Princeton, N.J.: Princeton University Press, 2015).

99. Pascoe, *What Comes Naturally*.

100. Allan W. Austin, *From Concentration Camp to Campus: Japanese American Students and World War II* (Urbana: University of Illinois Press, 2004).

101. Anthony Christian Ocampo, *The Latinos of Asia: How Filipino Americans Break the Rules of Race* (Stanford, Calif.: Stanford University Press, 2016).

102. Takaki, *Strangers from a Different Shore*.

103. Vinay Harpalani, "DesiCrit: Theorizing the Racial Ambiguity of South Asian Americans," *New York University Annual Survey of American Law* 69, no. 1 (2013): 77–183.

104. Brayboy, "Tribal Critical Race Theory."

105. Circe Sturm, *Blood Politics: Race, Culture, and Identity in the Cherokee Nation of Oklahoma* (Berkeley: University of California Press, 2002); Gerald Torres and Kathryn Milun, "Translating Yonnondio by Precedent and Evidence: The Mashpee Indian Case Frontiers of Legal Thought III," *Duke Law Journal* 4 (1990): 625–659.

106. Brayboy, "Tribal Critical Race Theory," 427.

107. Ibid., 432.

108. Jean M. O'Brien, "On Tracing the Origins of the Persistent Myth of the 'Vanishing Indian,'" in *Speaking of Indigenous Politics: Conversations with Activists, Scholars, and Tribal Leaders*, ed. J. Kehaulani Kauanui (Minneapolis: University of Minnesota Press, 2018), 242.

109. Sturm, *Blood Politics*; Eva Marie Garroutte, *Real Indians: Identity and the Survival of Native America* (Berkeley: University of California Press, 2003).

110. While immigration laws and policies are definitely a form of federal recognition, immigrants ultimately are associated with their home countries.

111. Garroutte, *Real Indians*.

112. Eva Marie Garroutte, "The Racial Formation of American Indians: Negotiating Legitimate Identities with Tribal and Federal Law," *American Indian Quarterly* 25, no. 2 (2001): 224–239.

113. Linda Tuhiwai Smith, *Decolonizing Methodologies: Research and Indigenous Peoples* (New York: Zed Books, 2012).

114. Ibid., 23.

115. Brayboy, "Tribal Critical Race Theory."

116. Bryan Brayboy, "Culture, Place, and Power: Engaging the Histories and Possibilities of American Indian Education," History of Education Quarterly 54, no. 3 (August 2014): 396.

117. Ibid. citing K. Tsianina Lomawaima and Teresa L. McCarty, *"To Remain Indian": Lessons in Democracy from a Century of Native American Education* (New York: Teachers College Press, 2006), 2.

118. Lesley Bartlett and Bryan Jones Brayboy, "Race and Schooling: Theories and Ethnographies," *Urban Review* 37, no. 5 (2005): 361–374; Brayboy, "Culture, Place, and Power," 395–402; Marisela Martinez-Cola, "Visibly Invisible: TribalCrit and Native American Segregated Schooling," *Sociology of Race and Ethnicity* 6, no. 4 (2019): 468–482; Jeanette Haynes Writer, "Unmasking, Exposing, and Confronting: Critical Race Theory, Tribal Critical Race Theory and Multicultural Education," *International Journal of Multicultural Education* 10, no. 2 (2008): 1–15.

119. Jacqueline Fear-Segal and Susan D. Rose, *Carlisle Indian Industrial School: Indigenous Histories, Memories, and Reclamations* (Lincoln: University of Nebraska Press, 2016), 5.

120. Evelyn Brooks Higginbotham, *Righteous Discontent: The Women's Movement in the Black Baptist Church, 1880–1920* (Cambridge, Mass.: Harvard University Press, 1993).

121. Marisela Martinez-Cola, "Sympathetic Symbols, Social Movements, and School Desegregation," *Journal of Law and Society* 45, no. 2 (2018): 177–204.

122. Collins, *Black Feminist Thought*, at 77.

123. Ibid.

124. bell hooks and Sut Jhally, dirs., *Cultural Criticism and Transformation* [video recording] (Northampton, Mass.: Media Education Foundation, 1997), 2:36.

125. Jean Kilbourne, *Deadly Persuasion: Why Women and Girls Must Fight the Addictive Power of Advertising* (New York: Free Press, 1999).

126. Molly Haskell, *Holding My Own in No Man's Land: Women and Men and Film and Feminists* (New York: Oxford University Press, 1997).

127. Mary Crawford and Rhoda Unger, *Women and Gender: A Feminist Psychology* (New York: McGraw Hill, 2004).

128. Tonya Maria Golash-Boza, *Race and Racisms: A Critical Approach* (New York: Oxford University Press, 2015), 111.

129. Ibid., 112.

130. Nazera Sadiq Wright, *Black Girlhood in the Nineteenth Century* (Urbana: University of Illinois Press, 2016).

131. Leigh Moscowitz and Micah Carpenter, "Girl Zines at Work: Feminist Media Literacy Education with Underserved Girls," *Girlhood Studies* 7, no. 2 (2014): 25–43.

132. Morgan Genevieve Blue, *Girlhood on Disney Channel: Branding, Celebrity, and Femininity* (New York: Routledge, 2017); Sarah Hentges, *Pictures of Girlhood: Modern Female Adolescence on Film* (Jefferson, N.C.: McFarland, 2006).

133. Kristine Moruzi and Michelle J. Smith, eds., *Colonial Girlhood in Literature, Culture, and History, 1840–1950* (New York: Palgrave Macmillan, 2014).

134. Mary E. Thomas, *Multicultural Girlhood: Racism, Sexuality, and the Conflicted Spaces of American Education* (Philadelphia: Temple University Press, 2011).

135. Kimberly Wallace-Sanders, *Mammy: A Century of Race, Gender, and Southern Memory* (Ann Arbor: University of Michigan Press, 2008).

136. Robin Bernstein, *Racial Innocence: Performing American Childhood from Slavery to Civil Rights* (New York: New York University Press, 2011), 3–4.

137. Ibid., 44, emphasis mine, quoting from Stowe's 1852 novel *Uncle Tom's Cabin*, 213.

138. Yung, *Unbound Feet.*

139. Ibid., 22.

140. Takaki, *Strangers from a Different Shore*, 104.

141. Jorae, *The Children of Chinatown*, 72.

142. Ibid.

143. While this research is largely historical, there are modern feminist pagans that do not necessarily carry the same meaning.

144. Takaki, *Strangers from a Different Shore*, 122.

145. Yung, *Unbound Feet*, 27.

146. Ibid., 17.

147. Jorae, *Children of Chinatown*; Peggy Pascoe, *Relations of Rescue: The Search for Female Moral Authority in the American West, 1874–1939* (New York: Oxford University Press, 1990); Takaki, *Strangers from a Different Shore*; Yung, *Unbound Feet.*

148. Yung, *Unbound Feet*, 32.

149. Ibid., 37.

150. Ibid.

151. Ibid., 18–19.

152. Ibid., 18.

153. Jorae explains, "This data is based on my survey of all Chinese children age sixteen and under in San Francisco. The category of clothing manufacturer in this table includes children whose occupations were listed as seamstress, tailor, embroiderer, sewing machine operator, pant and overall maker, shirt maker, button sewer, or underwear maker. The miscellaneous category included a number of the children employed in the food-service industry." *Children of Chinatown*, 81.

154. Pascoe, *Relations of Rescue*, 53.

155. Ibid., 121.

156. The author recognizes the problematic use of the word "squaw." In this book, it is used

as a term to describe a controlling image that is historically constructed. Use of the word is by no means an endorsement of its legitimacy. For an excellent article regarding the use of "squaw," please read Debra Merskin, "The S-Word: Discourse, Stereotypes, and the American Indian Woman," *Howard Journal of Communications* 21 (2010): 345–366.

157. David Wallace Adams, *Education for Extinction: American Indians and the Boarding School Experience* (Lawrence: University Press of Kansas, 1995); Lomawaima and McCarty, *"To Remain Indian"*.

158. Shyon Baumann and Kim de Laat, "Socially Defunct: A Comparative Analysis of the Underrepresentation of Older Women in Advertising," *Poetics* 40, no. 6 (2012): 536.

159. Wendy Griswold, "American Character and the American Novel: An Expansion of Reflection Theory in the Sociology of Literature," *American Journal of Sociology* 86 (1981): 740–65; Bernice A. Pescosolido, Elizabeth Grauerholz, and Melissa A. Milkie, "Culture and Conflict: The Portrayal of Blacks in U.S. Children's Books through the Mid- and Late-Twentieth Century," *American Sociological Review* 62, no. 3 (1997): 444 citing Herbert J. Gans, *Deciding What's News* (New York: Random House, 1979); Richard A. Peterson, *The Production of Culture* (Beverly Hills, Calif.: Sage, 1976).

160. Leanne Howe, Harvey Markowitz, and Denise K. Cummings, eds., *Seeing Red: Hollywood's Pixeled Skins* (East Lansing: Michigan State University Press, 2013); JoEllen Shively, "Cowboys and Indians: Perceptions of Western Films among American Indians and Anglos," *American Sociological Review* 57 (1992): 725–734; Sherry L. Smith, *Reimagining Indians: Native Americans through Anglo Eyes, 1880–1940* (New York: Oxford Publishing, 2000); Pauline Turner Strong, *American Indians and the American Imaginary: Cultural Representations across the Centuries* (Boulder, Colo.: Paradigm, 2013).

161. M. Elise Marubbio, *Killing the Indian Maiden: Images of Native American Women in Film* (Lexington: University Press of Kentucky, 2006).

162. Ibid., 29.

163. Ibid., 26.

164. Ibid., 36.

165. Ibid.

166. Ibid., 44–45 citing Kemp R. Niver and Bebe Bergsten, eds., *Biograph Bulletins: 1896–1908* (Los Angeles: Locare Research Group, 1971), 365, *emphasis mine*.

167. Marubbio, *Killing the Indian Maiden*, 45.

168. Ibid., 6.

169. Ibid., 7.

170. Mary Gloyne Byler, *American Indian Authors for Young Readers: A Selected Bibliography* (New York: Association on American Indian Affairs, 1999).

171. Jim Haskins, "Racism and Sexism in Children's Nonfiction," *Children's Literature* 5 (1976): 141–147; Opal Moore and Donnarae Maccann, "The Ignoble Savage: Amerind Images in the Mainstream Mind," *Children's Literature Quarterly* 13 (1988): 26–30; Michelle Pagni Stewart, "Judging Authors by the Color of Their Skin? Quality Native American Children's Literature," *MELEUS* 27 (2002): 179–196.

172. Byler, *American Indian Authors*, 47, 51.

173. Robert A. Trennert, "Educating Indian Girls at Nonreservation Boarding Schools, 1878–1920," *Western Historical Quarterly*, 13, no. 3 (1982): 271–290.

174. Laura Wexler, *Tender Violence: Domestic Visions of an Age of U.S. Imperialism* (Chapel Hill: University of North Carolina Press, 2000), 111.

175. Linda Peavy and Ursula Smith, *Full-Court Quest: The Girls from Fort Shaw Indian School, Basketball Champions of the World* (Norman: University of Oklahoma Press, 2008).

176. Ibid., 45.

177. Ibid., 155.

178. Ibid.

179. Pascoe, *What Comes Naturally*; Marubbio, *Killing the Indian Maiden*.

180. Fear-Segal and Rose, *Carlisle Indian Industrial School*.

181. N. Scott Momaday, "The Stones at Carlisle," in Fear-Segal and Rose, *Carlisle Indian School*, 45.

182. Fear-Segal and Rose, *Carlisle Indian School*, 11.

183. For more readings on boarding school experiences see Bethany R. Berger, "Red: Racism and the American Indian," *UCLA Law Review* 56, no. 3 (2009): 591–656; Lomawaima and McCarty, *"To Remain Indian"*; Jacqueline Fear-Segal, *White Man's Club: Schools, Race, and the Struggle of Indian Acculturation* (Lincoln: University of Nebraska Press, 2007); and Brenda Child, *Boarding School Seasons: American Indian Families, 1900–1940.* (Lincoln: University of Nebraska Press, 2012).

184. Clara E. Rodriguez, "Delores del Río and Lupe Vélez: Working in Hollywood, 1924–1944," *NorteAmérica* 6, no. 1(2011): 69–91.

185. Ibid., 73.

186. Ibid., 80.

187. Catherine S. Ramirez, *The Woman in the Zoot Suit: Gender, Nationalism and the Cultural Politics of Memory* (Durham, N.C.: Duke University Press, 2009).

188. Ibid., 38.

189. Ibid., 70–71.

190. Perea, "Buscando América," 1442.

191. Ibid., 1443.

192. George J. Sánchez, *Becoming Mexican American: Ethnicity, Culture and Identity in Chicano Los Angeles, 1900–1945* (New York: Oxford University Press, 1993), 102.

193. Perea, "Buscando América," 1442.

194. Peter Irons, *Jim Crow's Children: The Broken Promise of the "Brown" Decision* (New York: Penguin, 2002). At a history conference, a colleague suggested that Brown was selected as the lead plaintiff because of Kansas's middle American position that was neither North nor South. As a border state, Kansas does not represent the vitriol present in northern and southern extremes.

195. José M. Abreu, Estrella Ramirez, Bryan S. M. Kim, and Chris Haddy, "Automatic Activation of Yellow Peril Asian American Stereotypes: Effects on Social Impression Formation," *Journal of Social Psychology* 143, no. 6, (2003): 691–706; Erin Beeghly, "What's Wrong with Stereotypes? The Falsity Hypothesis," *Social Theory and Practice*, 47, no. 1 (January 2021): 33–61; Natalie Delia Deckard, Irene Browne, Cassaundra Rodriguez, and Marisela Martinez-Cola, "Controlling Images of Immigrants in Mainstream and Black Press: The Discursive Power of the 'Illegal Latino,'" *Latino Studies*, 18, no. 4 (2020); Golash-Boza, *Race and Racisms*; Graham Fuller, "All Violent on the Western Frontier: Reassessing Two Revisionist Native

American Westerns," *Cineaste* 46, no. 1 (2020): 30–36; Peter A. Leavitt, Rebecca Covarru-
bias, Yvonne A. Perez, and Stephanie A. Fryberg, "'Frozen in Time': The Impact of Native
American Media Representations on Identity and Self-Understanding," *Journal of Social Issues*
71, no. 1 (2015): 39–53; Jessica Tokos-Vasquez and Kathryn Norton-Smith, "Talking Back to
Controlling Images: Latinos' Changing Response to Racism over the Life Course," *Ethnic and
Racial Studies*, 40, no. 6: 912–930; Qin Zhang, "Asian Americans beyond the Model Minority
Stereotype: The Nerdy and the Left Out," *Journal of International and Intercultural Communi-
cation* 3, no. 1 (February 2010): 20–37.

196. Erin Delmore, "'Learn to Love Each Other': *Brown v. Board* Families Look Forward,"
last modified on May 16, 2014, http://www.msnbc.com/all/the-fight-their-lives-brown-v
-board-60-msna329621.

197. "Unknown Title," *Inyo Register* (Inyo County, Calif.), March 3, 1921; "Unknown Title,"
Inyo Register (Inyo County, Calif.), January 12, 1922; "Unknown Title," *Inyo Register* (Inyo
County, Calif.), September 6, 1923, 1; "Indians in Schools," *Inyo Register* (Inyo County, Calif.),
October 25, 1923, 1.

198. Baumann and de Laat, "Socially Defunct," 515; Ashley Mears, "Size Zero High-End Ethnic: Cultural Production and the Reproduction of Culture in Fashion Modeling," *Poetics* 38,
no. 1 (2010): 21–46.

199. Pescosolido, Grauerholz, and Milkie, "Culture and Conflict," 444.

CHAPTER 2. The 105 Bricks before *Brown*

1. Jacquelyn Dowd Hall, "The Long Civil Rights Movement and the Political Uses of the
Past," *Journal of American History* 91, no. 4 (2005): 1233–1263; Judith Stein, "Why American
Historians Embrace the 'Long Civil Rights Movement,'" *American Communist History* 11, no. 1
(2012): 55–58.

2. James D. Anderson, *The Education of Blacks in the South, 1860–1935* (Chapel Hill: University of North Carolina Press, 1988); Leslie Bow, *Partly Colored: Asian Americans and the Racial
Anomaly in the Segregated South* (New York: New York University Press, 2010); John L. Rury
and Shirley A. Hill, *The African American Struggle for Secondary Schooling, 1940–1980* (New
York: Teachers College Press, 2012); Guadalupe San Miguel Jr., *Brown, Not White: School Inte-
gration and the Chicano Movement in Houston* (Houston, Tex.: University of Houston, 2001);
Gilbert G. Gonzalez, *Chicano Education in the Era of Segregation* (Philadelphia: Balch Institute
Press, 1990).

3. Samuel Bowles and Herbert Gintis, *Schooling in Capitalist America: Educational Reform
and the Contradictions of Economic Life* (Chicago: Haymarket Books, 1976), 157.

4. Ibid.

5. Ibid.; Thomas Dublin, *Women at Work: The Transformation of Work and Community in
Lowell, Massachusetts, 1826–1860* (New York: Columbia University Press, 1979).

6. Bowles and Gintis, *Schooling in Capitalist America*, 167.

7. James Oliver Horton and Lois E. Horton, *Black Bostonians: Family Life and Community
Struggle in the Antebellum North* (New York: Holmes and Meier, 1979); John Hope Franklin
and Evelyn Brooks Higginbotham, *From Slavery to Freedom: A History of African Americans*,
9th ed. (New York: McGraw Hill, 2011).

8. Franklin and Higginbotham, *From Freedom to Slavery*; Leon Litwack, *North of Slavery: The Negro Free States, 1790–1860* (Chicago: University of Chicago Press, 1965); Hilary J. Moss, *Schooling Citizens: The Struggle for African American Education in Antebellum America* (Chicago: University of Chicago Press, 2009).

9. Ronald Takaki, *A Different Mirror: A History of Multicultural America* (New York: Back Bay Books, 2008), 99.

10. David Nasaw, *School to Order: A Social History of Public Schooling in the United States* (New York: Oxford University Press, 1979).

11. *Roberts v. Boston*, 59 Mass. 198 (1849), 200.

12. Waldo E. Martin Jr., *"Brown v. Board of Education": A Brief History with Documents* (Boston: Bedford / St. Martin's, 1998).

13. *Roberts v. Boston*, 203.

14. Martin, *"Brown v. Board,"* 56.

15. *Roberts v. Boston*, 209, emphasis mine.

16. Black (B), Asian (A), Native American (N), Male (M), Female (F), Both (B).

17. *Clark v. Board of Directors*, 24 Iowa 266 (1868), 273.

18. *Clark v. Board*, 272 and 277.

19. *Dove v. Independent School District*, 41 Iowa 689 (1875); *Smith v. Directors of the Independent School District of Keokuk*, 40 Iowa 518 (1875), 518.

20. *Van Camp v. Board of Education*, 9 Ohio St. 406 (1859), 414.

21. *State ex rel. Garnes v. McCann*, 21 Ohio St. (1871), 211.

22. *State ex rel. Lewis v. Board of Education of Cincinnati*, 1876 Ohio Misc., 3.

23. Davison M. Douglas, "The Struggle for School Desegregation in Cincinnati before 1954," *University of Cincinnati Law Review* 71 (2003): 979); Paul Finkelman, "The Hidden History of Northern Civil Rights Law and the Villainous Supreme Court, 1875–1915," *University of Pittsburgh Law Review* 357 (2018); Russell E. Lovell II, "Shine On, You Bright Radical Star: Clark v. Board of School Directors (of Muscatine)—the Iowa Supreme Court's Civil Rights Exceptionalism," *Drake Law Review* 67 (2019): 175; Earl "Marty" Martin, Russell E. Lovell II, Robert G. Allbee, David S. Walker, Mark S. Cady, Brent Appel, Edward Mansfield, Alfredo Parrish, and Johnny C. Taylor Jr., et al., *"Clark v. Board of School Directors*: Reflections after 150 Years," *Drake Law Review* 67 (2019): 170; Molly O'Brien, "The Ohio Constitution—Then and Now: An Examination of the Law and History of the Ohio Constitution on the Occasion of its Bicentennial: The Constitutional Common School," *Cleveland State Law Review* 51 (2004): 581.

24. "WSB-TV Newsfilm Clip of Demonstrators Protesting against De Facto School Segregation and of African American Leaders Malcolm X and Adam Clayton Powell Speaking in Favor of the School Boycott in New York City, New York," March 16, 1964, WSB-TV Newsfilm Collection, reel 0802, 53:34/55:26, Walter J. Brown Media Archives and Peabody Awards Collection, University of Georgia Libraries, Athens.

25. Richard Kluger, *Simple Justice: The History of "Brown v. Board of Education" and Black America's Struggle for Equality* (1975; repr., New York: Vintage Books, 2004); Michael J. Klarman, *"Brown v. Board of Education" and the Civil Rights Movement* (New York: Oxford University Press, 2007).

26. *Weaver v. Board of Trustees of Ohio State University*, 126 Ohio St. 290, 185 N.E. 196 (1933), 296.

27. Ibid., 297–98.

28. Derrick Bell Jr., *Silent Covenants: "Brown v. Board of Education" and the Unfulfilled Hopes of Racial Reform* (New York: Oxford University Press. 2004); Klarman, *"Brown v. Board"*; Michael J. Klarman, *From Jim Crow to Civil Rights: The Supreme Court and the Struggle for Racial Equality* (New York: Oxford University Press, 2004); Kluger, *Simple Justice*; Charles M. Payne and Adam Green, eds., *Time Longer Than Rope: A Century of African American Activism, 1850–1950* (New York: New York University Press, 2003).

29. For a more detailed analysis of all five cases, see Marisela Martinez-Cola, "Visibly Invisible: TribalCrit and Native American Segregated Schooling," *Sociology of Race and Ethnicity* 6, no. 4 (2019): 468–482. Portions of the article are reproduced in this section.

30. David Wallace Adams, *Education for Extinction: American Indians and the Boarding School Experience* (Lawrence: University Press of Kansas, 1995).

31. John W. Wertheimer, Jessica Bradshaw, Allyson Cobb, and Harper Addison, "The Law Recognizes Racial Instinct: *Tucker v. Blease* and the Black-White Paradigm in the Jim Crow South," *Law and History Review* 29 no. 2 (2011): 476.

32. *McMillan v. School Committee District No. 4*, 107 N.C. 609; 12 S.E. 330 (1890), 613. The Croatans became the "Indians of Robeson County" in 1911, the "Cherokee Indians of Robeson County" in 1913, and the present-day "Lumbee Indians" beginning in 1953. From Wertheimer et al., "Law Recognizes Racial Instinct," 477.

33. *McMillan v. School Committee*, 613.

34. Anna Bailey, "How Scuffletown Became Indian Country: Political Change and Transformation in Indian Identity in Robeson County, North Carolina, 1865–1956" (PhD diss., University of Washington, 2008), 92, https://www.proquest.com/openview/699522a706f7caf910 2f49eac73cf319/1?pq-origsite=gscholar&cbl=18750&diss=y.

35. *McMillan v. School Committee*, 609.

36. Ibid.

37. Bailey, "How Scuffletown Became Indian Country," 95.

38. Ibid., 615.

39. Ibid.

40. *Crawford v. School District No. 7*, 68 Ore. 388 (1913), 390.

41. Peggy Pascoe, *What Comes Naturally: Miscegenation Law and the Making of Race in America* (Oxford: Oxford University Press, 2010).

42. Ibid.

43. *Crawford v. School District*, 393.

44. Ibid., 390.

45. Ibid., 395.

46. Ian F. Haney López, *White by Law: The Legal Construction of Race* (New York: New York University Press, 1996); Ariela J. Gross, *What Blood Won't Tell: A History of Race on Trial in America* (Cambridge, Mass.: Harvard University Press, 2008).

47. Paige Raibmon, *Authentic Indians: Episodes of Encounter from the Late-Nineteenth Century Northwest Coast* (Durham, N.C.: Duke University Press, 2005), 183.

48. *Crawford v. School District*, 397.

49. Morton J. Horowitz, *The Warren Court and the Pursuit of Justice* (New York,: Hill and Wang, 1998).

50. *Pierce v. Society of Sisters*, 268 U.S. 510 (1925).

51. *Moreau v. Grandich*, 114 Miss. 560; 75 So. 434 (1917), 570.

52. Ibid., 560.

53. Ibid.

54. Ibid., 572.

55. Ibid., 575.

56. Ibid., 573.

57. Ibid.

58. Ibid.

59. Gross, *What Blood Won't Tell*.

60. Heidi Ardizzone and Earl Lewis, *Love on Trial: An American Scandal in Black and White* (New York: W. W. Norton, 2002).

61. Gross, *What Blood Won't Tell*.

62. Ardizzone and Lewis, *Love on Trial*.

63. *Moreau v. Grandich*, 574.

64. Ibid.

65. Ibid.

66. Katherine M. B. Osburn, "The 'Identified Full-Bloods' in Mississippi: Race and Choctaw Identity, 1898–1918," *Ethnohistory* 56, no. 3 (2009): 423–227.

67. Katherine M. B. Osburn, *Choctaw Resurgence in Mississippi: Race, Class, and Nation Building in the Jim Crow South, 1830–1977* (Lincoln: University of Nebraska Press, 2014), 43.

68. Ibid., emphasis mine.

69. *Peters v. Pauma*, 91 Cal. App. 792; 267 P. 576 (1928), 577.

70. Ibid.

71. Ibid., 793.

72. Ibid., 794.

73. *Wong Him v. Callahan*, 119 F. 381 (1902), 382.

74. Ibid.

75. Ibid.

76. Charles Wollenberg, *All Deliberate Speed: Segregation and Exclusion in California Schools, 1855–1975* (Berkeley: University of California Press, 1976).

77. Ibid.

78. Ibid., 44–45.

79. James W. Loewen, *The Mississippi Chinese: Between Black and White*, 2nd ed. (Long Grove, Ill.: Waveland, 1988); Robert Seto Quan, *Lotus among the Magnolias: The Mississippi Chinese* (Jackson: University Press of Mississippi, 2007); John Jung, *Chopsticks in the Land of Cotton: Lives of Mississippi Delta Chinese Grocers* (Long Beach, Calif.: Ying and Yang, 2011).

80. Jung, *Chopsticks*, 4.

81. *Gong Lum v. Rice*, 275 U.S. 78; 48 S. Ct. 91 (1927), 87.

82. Joyce Kuo, "Excluded, Segregated, and Forgotten: A Historical View of the Discrimination of Chinese Americans in Public Schools," *Asian American Law Journal* 5, no. 7 (1998): 181–212.

83. Adrienne Berard, *Water Tossing Boulders: How a Family of Chinese Immigrants Led the First Fight to Desegregate Schools in the Jim Crow South* (Boston: Beacon, 2016).

84. *Bond v. Tij Fung*, 148 Miss. 462 (1927), 462, *emphasis mine.*

85. Ibid., 471.

86. Ibid.

87. Ibid., 470.

88. Eileen H. Tamura, "Introduction: Asian Americans and Educational History," *History of Education Quarterly* 43, no. 1 (2003): 9.

89. Eileen O'Brien, *The Racial Middle: Latinos and Asian Americans Living beyond the Racial Divide* (New York: New York University Press, 2008); Jennifer C. Ng, Sharon S. Lee, and Yoon K. Pak, "Contesting the Model Minority and Perpetual Foreigner Stereotypes: A Critical Review of Literature on Asian Americans in Education," *Review of Research Education* 3, no. 1 (2007): 95–130; Diane C. Okamoto, *Redefining Race: Asian American Panethnicity and Shifting Ethnic Boundaries* (New York: Russell Sage Foundation, 2014); Rosalind S. Chou and Joe R. Feagin, *The Myth of the Model Minority: Asian Americans Facing Racism* (Boulder, Colo.: Paradigm, 2015); Ronald Takaki, *Strangers from a Different Shore: A History of Asian Americans*, updated and rev. ed. (New York: Back Bay Books, 1998); Mia Tuan, *Forever Foreigners or Honorary Whites? The Asian Ethnic Experience Today* (New Brunswick, N.J.: Rutgers University Press, 2005).

90. I did not include *Salvatierra* because it was brought on behalf of taxpayers rather than a particular family for whom I could identify the race, gender, and age of the plaintiffs. *Delgado* and *Alvarez* were cases that were never appealed, so they did not show up in my electronic research and therefore were not included.

91. José M. Alamillo, *Making Lemonade out of Lemons: Mexican American Labor and Leisure in a California Town, 1880–1890* (Urbana: University of Illinois Press, 2006); Brian D. Behnken, *Fighting Their Own Battles: Mexican Americans, African Americans, and the Struggle for Civil Rights in Texas* (Chapel Hill: University of North Carolina Press, 2011); Anaida Cólon-Muñiz and Magaly Lavandez, *Latino Civil Rights in Education:* La Lucha Sigue (New York: Routledge, 2016); Mario García, *Mexican Americans: Leadership, Ideology & Identity, 1930–1960* (New Haven, Conn.: Yale University Press, 1989); Miguel Guajardo and Francisco Guajardo, "The Impact of *Brown* on the Brown of South Texas: A Micropolitical Perspective on the Education of Mexican Americans in a South Texas Community," *American Education Research Journal* 41, no. 3 (2004): 501–526; Laura K. Muñoz, "Separate but Equal? A Case Study of *Romo v. Laird* and Mexican American Education," *OAH Magazine of History* 15, no. 2 (2001): 28–35; Maria Josefina Saldana-Portillo, "How Many Mexicans Is a Horse Worth? The League of United Latin American Citizens, Desegregation Cases, and Chicano Historiography," *South Atlantic Quarterly* 107, no. 4 (2008): 4; George J. Sánchez, *Becoming Mexican American: Ethnicity, Culture and Identity in Chicano Los Angeles, 1900–1945* (New York: Oxford University Press, 1993); San Miguel, *Brown, Not White*; Guadalupe San Miguel Jr., *"Let Them All Take Heed": Mexican Americans and the Campaign for Educational Equality in Texas, 1910–1981* (Austin: University of Texas Press, 1987); Steven H. Wilson, "Brown over 'Other White': Mexican Americans' Legal Arguments and Litigation Strategy in School Desegregation Lawsuits," *Law and History Review* 21, no. 1 (2003): 145–194.

92. Gross, *What Blood Won't Tell.*

93. Carlos Blanton, "George I. Sánchez, Ideology, and Whiteness in the Making of the Mexican American Civil Rights Movement, 1930–1960," *Journal of Southern History* 72, no. 3

(2006): 569–604; Michael Calderon-Zaks, "Debated Whiteness amid World Events: Mexican and Mexican American Subjectivity and the U.S. Relationship with the Americas, 1924–1936," *Mexican Studies* 27, no. 2 (2011): 325–359; Thomas Guglielmo, "Fighting for Caucasian Rights: Mexicans, Mexican Americans, and the Transnational Struggle for Civil Rights in World War II Texas," *Journal of American History* 92, no. 4 (2006): 1212–1237.

94. Robert R. Alvarez, "Jim and José Crow: Conversations on the Black/Brown Dialogue," *Journal of Asian and African Studies* 51, no. 3 (2016): 346–357.

95. Mai Ngai, *Impossible Subjects: Illegal Aliens and the Making of Modern America* (Princeton, N.J.: Princeton University Press, 2004), 129.

96. The Bracero Program was the result of a 1942 agreement between the United States and Mexico effectively "leasing" manual labor, allowing Mexicans to work in the United States to make up for the labor shortage created by World War II. *Braceros* literally translated means "one who works with his arms" (a.k.a. manual labor).

97. *Gonzales v. Sheely*, 96 F. Supp. 1004 (1951): 1006.

98. Ibid., 1008.

99. Ellis O. Knox, "Racial Integration in the Public Schools of Arizona, Kansas, and New Mexico," *Journal of Negro Education* 23, no. 3 (1954), 292.

100. Jeanne M. Powers and Lirio Patton, "Between *Mendez* and *Brown*: *Gonzales v. Sheely* (1951) and the Legal Campaign against Segregation," *Law and Social Inquiry* 33, no. 1 (2008): 128.

101. Nikole Hannah-Jones, "The Resegregation of America's Schools." *ProPublica* accessed December 11, 2016, https://www.propublica.org/series/segregation-now.

102. Marisela Martinez-Cola, "The Long Battle Against Jim Crow: African American Activism and the History of Segregation," in *African American Activism and Political Engagement: An Encyclopedia of Empowerment*, ed. Angela Jones (Santa Barbara, Calif.: ABC-CLIO, forthcoming).

CHAPTER 3. *Tape v. Hurley*—the Omitted

1. Mae Ngai, *The Lucky Ones: One Family and the Extraordinary Invention of Chinese America* (Princeton, N.J.: Princeton University Press, 2010).

2. Leland Gamble, "What a Chinese Girl Did: An Expert Photographer and Telegrapher," *Morning Call* (San Francisco), November 19, 1982, 12 and 18.

3. Wendy Rouse Jorae, *The Children of Chinatown: Growing Up Chinese American in San Francisco, 1850–1920* (Chapel Hill: University of North Carolina Press, 2009); Peggy Pascoe, *Relations of Rescue: The Search for Female Moral Authority in the American West, 1874–1939* (New York: Oxford University Press, 1990); Ronald Takaki, *Strangers from a Different Shore: A History of Asian Americans*, updated and rev. ed. (New York: Back Bay Books, 1998); Judy Yung, *Unbound Feet: A Social History of Chinese Women in San Francisco* (Berkeley: University of California Press, 1995).

4. Gamble, "What a Chinese Girl Did."

5. D. Krah, *Finding Aid to the San Francisco Ladies' Protection and Relief Society Records* [background information] (2007), San Francisco Ladies' Protection and Relief Society Records(MS 3576), California Historical Society, San Francisco.

6. Box 2, Volume 3, Minutes 1865 July–1878 May, 191, San Francisco Ladies' Protection and Relief Society Records, 1854–1869, MS 3576, California Historical Society.

7. Pascoe, *Relations of Rescue*.

8. Box 2, Volume 3, Minutes 1865 July–1878 May, 223, San Francisco Ladies' Protection and Relief Society Records, 1854–1869, MS 3576.

9. Ibid., at 237–238.

10. Gamble, "What a Chinese Girl Did."

11. Pascoe, *Relations of Rescue*.

12. Ngai, *Lucky Ones*.

13. Ibid., at 25.

14. "No Chinese Need Apply," *Daily Alta California* (San Francisco), September 17, 1884, 1.

15. Ibid.

16. "Chinese Question Again—the Board Refuses to Listen to Petition for Admitting Native-Born Chinese Children in Public Schools," *Daily Alta California* (San Francisco), October 22, 1884, 1.

17. Ngai, *Lucky Ones*.

18. Charles J. McClain, *In Search of Equality: The Chinese Struggle against Discrimination in Nineteenth-Century America* (Berkeley: University of California Press, 1994), 163.

19. "Look Tin Sing: An Important Case Argued in the Circuit Court Yesterday," *Daily Alta California* (San Francisco), September 28, 1884, 1.

20. "Chinese Question Again," 1.

21. "A Test Case: Shall the Child of Chinese Parents Be Admitted to the Public Schools?," *Daily Alta California* (San Francisco), October 29, 1884, 1.

22. *Daily Alta California* (San Francisco), September 17, 1884, 1.

23. "Chinese in Our Schools—Judge Maguire Says They Have Same Rights as Others," *Daily Alta California* (San Francisco), January 10, 1885, 1.

24. Ibid., emphasis mine.

25. Ibid.

26. "The Chinese Question: An Exhaustive Communication from State Superintendent Welcker—Committee Reports and Recommendations," *Daily Alta California* (San Francisco), January 15, 1885, 8.

27. Ibid.

28. Ibid.

29. *Ward v. Flood*, 48 Cal. 36 (1874), 57.

30. *Tape v. Hurley*, 66 Cal. 36 (1885), 474.

31. Ibid., 474, emphasis theirs.

32. "Strong Anti-Chinese Speech Delivered by Director Culver," *Daily Alta California* (San Francisco), April 2, 1885, 1.

33. Ibid., 1.

34. Ibid.

35. Ibid.

36. "Mamie Tape Outwitted," *Daily Alta California* (San Francisco), April 8, 1885, 1.

37. "Mamie Tape Outwitted," 1.

38. "Mamie Tape Outwitted," 1.

39. Elmer Clarence Sandmeyer, *The Anti-Chinese Movement in California* (Urbana: University of Illinois Press, 1973), 30.

40. Ibid., 90.

41. Center for Inquiry, "Meet the Most Remarkable American Most People Never Heard Of," September 11, 2008, YouTube Video, 7:59, https://www.youtube.com/watch?v=O2M1Ekltg4M.

42. "The Chinese School. To Be Formally Opened on Next Monday—the Tape Girl Not to Attend," *Daily Alta California* (San Francisco), April 10, 1885, 8.

43. "The Chinese School. Opened Yesterday with an Attendance of Six Children," *Daily Alta California* (San Francisco), April 14, 1885, 1.

44. Ibid.

45. Ibid.

46. Ibid., emphasis mine.

47. Ibid. According to the 1885 *American Newspaper Annual*, San Francisco's *Daily Alta California* had a circulation of at least seventeen thousand subscribers, a number that does not include everyday readers.

48. "A Chinese Mother's Letter. A Letter from Mrs. Tape," *Daily Alta California* (San Francisco), April 16, 1885, 1.

49. Ibid.

50. Ibid.

51. "Twenty-Five Years Ago, Today. March 4, 1885," *Sacramento Union*, March 4, 1910, 6.

52. Joyce Kuo, "Excluded, Segregated, and Forgotten: A Historical View of the Discrimination of Chinese Americans in Public Schools," *Asian American Law Journal* 5, no. 7 (1998): 199.

53. S. W. John, *Exclusive Citizenship: Immigration, Asian Americans, and the Paradox of Civil Rights* (New York: New York University Press, 2004); Mark E. Steiner, "Inclusion and Exclusion in American Legal History," *Asian American Law Journal* 23 (2016): 69–98.

54. Robert Chang, "Toward an Asian American Legal Scholarship: Critical Race Theory, Post-structuralism, and Narrative Space," *California Law Review* 81, no. 5 (1993); Gary Okihiro, *Margins and Mainstreams: Asians in American History and Culture* (Seattle: University of Washington Press, 1994); Frank H. Wu, "Neither Black nor White: Asian Americans and Affirmative Action," *Boston College Third World Law Journal* 15, no. 2 (1995): 225–284; Janine Young Kim, "Are Asians Black? Asian-American Civil Rights Agenda and the Contemporary Significance of the Black/White Paradigm," in *Contemporary Asian America: A Multidisciplinary Reader*, ed. Min Zhou and J. V. Gatewood, 2nd ed. (New York: New York University Press, 2007).

55. Leslie Bow, *Partly Colored: Asian Americans and the Racial Anomaly in the Segregated South* (New York: New York University Press, 2010), 11 and 42.

56. "Chinese in Our Schools," 1.

57. "Chinese Question: An Exhaustive Communication," 8; "Mongolian Children: Shall They Be Admitted to Our Public School?," *Sacramento Daily Record-Union*, January 16, 1885, 1.

58. "Chinese Question: An Exhaustive Communication," *Daily Alta California* (San Francisco), January 15, 1885, 8.

59. McClain, *In Search of Equality*; William H. Watkins, *The White Architects of Black Education: Ideology and Power in America, 1865–1954* (New York: Teachers College Press, 2001).

60. "Chinese in Our Schools," 1, emphasis mine.

61. Ibid.

62. " Chinese Question: An Exhaustive Communication," *Daily Alta California* (San Francisco), January 15, 1885, 8.

63. Ibid.

64. "The Chinese Problem," *Daily Alta California* (San Francisco), January 11, 1885, 1; " Chinese Question: An Exhaustive Communication," *Daily Alta California* (San Francisco), January 15, 1885, 8; "The Chinese School Problem," *Daily Alta California* (San Francisco), March 5, 1885, 1; "The Chinese Problem," *Daily Alta California* (San Francisco), April 11, 1885, 1.

65. "The Chinese Problem," *Daily Alta California* (San Francisco), January 11, 1885, 1.

66. "Chinese School Problem," 1.

67. Ibid.

68. "The Chinese School—Director Culver's Speech," *Daily Alta California* (San Francisco), April 2, 1885, 1.

69. Ibid.

70. Ibid.

71. Ibid. *Phylloxera* is a parasite that infests vineyards and can destroy entire crops.

72. Ibid.

73. Ibid.

74. "San Francisco Items: The Chinese and the Schools," *Sacramento Daily Record Union*, October 10, 1884, 2

75. "Chinese in Our Schools," 1; "Mongolian Children," 1.

76. " Chinese Question: An Exhaustive Communication," *Daily Alta California* (San Francisco), January 15, 1885, 8.

77. Ibid.

78. "Chinese School Problem," 1.

79. "The Chinese School," *Daily Alta California* (San Francisco), April 10, 1885, 1.

80. "No Chinese Need Apply," 1; "Chinese Question Again," 1; "Chinese Question Again—the Board Refuses to Petition for Admitting Native Born Chinese Children in the Public Schools," *Daily Alta California* (San Francisco), December 24, 1884, 1.

81. "Chinese in Our Schools," 1.

82. "The Chinese School. Opened Yesterday," 1.

83. Ibid.

84. Ibid.

85. "San Francisco Items," *Sacramento Daily Record Union*, April 10, 1885, 1.

86. "Chinese Mother's Letter," 1.

87. Ibid.

88. Ibid.

89. Gamble, "What a Chinese Girl Did," 2.

90. Ibid., 18.

91. Ibid.

92. Ibid.

93. Ibid.

94. Ibid.

95. "Chinese in Our Schools," 1.

96. "Chinese School—Director Culver's Speech," 1.

97. Ibid.

98. Gamble, "What a Chinese Girl Did," 18.

99. Ibid.

100. Ngai, *Lucky Ones*, ix.

101. "Chinese School. To Be Formally Opened," 8.

102. "Chinese Question: An Exhaustive Communication," 8.

103. "Chinese School—Director Culver's Speech," 1.

104. "Chinese Mother's Letter," 1.

105. Ngai, *Lucky Ones*.

106. "Chinese School—Director Culver's Speech," 1.

107. "Chinese Question: An Exhaustive Communication," 8.

108. Ibid., 8, emphasis mine.

109. "Mamie Tape Outwitted," 1.

110. "The Chinese School. Opened Yesterday," 1.

111. "Chinese Question Again—the Board Refuses to Listen to Petitions for Admitting Native-Born Chinese Children to the Public Schools," *Daily Alta California* (San Francisco), October 22, 1884, 1.

112. "Board of Education," *Daily Alta California* (San Francisco), December 24, 1884, 1.

113. Gamble, "What a Chinese Girl Did," 12.

114. Laura Wexler, *Tender Violence: Domestic Visions in An Age of U.S. Imperialism* (Chapel Hill: University of North Carolina Press, 2000).

115. Ibid., 40.

116. Ibid.

117. Gamble, "What a Chinese Girl Did," 12.

118. Ibid., 18.

119. Ibid.

120. Ibid.

121. Ibid.

122. Ibid.

123. Ibid.

124. Ibid.

125. Ibid.

126. Ibid., emphasis mine.

CHAPTER 4. *Piper v. Big Pine*—the Forgotten

1. Nicole Blalock-Moore, "*Piper v. Big Pine School District of Inyo County*: Indigenous Schooling and Resistance in the Early Twentieth Century," *Southern California Quarterly* 94, no. 3 (2012): 346–377; Charles Wollenberg, *All Deliberate Speed: Segregation and Exclusion in California Schools, 1855–1975* (Berkeley: University of California Press, 1976).

2. Leo Killsback, "Indigenous Perceptions of Time: Decolonizing Theory, World History, and the Fates of Human Societies," *American Indian Culture and Research Journal* 37 no. 1 (2013): 134.

3. Linda Tuhiwai Smith, *Decolonizing Methodologies: Research and Indigenous Peoples* (New York: Zed Books, 2012), 29, emphasis hers.

4. Ibid., 29–30.

5. Chantal Walker, "Piyahu Nadu—Land of Flowing Waters: The Water Transfer from Owens Valley to Los Angeles, 1913–1939," (MA thesis, UCLA, 2014).

6. Walker, "Piyahu Nadu," 43.

7. For a more in-depth review and discussion of the history of Owens Valley water rights, please see William Bauer Jr., "The Giant and the Waterbaby. Paiute Oral Traditions and the Owens Valley Water Wars," *Boom: A Journal of California* 2, no. 4 (2012): 104–117; Abraham Hoffman, "Mary Austin, Stafford Austin, and the Owens Valley," *Journal of the Southwest* 54, nos. 3–4 (2011): 304–322; William Kahrl, "The Politics of California Water: Owens Valley and the Lost Angeles Aqueduct, 1900–1927 (Part 1)," *Hastings West-Northwest Journal of Environmental Law and Policy* 6, nos. 2–3 (2000): 239–253; and Walker, "Piyahu Nadu."

8. Ronald Takaki, *A Different Mirror: A History of Multicultural America* (New York: Back Bay Books, 2008), 222.

9. Jon Reyhner and Jeanne Eder, *American Indian Education: A History* (Norman: University of Oklahoma Press, 2004).

10. David Wallace Adams, *Education for Extinction: American Indians and the Boarding School Experience* (Lawrence: University of Kansas Press, 1995), 320.

11. *Ward v. Flood* 48 Cal. 36 (1874).

12. Blalock-Moore, "*Piper v. Big Pine.*"

13. Ibid.

14. Ibid., 355.

15. Marisela Martinez-Cola interview with Pamela Jones, Sage Andrew Romero, and Danelle Gutierrez, March 7, 2017.

16. *Piper v. Big Pine*, 193 Cal. 664; 226 P. 926 (1924), at 674.

17. Martinez-Cola interview with Jones, Romero, and Gutierrez.

18. *Piper v. Big Pine*, 668.

19. Ibid., 674.

20. Ibid., 671, emphasis mine.

21. Ibid., 672.

22. Jess Hession to L. L. Goen, June 24, 1924, privately held.

23. Blalock-Moore, "*Piper v. Big Pine.*"

24. Martinez-Cola interview with Jones, Romero, and Gutierrez.

25. All of the informants wanted it known that, while Alice Piper was the named plaintiff, there were six other children and families involved in the case. Their names remain unknown, but their sacrifice is not. During the interview, however, Sage and Danelle surmise that Jeff Tibbets and Ike Baker might have been co-plaintiffs. They are pictured in the integrated school photograph featured in Figure 4.1.

26. Annie Piper, "Office of Indian Affairs Application for Enrollment," United States Department of Interior, application number redacted for protection against identity theft,

1930, 2, privately held; Pike Piper, "Office of Indian Affairs Application for Enrollment," United States Department of Interior, application number redacted for protection against identity theft, 1930, at 2 and 4, privately held.

27. Ibid.

28. Martinez-Cola interview with Jones, Romero, and Gutierrez.

29. Pike Piper, "Office of Indian Affairs Application," 2.

30. Alice Piper's application for employment, United States Department of Interior, Office of Indian Affairs, October 20, 1938, 2. Alice Piper's federal employee records were supplied by the National Personnel Records Center in Valmeyer, Illinois. The author sent copies with a detailed timeline to the tribal historian.

31. Bonnie Thompson, "The Student Body: A History of Stewart Indian School, 1890–1940" (PhD diss., Arizona State University, 2013).

32. From my interview, I was informed that Alice Piper never married. Her employment record, however, shows that she left Stewart to marry Ray Antelope in 1939. She returned to Stewart in 1944 under the name Alice Antelope but wrote in 1948 that she was separated. She changed her name back to Alice Piper in 1960.

33. "Experience and Qualifications Sheet," Alice Piper's employment record, United States Department of Interior, July 13, 1953, 1, National Personnel Records Center, Valmeyer, Ill.

34. "Application for Federal Employment," Alice Piper's employment record, United States Department of Interior, March 20, 1961, 2, National Personnel Records Center, Valmeyer, Ill.

35. "What Makes the Stewart Indian School Unique," Stewart Indian School Cultural Center & Museum, revised March 27, 2018, https://stewartindianschool.com/wp-content /uploads/2018/05/What_makes_Stewart_Indian_School_Unique.pdf.

36. Ibid., 7.

37. Collected interviews with Evelyn Cook, Ruthe Abbie, Beatrice Allen, Thomas Benjamin, Rolf Brown, Carlene Burton, Rudy Clark, Delbert Holly, JoAnn Nevers, Reynese Peterson, Roger Sam, Rupert Steele, Bill Turner, Robey Willis, and Ron Wopsock, 2016–2018, Stewart Indian School Oral History Project, held in the Special Collections and University Archives Collection at the University of Nevada, Reno. Available online at https://unr.dgicloud.com /islandora/object/stewart%3Aroot.

38. Mary Annette Pember, "A Painful Remembrance," *Diverse Issues in Higher Education* 24, no. 21 (November 28, 2007): 26.

39. Jacqueline Fear-Segal and Susan D. Rose, *Carlisle Indian Industrial School: Indigenous Histories, Memories, and Reclamations* (Lincoln: University of Nebraska Press, 2016); Joseph P. Gone and Joseph E. Trimble, "American Indian and Alaska Native Mental Health: Diverse Perspectives on Enduring Disparities," *Annual Review of Clinical Psychology* 8 (2012): 131–160; William E. Hartmann, Dennis C. Wendt, Rachel L. Burrage, Andrew Pomerville, and Joseph P. Gone, "American Indian Historical Trauma: Anticolonial Prescriptions for Healing, Resilience, and Survivance," *American Psychologist*, 74, no. 1 (2019): 6–19.

40. *Desert Braves, 1946* (Stewart, Nev.: Senior class of the Carson Indian School, 1946), available at Stewart Indian Cultural Center & Museum website, https://stewartindianschool .com/wp-content/uploads/2019/05/1946.pdf.

41. "Notice of Personnel Action," Alice Piper employment records, 6–28–68, National Personnel Records Center, Valmeyer, Ill.

42. To demonstrate my respect to Alice and her family, I asked to visit their gravesite so that I might place flowers nearby. Sage Andrew Romero and I found Pike and Annie Piper's site but not Alice's. There was an unmarked grave, but Romero was not certain whether it was hers. Danelle Gutierrez surmised that because Alice was an only child who never married and never had kids, she did not have descendants who would maintain her burial site. It was also surmised that she might not have been buried there but near Fish Valley, where she was born.

43. Martinez-Cola interview with Jones, Romero, and Gutierrez.

44. DigitalNdn (YouTube user), "Alice Piper vs. Big Pine School Facts," accessed November 22, 2017, https://www.youtube.com/watch?v=TuAq_LKOzKg; DigitalNdn, "Alice Piper Memorial Project Video—1," accessed November 22, 2017, https://www.youtube.com/watch?v=nO44ZAUDFws; DigitalNdn, "Alice Piper Memorial Project Video—2," accessed November 22, 2017, https://www.youtube.com/watch?v=wsPAhIn5TUY ; DigitalNdn, "A Quiet Hero—Alice Piper," accessed November 22, 2017, https://www.youtube.com/watch?v=bOAfmwzp7hk; DigitalNdn, "The Alice Piper Journey," accessed November 22, 2017, https://www.youtube.com/watch?v=vlsNsnWB2rU&t=4s.

45. "Alice Piper vs. Big Pine School Facts," at 1:51.

46. *Piper v. Big Pine*, 666.

47. Ariela J. Gross, *What Blood Won't Tell: A History of Race on Trial in America* (Cambridge, Mass.: Harvard University Press, 2008), 13. See also Mikaela Adams, *Who Belongs? Race, Resources and Tribal Citizenship in the Native South* (New York: Oxford University Press, 2016).

48. Bryan McKinley Jones Brayboy, "Toward a Tribal Critical Race Theory in Education," *Urban Review* 37, no. 5 (2014): 432.

49. Gloria Anzaldúa, *Borderlands / La Frontera: The New Mestiza*, 4th ed. (San Francisco: Aunt Lute Books, 2012).

50. *Piper v. Big Pine*, 666, emphasis mine.

51. Ibid., 671.

52. Ibid., 672.

53. Paige Raibmon, *Authentic Indians: Episodes of Encounter from the Late-Nineteenth Century Northwest Coast* (Durham, N.C.: Duke University Press, 2005).

54. Jones, Romero, and Gutierrez interview.

55. Ibid.

56. Brayboy, "Tribal Critical Race Theory," 434.

57. Ibid.

58. "Alice Piper vs. Big Pine School Facts," at 1:31.

59. Audre Lorde, *Sister Outsider: Essays and Speeches* (Berkeley, Calif.: Crossing, 1984).

60. *Piper v. Big Pine*, 666.

61. Charles J. McClain, *In Search of Equality: The Chinese Struggle against Discrimination in Nineteenth-Century America* (Berkeley: University of California Press, 1994); Ronald Takaki, *Strangers from a Different Shore: A History of Asian Americans*, updated and rev. ed. (New York: Back Bay Books, 1998); Wollenberg, *All Deliberate Speed*.

62. Lisa J. Ellwood, "Native American Students Face Ongoing Crisis in Education," Indian Country Today, September 3, 2017, https://indiancountrymedianetwork.com/education/native-education/native-american-students-face-ongoing-crises-education/; Charles James,

"Long-Awaited Honor Unveiled at Big Pine Schools," *Inyo Register* (Inyo County, Calif.) 144, no. 68 (2014): 1–2; "Native American Civil Rights Hero Honored in Big Pine," Sierra Wave Media, accessed May 31, 2014, https://sierrawave.net/native-american-civil-rights/.

63. Richard H. Chused, "Late Nineteenth Century Married Women's Property Law: Reception of the Early Married Women's Property Act by Courts and Legislatures," *American Journal of Legal History* 29, no. 1 (1985): 3–35.

CHAPTER 5. The Mendezes—the Understated

Permission to reprint the epigraphs provided by the Denver Public Library.

1. *Gonzalo Mendez et al. v. Westminster School District of Orange County et al.* trial transcript, July 5, 1945, at 8, National Archives identifier 6377736, Records Group 21, Civil Case Files, 1938–2001, National Archives at Riverside, Perris, Calif. Hereafter, this source is cited as *Mendez* trial transcript.

2. While the Supreme Court would later clarify in *Plyler v. Doe* (1982) that discrimination based on national origin was the same as discrimination based on race, it is clear from the *Mendez* case that descent and race were different protected classes.

3. Christopher Arriola, "Knocking on the Schoolhouse Door: *Mendez v. Westminster*, Equal Protection, Public Education, and Mexican Americans in the 1940s," *Berkeley* La Raza *Law Journal* 8 (1995): 166–207.

4. I am not arguing that *Mendez* receives no attention, just that it makes up a relatively small portion of the literature on school desegregation. For example, there is only one whole book on *Mendez v. Westminster*, and fewer than twenty books include chapter treatments of the case. While the list of resources is growing, *Mendez* should be much more well known. While not exhaustive, please see this list of scholarly treatments: Maria Blanco, *Before "Brown," There Was "Mendez": The Lasting Impact of "Mendez v. Westminster" in the Struggle for Desegregation*, Perspectives: Immigration Policy Center (American Immigration Council, 2010); Kristi L. Bowman, "The New Face of School Desegregation (Latino Segregation in Public Schools)" *Duke Law Journal* 50, no. 6 (2001): 1751–1808; Kristi L. Bowman and James E. Ryan, eds., *The Pursuit of Racial and Ethnic Equality in American Public Schools: "Mendez," "Brown," and Beyond* (East Lansing: Michigan State University Press, 2015); Frank Dimaria, "Road to *Brown v. Board of Education* Partially Paved by Hispanics," *The Hispanic Outlook in Higher Education* 18, no. 5 (2007): 32–34; Rubén Donato, *The Other Struggle for Equal Schools: Mexican Americans during the Civil Rights Era* (New York: SUNY Series, 1997); Gilbert G. Gonzalez, "Segregation of Mexican Children in a Southern California City: The Legacy of Expansionism and the American Southwest," *Western Historical Quarterly* 16, no. 1 (1985): 55–76; Paul Hoogeveen, "In Search of Equality *Mendez v. Westminster*," *The Hispanic Outlook in Higher Education* 18, no. 2 (2007): 41; Margaret Montoya, "A Brief History of Chicana/o Segregation: One Rationale for Affirmative Action," *Berkeley* La Raza *Law Journal* 12, no. 2 (2001): 159–172; Lisa Y. Ramos, "Dismantling Segregation Together: Interconnections between *Mendez v. Westminster* (1946) and *Brown v. Board of Education* (1954) School Segregation Cases," *Equity and Excellence in Education* 37, no. 3 (2004): 247–254; Vicki Ruiz, "'We Always Tell Our Children They Are Americans': *Mendez v. Westminster* and the California Road to *Brown v. Board of Education*," *College Board Review* 200 (2003): 20–27; Mabel Santiago, "*Mendez v. Westminster*, 1947:

Teaching a New Chapter of History" *Phi Delta Kappa International* 94, no. 6 (2013): 35–38; Richard R. Valencia, "The Mexican American Struggle for Equal Educational Opportunity in *Mendez v. Westminster*: Helping to Pave the Way for *Brown v. Board of Education,*" *Teachers College Record* 107, no. 3 (2005): 389–423; Richard R. Valencia, *Chicano Students and the Courts: The Mexican American Legal Struggle for Educational Equality* (New York: New York University Press, 2008); Charles Wollenberg, "*Mendez v. Westminster*: Race, Nationality and Segregation in California Schools," *California Historical Quarterly* 53, no. 4 (1974): 317–332.

5. Philippa Strum, *"Mendez v. Westminster": School Desegregation and Mexican-American Rights* (Lawrence: University Press of Kansas, 2010).

6. Ana Elizabeth Rosas, Abrazando el Espiritu*: Bracero Families Confront the U.S.-Mexico Border* (Oakland: University of California Press, 2014).

7. Jennifer McCormick and César Ayala, "Felícita 'La Prieta' Mendez (1916–1998) and the end of Latino School Segregation in California," *CENTRO Journal* 29, no. 2 (2007): 15.

8. Ibid., 16.

9. Ibid. citing Carey McWilliams, *Ill Fares the Land: Migrants and Migratory Labor in the United States* (New York: Barnes and Noble, 1967), 80.

10. McCormick and Ayala, "Felícita 'La Prieta' Mendez," 19.

11. Strum, *"Mendez v. Westminster,"* 36.

12. Ibid.

13. Ibid.

14. Ibid., 24; Molly Nance, "The Landmark Decision that Faded into Historical Obscurity," *Diverse: Issues in Higher Education* 24, no. 22 (2007): 28–31.

15. McCormick and Ayala, "Felícita 'La Prieta' Mendez," 26, citing Luis Arríola, "Hace 50 Años Se Derrotó la Segregación Racial de Mexicanos, *Unión Hispana*, June 16, 1995, 3.

16. McCormick and Ayala, "Felícita 'La Prieta' Méndez," 24.

17. Ibid., 26.

18. *Lopez v. Seccombe*, 71 F. Supp. 769 (S.D. Cal. 1944).

19. Strum, *"Mendez v. Westminster."*

20. Ibid.

21. McCormick and Ayala, "Felícita 'La Prieta' Méndez."

22. Strum, *"Mendez v. Westminster,"* 61.

23. McCormick and Ayala, "Felícita 'La Prieta' Mendez."

24. George J. Sánchez, *Becoming Mexican American: Ethnicity, Culture and Identity in Chicano Los Angeles, 1900–1945* (New York: Oxford University Press, 1993).

25. Catherine S. Ramirez, *The Woman in the Zoot Suit: Gender, Nationalism and the Cultural Politics of Memory* (Durham, N.C.: Duke University Press, 2009).

26. Ibid., 4–5.

27. "Who Is Really Stirring Up the Racial Prejudice?," *Los Angeles Times*, June 15, 1943, A4.

28. "Trade Schools Advocated for Mexican American Youths," *Los Angeles Times*, May 10, 1943, A2.

29. "Los Angeles School Workshop Points Course to Racial Accord," *Christian Science Monitor*, July 29, 1943, 12.

30. Juan Perea, "Buscando América: Why Integration and Equal Protection Fail to Protect Latinos," *Harvard Law Review* 117, no. 5 (2004): 1442.

31. *Mendez* trial transcript, July 5, 1945, 80.

32. Ibid., 81.

33. Ibid.

34. Ibid., 14.

35. Ibid., 108.

36. Ibid., 109.

37. Ibid., 85.

38. Ibid., 116. According to the National Institutes of Health, impetigo is a common skin infection caused by *Staphylococcus* (staph). It is most common in children who are in unhealthy living conditions.

39. Ibid.

40. Ibid., 122.

41. Sylvia Mendez and Sandra Mendez Duran, "Sylvia Mendez and Sandra Mendez Duran," *StoryCorps*, produced by Nadia Reiman, National Public Radio, original airdate March 26, 2010.

42. *Mendez* trial transcript, July 5, 1945, at 128.

43. *Mendez* trial transcript, July 6, 1945, at 225, National Archives identifier 6377736, Records Group 21, Civil Case Files, 1938–2001, National Archives at Riverside, Perris, Calif.

44. Ibid., 229–230.

45. Ibid., 311.

46. Ibid., 320.

47. Ibid., 322.

48. Ibid., at 326–327.

49. *Mendez* trial transcript, July 9, 1945, at 350, National Archives identifier 6377737, Records Group 21, Civil Case Files, 1938–2001, National Archives at Riverside, Perris, Calif.

50. Ibid., 358, 360, 361–367.

51. Ibid., 376.

52. Ibid.

53. Ibid., 379, 382.

54. Ibid., 382.

55. Ibid.

56. Bess M. Wilson, "Problems of School Child of Latin Lineage Studied," *Los Angeles Times*, July 3, 1944, A5.

57. Ibid.

58. Ibid.

59. Ibid.

60. "Demanda de Cinco Mil Mexicanos," *La Prensa* (San Antonio, Tex.), March 10, 1945, 1; "Termina la Segregación de Escolares de Origen Mexicano en Los Planteles del Condado de Orange, California," *La Prensa* (San Antonio, Tex.), March 26, 1946, 1; "Los Angeles Judge Rules Discrimination by Schools Illegal," *Baltimore Afro-American*, May 18, 1946, 3.

61. Six witnesses did not spend a great deal of time on the stand or were prematurely taken from the stand because the judge upheld various objections put forth by the school's attorney. Among them were seventeen-year-old Isabel Ayala, who was there to testify on behalf of her younger sisters (*Mendez* trial transcript, July 11, 1945, 637–642, National Archives identifier

6377739, Records Group 21, Civil Case Files, 1938–2001, National Archives at Riverside, Perris, Calif.), and Jane Sianez, married mother of five who traveled three miles to attend the Mexican school when the white school was only half a mile away from her home (*Mendez* trial transcript, July 5, 1945, 56).

62. Ariela J. Gross, *What Blood Won't Tell: A History of Race on Trial in America* (Cambridge, Mass.: Harvard University Press, 2008), 254.

63. *Mendez* trial transcript, July 5, 1947, 63.

64. *Mendez* trial transcript, July 6, 1945, 212.

65. Ibid., 252.

66. *Mendez* trial transcript, July 9, 1945, 351.

67. *Mendez* trial transcript, July 5, 1945, 138–139.

68. Ibid., 120.

69. Ibid., 124.

70. Ibid.

71. Manuela Ochoa, *Mendez* trial transcript, July 5, 1945, 13.

72. Ibid., 48.

73. *Mendez* trial transcript, July 10, 1945, 469, National Archives identifier 6377738, Records Group 21, Civil Case Files, 1938–2001, National Archives at Riverside, Perris, Calif.

74. David G. Gutiérrez, *Walls and Mirrors: Mexican Americans, Mexican Immigrants, and the Politics of Ethnicity* (Los Angeles: University of California Press, 1995), 73; Vicki Ruiz, "Morena/o, Blanca/o, y Café con Leche: Racial Constructions in Chicana/o Historiography," *Mexican Studies* 20, no. 2 (2004): 667.

75. Mario García, *Mexican Americans: Leadership, Ideology & Identity, 1930–1960* (New Haven, Conn.: Yale University Press, 1989).

76. *Mendez* trial transcript, July 5, 1945, 10.

77. Ibid., 24.

78. Ibid.

79. Ibid., 29.

80. Ibid., 150.

81. Ibid., 151.

82. Ibid., 142.

83. Felícitas Fuentes, *Mendez* trial transcript, July 5, 1945, 152.

84. García, *Mexican Americans*, 283.

85. Petitioner's opening brief, *Gonzalo Mendez et al v. Westminster School District of Orange County et al.*, September 29, 1945, 45, National Archives identifier 294942, Records Group 21, Civil Case Files, 1938–2004, National Archives at Riverside.

86. Strum, "*Mendez v. Westminster*," 28 quoting an interview printed in the *Santa Ana (Calif.) Register*, dates unknown.

87. *Mendez* trial transcript, July 5, 1945, 65.

88. Ibid., 67.

89. *Mendez* trial transcript, July 10, 1945, 469.

90. *Mendez* trial transcript, July 5, 1945, 45.

91. Ibid., 161.

92. *Mendez* trial transcript, July 10, 1945, 471.

93. Ibid., 476–477.

94. *Mendez* trial transcript, July 6, 1945, 281.

95. Ibid.

96. Ibid., 282.

97. Ibid.

98. Ibid., 167.

99. Ibid., 176.

100. *Mendez* trial transcript, July 5, 1945, 10 and 68; *Mendez* trial transcript, July 6, 1945, 172, 189, 269, and 278; *Mendez* trial transcript, July 9, 1945, 422.

101. *Mendez* trial transcript, July 6, 1945, 288–289.

102. Ibid., 272.

103. Ibid., 204–210.

104. *Mendez* trial transcript, July 10, 1945, 467–470.

105. Ibid., 258.

106. Ibid., 264.

107. Ibid., 265.

108. Ibid., 267.

109. *Mendez* trial transcript, July 6, 1945, 184 and 201.

110. Ibid., 190.

111. *Mendez* trial transcript, July 9, 1945, 421.

112. Ibid., 437–438.

113. Ibid., 434–435.

114. Ibid., 444.

115. Ibid., 446.

116. Ibid., 448.

117. Ibid., 345.

118. *Mendez* trial transcript, July 6, 1945, 188.

119. Ibid., 265.

120. *Mendez* trial transcript, July 10, 1945, 470.

121. *Mendez* trial transcript, July 11, 1945, 676.

122. Ibid., 690–691.

123. "Ruling Gives Mexican Children Equal Rights," *Los Angeles Times*, February 20, 1946, 1.

124. "Termina la Segregación," 1.

125. "Court Ruling Bars California School Bias," *Baltimore Afro-American*, May 18, 1946, 1; "Judge Rules against Jim Crow," *New England Journal and Guide*, March 2, 1946, 1; Ira De A. Reid, "Persons and Places," *Phylon* 7, no. 2 (2nd Quarter 1946): 200; "Anti-Bias Ruling Upheld by Court," *Chicago Defender*, May 17, 1947, 3.

126. Carey McWilliams, "Is Your Name Gonzalez?," *Nation*, March 15, 1947, 302.

127. Lester H. Phillips, "Segregation in Education: A California Case Study," *Phylon* 4 (1949): 407.

128. McWilliams, "Is Your Name Gonzalez?," 304.

129. *Westminster School District of Orange County v. Mendez* 9th Cir. (1947).

130. Frederick P. Aguirre, "*Mendez v. Westminster School District*: How It Affected *Brown v. Board of Education*," *Journal of Hispanic Higher Education* 4, no. 2 (2005): 321–332; Frederick P. Aguirre, Kristi L. Bowman, Gonzalo Mendez, Sandra Robbie, and Philippa Strum, "*Mendez v. Westminster*: A Living History (Pursuing the Dreams of *Brown* and the Civil Rights Act: A Living History of the Fight for Educational Equality) (Discussion)," *Michigan State Law Review* 3 (2014): 401–427.

131. Toni Robinson and Greg Robinson, "*Mendez v. Westminster*: Asian-Latino Coalition Triumphant?," *Asian Law Journal* 10, no. 2 (2003): 161–184.

132. Strum, "*Mendez v. Westminster*," at 135.

133. Sandra Robbie, "Sandra Robbie's *Mendez v. Westminster: For All the Children*," July 9, 2020, YouTube Video, 4:21, https://www.youtube.com/watch?v=F46Mlzt2tFc.

134. McCormick and Ayala, "Felícita 'La Prieta' Mendez," 21 citing McWilliams, "Is Your Name Gonzalez?," *Nation*, 302.

135. McCormick and Ayala, "Felícita 'La Prieta' Mendez," 22 citing a 1975 interview with Felícitas.

136. Vincent N. Parrillo, "The Immigrant Family: Securing the American Dream," *Journal of Comparative Family Studies* 22, no. 2 (1991): 131–145.

137. McCormick and Ayala, "Felicita 'La Prieta' Mendez," 13.

138. Ibid., 26.

139. Garcia, *Mexican Americans*; Carlos Blanton, "George I. Sánchez, Ideology, and White-ness in the Making of the Mexican American Civil Rights Movement, 1930–1960," *Journal of Southern History* 72, no. 3 (2006): 569–604.

140. Mendez trial transcript, June 26, 1945, 7–8, 12, 22,34, 44, 45.

141. Ibid., 46.

142. *Mendez* trial transcript, July 5, 1945, 29.

143. Juan Muñoz, *Mendez* trial transcript, July 5, 1945, 65.

144. Ibid.

145. James Kent, *Mendez* trial transcript, July 5, 1945, 85.

146. Ibid., 100.

147. Ibid., 123.

148. Ibid., 138–139.

149. George Lipsitz, "The Possessive Investment in Whiteness: Racialized Social Democracy and the 'White' Problem in American Studies," *American Quarterly* 47, no. 3 (1995): 371.

150. *Mendez* trial transcript, July 6, 1945, 301.

151. Ibid., 311.

152. *Mendez* trial transcript, July 9, 1945, 382.

153. Ibid., 384.

154. Ibid., 434–435.

155. McCormick and Ayala, "Felicita 'La Prieta' Mendez," 25–26.

156. Mendez and Duran, "Sylvia Mendez and Sandra Mendez Duran."

157. Caitlin Yoshiko Kandil, "Mendez vs. Segregation: 70 Years Later, Famed Case Isn't Just about Mexicans. It's about Everybody Coming Together," *Los Angeles Times*, April 17, 2016, https://www.latimes.com/socal/daily-pilot/tn-wknd-et-0417-sylvia-mendez-70-anniversary-20160417-story.html.

158. Sylvia Mendez visited Utah State University on September 18, 2019. Prior to her remarks, she shared the meaning behind the photograph with the author.

159. Mary MacVean, "The Piano's Status in U.S. Living Rooms Is Declining," *Los Angeles Times*, May 16, 2009, https://www.latimes.com/home/la-hm-pianos16-2009may16-story.html.

160. This information was discovered by Jae Hoon Chae, an undergraduate student at Emory University.

161. *Mendez* trial transcript, July 10, 1945, 468–469.

162. *Orange Daily News* (Orange County, Calif.), April 14, 1947.

163. "Demanda de Cinco Mil Mexicanos," 6.

164. "Judge Rules against Jim Crow," 1.

165. "Court Ruling Bars California School Bias," 3.

166. They were also referred to as "the five fathers" a second time in the *Orange Daily News* (Orange County, Calif.), February 20, 1946, 1.

167. *Mendez* trial transcript, July 5, 1945, 44.

168. Ibid., 52.

169. *Mendez* trial transcript, July 9, 1945, 437.

170. Ibid., 441.

171. Ibid.

172. Ibid., 439–440.

173. Ibid., 443.

174. Ibid., 444, emphasis mine.

175. *Mendez* trial transcript, July 10, 1945, 465–467.

176. Ibid., 469.

177. Joe Rodriguez, "*Brown v. Board* Ruling Stood on Sylvia Mendez's Shoulders," *San Jose (Calif.) Mercury*, April 20, 2004, reprinted in *Equal Justice: An Official Publication of the Washington State Minority and Justice Commission* 8, no. 2 (December 2004): 6–7.

178. Maria Luisa Arrendondo, "Sylvia Méndez, a Champion of Racial Tolerance and Equality in Education," October 14, 2011, https://www.huffingtonpost.com/maria-luisa-arredondo/sylvia-mendez-a-champion-_b_1010975.html.

179. Gilbert G. Gonzalez, *Chicano Education in the Era of Segregation* (Philadelphia: Balch Institute Press, 1990), 151.

180. Strum, "*Mendez v. Westminster*," at 42.

CONCLUSION

1. For more information on the *Roberts* case, see Stephen Kendrick and Paul Kendrick, *Sarah's Long Walk: The Free Blacks of Boston and How Their Struggle for Equality Changed America* (Boston: Beacon, 2004).

2. Brian J. Daugherity, *Keep On Keeping On: The NAACP and the Implementation of "Brown v. Board of Education" in Virginia* (Charlottesville: University of Virginia Press, 2016); Ophelia De Laine, *Dawn of Desegregation: J. A. De Laine and "Briggs v. Elliott"* (Columbia: University of South Carolina Press, 2011); Brett V. Gadsden, *Between North and South: Delaware, Desegregation, and the Myth of American Sectionalism* (Philadelphia: University of Pennsylvania Press,

2013); Kendrick and Kendrick, *Sarah's Long Walk*; Charles Wollenberg, "*Mendez v. Westminster*: Race, Nationality and Segregation in California Schools," *California Historical Quarterly* 53, no. 4 (1974): 317–332.

3. Rachel Devlin, *A Girl Stands at the Door: The Generation of Young Women Who Desegregated America's Schools* (New York: Basic Books, 2018).

4. Cheryl Elizabeth Brown Wattley, *A Step toward "Brown v. Board of Education": Ada Lois Sipuel Fisher and Her Fight to End Segregation* (Norman: University of Oklahoma Press, 2014).

5. Steven J. Crossland, "*Brown's* Companion: *Briggs, Belton,* and *Davis*," *Washburn Law Review* 43, no. 2 (2004): 381–428; Gadsden, *Between North and South*; Matthew D. Lassiter and Andrew B. Lewis, eds., *The Moderates' Dilemma: Massive Resistance to School Desegregation in Virginia* (Norfolk: University of Virginia Press, 1998).

6. Douglas M. Davison, *Jim Crow Moves North: The Battle over Northern School Desegregation, 1865–1954* (Cambridge: Cambridge University Press, 2005).

7. Marlon E. Riggs, dir. and prod., *Ethnic Notions: Documentary*, directed/produced by Marlon Riggs (San Francisco: California Newsreel, 1986), DVD.

8. William Barry Furlong, "The Case of Linda Brown; Now a High-School Senior, a Girl Who Made History at 9 Looks Back on the Trying Days of '*Brown vs. the Board of Education*,'" *New York Times*, February 12, 1961, section SM, 63.

9. It would have been too perfect if Alice Piper had ended up playing the piano as well. Unfortunately, there is no evidence that this was a skill she learned or that was required of her at Stewart Indian School.

10. Ronald Takaki, *A Different Mirror: A History of Multicultural America* (New York: Back Bay Books, 2008), 4.

APPENDIX C. Methodology

1. In order to confirm these results, I need to conduct the same search in Westlaw, another electronic legal database.

2. Samuel Bowles and Herbert Gintis, *Schooling in Capitalist America: Educational Reform and the Contradictions of Economic Life* (Chicago: Haymarket Books, 1976); Richard A. Peterson, *The Production of Culture* (Beverly Hills, Calif.: Sage, 1976).

3. *Roberts v. Boston*, 59 Mass. 198 (1849); *Van Camp v. Board of Education*, 9 Ohio St. 406 (1859); and *Clark v. Board of Directors*, 24 Iowa 266 (1868).

4. *Claybrook v. Owensboro* (1884), *Maddox v. Neal* (1885), *Davenport v. Clover Port* (1896), and *Cumming v. Richmond* (1899).

5. *Berea College v. Kentucky*, 211 U.S. 45 (1908); *Pierce v. Society of Sisters*, 268 U.S. 510 (1925); *Butler v. Wilemon*, 86 F. Supp. 397 (1949); and *Pitts v. Board*, 84 F. Supp. 975 (1949).

6. *Medlin v. Board*, 167 N.C. 239 (1914).

7. *Del Rio Independent School District v. Salvatierra* (1930), *Alvarez v. Lemon Grove School District* (1931), *Delgado v. Bastrop Independent School District* (1948).

8. *Jones v. City of Ketchikan Alaska* (1929) was a case involving an Alaskan Native child who was prohibited from attending her local white school.

INDEX

Printed in the USA
CPSIA information can be obtained
at www.ICGtesting.com
CBHW011101280624
10807CB00010B/346

9 780820 362038